APPROACHES TO GRAMSCI

edited
by
Anne Showstack Sassoon

Published 1982 by
Writers and Readers Publishing Cooperative Society Ltd.,
London, England

Typeset by
Shanta Thawani, 25 Natal Road, London N11 2HU 01-889 0079

Paste up by
Anthony Richard Associates

Designed by
Cassandra Wedd

Edited by
Lisa Appignanesi

Printed and Bound by **Grijelmo, S. A.**, *Spain.*

ISBN 0 906495 56 3 p/b
ISBN 0 906495 55 5 h/b

ACKNOWLEDGEMENTS

I would like to thank Lawrence and Wishart for permission to quote from Antonio Gramsci, *Selections from the Prison Notebooks* (London, 1971), translated by Quintin Hoare and Geoffrey Nowell Smith; Antonio Gramsci, *Selections from Political Writings, 1910-1921* (London, 1977), translated by John Mathews; Antonio Gramsci, *Selections from Political Writings, 1921-1926* (London, 1978), translated by Quintin Hoare. I would also like to thank the following for allowing me to reproduce material which they first published: Einaudi, Alberto Maria Cirese, *Intellettuali, folklore, istinto di classe. Note su Verga, Deledda, Scotellaro, Gramsci* (Turin, 1976); De Donato, Franco De Felice, *Serrati, Bordiga, Gramsci e il problema della rivoluzione in Italia, 1919-1920* (Bari, 1971) and Luis Razeto Migliaro and Pasquale Misuraca, *Sociologia e marxismo nella critica di Gramsci* (Bari, 1978); Editori Riuniti, Giuseppe Vacca, 'La "quistione politica degli intellettuali" e la teoria marxist dello Stato nel pensiero di Gramsci' in *Politica e storia in Gramsci*. Vol. I, edited by Franco Ferri, (Rome 1977); *Problemi del socialismo*, Mario Telò, 'Strategia consiliare e sviluppo capitalistico in Gramsci' (Rome, 1976); Croom Helm, Anne Showstack Sassoon, *Gramsci's Politics* (London, 1980); Garzanti Editore, for the extract from Pier Paolo Pasolini, 'Laboratorio' in *Nuovi Argumenti*, N.1.

Lisa Appignanesi has been of invaluable help to me in editing this book. Derek Boothman, Michael Caesar, Richard Appignanesi and John Fraser provided the translations. I particularly want to thank Christine Buci-Glucksmann, Franco De Felice, Luis Razeto Migliaro, Pasquale Misuraca, Mario Telò and Giuseppe Vacca for allowing me to edit their work considerably for reasons of space and in the attempt to cross cultural frontiers.

CONTENTS

PREFACE

As Bernard Crick recently remarked in the *London Review of Books*, authoritarian, mechanical Marxists are now few and far between. The old assumptions of what for many years was widely considered Marxism have been thrown aside: the economy as the direct source of historical change with ideas and culture the mere reflection of economics; the state as an instrument of a class; the great 'bang' or crisis theory of the downfall of capitalism; ideology as something which is used to blind the population to its 'true' interest; the vanguard party, the dictatorship of the proletariat, etc., etc. In the bad old days we used to know where we stood — partisans and enemies of Marxism. Now the 'crisis of Marxism' has arrived where the only certainty seems to be that we aren't sure of anything. The hope of a 'third way' — avoiding the drawbacks of both social democracy and the really existing socialism of the socialist countries, particularly the growth and reinforcement of the state — which seemed to many to be represented by Euro-Communism, has itself been undermined because of the varying fortunes and twists and turns of the French, Spanish and Italian Communist parties. At the same time the advance of a 'new conservatism', throwing aside any belief in equality, questioning the very basis of consensus politics has challenged liberal and social-democratic assumptions in many countries. In the socialist countries, a particular model of socialist development is now being challenged internally. Poland is only the most recent dramatic example of this.

Against this background an interest in the work of Antonio Gramsci continues. His ideas are referred to in a wide range of political discussions. In history, sociology, literature, politics and cultural studies courses, his work regularly forms part of the reading list. I would argue that this is not simply a question of fashion. Read with a critical spirit, with the realization that the problems of each age cannot possibly be resolved on the basis of any bible or dogma, Gramsci's work helps us to reflect on socialism, to understand Marx and Lenin and their theories of the state and politics. Perhaps, too, Gramsci appears particularly interesting today precisely because he argued against a dogmatic reading of Marxism.

This selection of articles on various aspects of Gramsci's thought is a personal choice. Most of the interpretations try to suggest a reading of Gramsci which shows his originality and usefulness for understanding contemporary problems. Particular stress is put on his anti-statism and his attempt to analyze actual political institutions. None of the articles argue that we can find ready-made solutions in his writings.

A theme running through the book is the concept of hegemony, the notion that any ruling class which moulds a society has to represent more than its narrow corporate interests. This is true of both the bourgeoisie and the proletariat. The state as force plus consent, the crucial nature of social relations, ideas, culture for the survival of a particular society appears over and over. The crisis of the liberal democratic state, the vast expansion of the intellectuals in modern society, the new relationship between the state and the economy, the need to study the concrete relationship between leaders and led are themes running through several articles. Underlying most of them is the question: what is the relationship between democracy — or political and economic control by the mass of the population — and the building of socialism? It is a question which is being posed widely today, both by critics of socialism who reject it altogether and by socialist critics of traditional left organizations like socialist feminists.

This anthology, then, is meant as a companion to reading Gramsci. It aims to suggest some of the questions which can be asked of his work. Because so much of interest has hitherto been unavailable in English, many of the articles are translations in which the original piece has been edited considerably in order to overcome the distance between discussions in the Anglo-Saxon world and those in France and

Italy. There are brief introductions to each article to help the reader enter what for many is unknown territory. A glossary and extended bibliography are also included. A brief biographical sketch accompanies a photographic insert to give a sense of Gramsci's historical setting.

It is hoped that both those who have never read Gramsci and those who have already studied his writings will find stimulating and useful material in this critical assessment of one of the principal thinkers of our century.

Anne Showstack Sassoon

A GRAMSCI DICTIONARY

These are some of the terms used by Gramsci and referred to in this book.
Since the exact meaning of many of them is the subject of some debate,
the following must be considered working definitions only.

Americanism and Fordism: This refers to the development
of assembly line production in the United States most notably
by Henry Ford. Gramsci was concerned with the significance
for the working class movement of the introduction of the
techniques of 'scientific management' as elaborated by the
American Frederick W. Taylor (thus 'Taylorism') in a period
in which this kind of rationalization of production was much
admired in the Soviet Union.

Civil Society: Gramsci defines this as 'the ensemble of
organisms commonly called "private" and contrasts it to
"political society" or "the State"'. (*SPN* 12) While he
differentiates the two areas, the relationship between the two
varies in his writings. The State at times seems to encompass or
at least balance the two areas of society; while the economy is
included within civil society. Although Gramsci's frequent use
of the term is evidence of Hegel's influence, he gives the term
new meaning. He is interested, on the one hand, in the
increasing complexity of social organization and social classes
in the private or non-political arena in advanced capitalist
societies; and, on the other, in the consequences of greater
state intervention in the economy and society in general.

Collective Will: This is organized, collective human activity which intervenes in the historical process given certain material conditions. Gramsci uses the term, which refers to what he calls 'collective man' rather than the individual, to refer to the creation of a new national-popular identity and the need for a wide, active popular intervention in the process of creating a new kind of state.

Common Sense: The incoherent and at times contradictory set of assumptions and beliefs held by the mass of the population at any one time. Common sense is differentiated by Gramsci from 'good sense' which refers to practical common sense in its English meaning. Gramsci investigates the relationship between this popular conception of the world and philosophy, religion and science.

Corporatism: Gramsci uses this term to indicate political or trade union activity which seeks to protect the narrow, particular, sectional interests of a group rather than the more general interests of the whole of society. Also known as economic-corporatism, it is related to economism.

Economism: A term which has a wide range of applications, it refers to the belief that the economy, understood in a simple way, is the primary factor determining historical development and all other aspects of society such as culture and politics. It is associated on the practical level with the defence of narrow, corporate interests. Put simply, an economistic or mechanistic view of history assumes that history unfolds automatically, going in a straight line of progress as the economy develops. Economism is one of the main objects of Gramsci's criticism in prison because, according to him, it prevents an adequate understanding of the state and of social groups and classes and thus prevents the working class movement from intervening effectively.

Hegemony: Probably Gramsci's key concept and the one which is the most controversial, hegemony is used in the sense of influence, leadership, consent rather than the alternative and opposite meaning of domination. It has to do with the way one social group influences other groups, making certain compromises with them in order to gain their consent for its leadership in society as a whole. Thus particular, sectional interests are transformed and some concept of the general interest is promoted. Hegemony has cultural, political and economic aspects and is the foundation of Gramsci's argument that the modern state is not simply an instrument of a class which it uses for its own narrow interest.

Historic Bloc: Gramsci uses this term to describe the complex way in which classes and factions of classes are related in society and the complicated relationship between economic, political and cultural aspects of reality. In Gramsci's writing it replaces any simple notion of an economic base or structure giving rise to a political and ideological superstructure, which is the traditional Marxist metaphor. An historic bloc is specific to a national context in which a different historic bloc may be created under the leadership of a revolutionary class. The hegemony of a class is the 'glue' which binds together the various parts of an historic bloc.

Intellectual and Moral Reform: This is a transformation of the way in which the mass of the population conceptualizes the role of the individual, his/her place in society and relationship to other human beings, to God, to the economy, and to politics. It is a change in the conception of the world held by most people comparable to that brought about by the Protestant Reformation or the French Revolution.

Intellectuals (organic, traditional): First, Gramsci uses the term intellectual in a broad sense, to indicate all those people who have an organizational or ideological-cultural role in society, *e.g.* school teachers, factory technicians and managers, civil servants, social workers, university professors, journalists *etc.* He then differentiates between organic intellectuals who perform tasks essential to the reproduction of a particular society, *e.g.* a capitalist one; and traditional intellectuals whose function derives from an earlier historical period, *e.g.* priests, but who continue to exist. Moreover, Gramsci relates the functions of all intellectuals to a capacity inherent in every human being, the ability to think and reason, which becomes a technical skill in certain people through study and practice.

Jacobinism: A term derived from the kind of leadership exerted by the Jacobins in the French Revolution. Its use by Gramsci and his attitude to it change as his view of bourgeois revolutions changes. In his earlier writings, he criticizes the authoritarian nature of Jacobinism viewed as the imposition of leadership by an élite. Later, while still criticizing what he considers a deleterious version of Jacobinism, he emphasizes the ability of the Jacobins to forge alliances and to establish a new state enjoying the consent of the mass of the population and engaged in constructing a new society.

National-popular: This refers on the one hand to the ability or inability of intellectuals in the wide sense to relate to the needs and aspirations of the mass of the population; and on the other to a view of the revolution as a struggle to unite a whole people against a small minority of exploiters and oppressors, thereby creating a new national identity. The question of the nation and of specific national traditions, and the needs of people at large are thus essential to the working class rather than marginal. Revolutionary transformation is redefined to indicate a change in which a variety of groups participate under the hegemony of a working class which is able to forge a new historic bloc and go beyond its own narrow, sectional interests.

Passive Revolution: This is a notion derived from conservative tradition going back to Edmund Burke who argued that society had to change in order to stay the same, *i.e.* to preserve its most essential features. It indicates historical changes which take place without widespread popular initiative, from 'on high'. Gramsci uses it to describe both specific historic developments, for example the establishment of an Italian nation-state, and a style of politics which preserves control by a relatively small group of leaders while at the same time instituting economic, social, political, and ideological changes.

Revolution as Process: Rather than viewing revolution as a dramatic break after which the new society begins to develop from scratch, Gramsci maintains that revolution must be understood as a process which begins within the old society and continues after moments of dramatic change. An old society will be destroyed in all its aspects only insofar as a new one is built and consolidated. Put differently, a revolutionary movement will be able to destroy the old only by building qualitatively new social relationships. In addition to this notion of construction-destruction, revolution as a process is related to Gramsci's view that a socialist revolution must be made by the mass of the population, not by a small élite.

Spontaneity: Gramsci argues that what appears to be spontaneous social or political activity, *i.e.* without any leadership, is always under the *de facto,* even if only implicit, influence of one or more sets of ideas, leaders, *etc.*; and therefore that true spontaneity does not exist. At the same time, he suggests that political leadership can only be effective if rooted in a mass movement whose complex and contradictory 'spontaneous' ideas and actions are understood and whose positive attributes are developed.

Statolatry: Literally meaning state worship, Gramsci uses this term to indicate an almost religious belief in the state's ability to bring about social transformation rather than the self-governing activities of the mass of the population. A contemporary term which is related is statism, or the giving to the state of enormous social and economic tasks.

Subaltern/Subordinate: This does not just mean oppressed, although that may be the case, but lacking autonomy, subjected to the influence or hegemony of another social group, not possessing one's own hegemonic position.

War of Movement (War of Manoeuvre): This is one of Gramsci's frequent military metaphors. It indicates a frontal confrontation or the kind of struggle associated with the 1848 revolutions in Europe or the 1917 revolution in Russia. The image is of manning the barricades and destroying the enemy as a result of a sharp clash between easily definable forces. Gramsci argues that this kind of strategy is appropriate where the state and civil society are less developed so that political power is more fragile, and mass trade unions, pressure groups, and party organizations are not yet developed. It is not a suitable strategy, he says, when faced with the more complex conditions of the interventionist state and mass organizations of modern advanced capitalist societies, where state authority is based on some degree of mass consent. The war of movement or dramatic and possibly violent struggle may still occur, but it recedes to being a moment within an overall strategy of war of position.

War of Position: Gramsci argues that a war of position or a kind of political trench warfare is necessary because of the nature of modern state power. It is a struggle which engages on a wide range of fronts in which the state as normally defined (government, parliament, *etc.*) is only one aspect. Involving all aspects of society, it is the only decisive form of engagement, not least because it is the form in which bourgeois power is exercised. It involves wide-ranging social organization and cultural influence, and it is only victory on these fronts which makes possible or conclusive a frontal attack or war of movement. Gramsci says that a war of position continues after the transformation of state power and while a new society is built and consolidated.

APPROACHES TO
GRAMSCI

I
A NEW SCIENCE OF POLITICS

GRAMSCI AND MARXIST
POLITICAL THEORY
Eric J. Hobsbawm

In this paper, read at a conference 40 years after Gramsci's death, Eric Hobsbawm discusses what he considers Gramsci's major contribution to Marxism - his political theory. While Marx considered politics primary and while there is an implied political theory in his writings, he never studied politics as an autonomous subject. Gramsci, Hobsbawm suggests, not only developed Marx's ideas but goes beyond him by redefining the very meaning of politics. His work concerns both a strategy for the transformation of capitalism and for building socialism. Gramsci poses the question of what is preserved from the past and what is changed. For him, as for Marx, there is a continuum between the over-throw of capitalism and the construction of socialism. But Gramsci went beyond both Marx and Lenin in his analysis of the political and not just organizational nature of the party and its task in helping to construct elements of a new society; as well as in the attention he paid to the relations between leaders, party and masses. He is, moreover, original in his thinking about the relationship between the working class and the nation: 'the national question' is for him not external to the working class movement, but integral to its task. The revolution is a struggle to lead and represent the whole people and to isolate the minority of exploiters and the oppressors.

Hobsbawm points out that Gramsci's concept of hegemony is not just relevant for advanced Western countries but for every revolutionary situation since the problem of winning and maintaining the consent of the vast majority of the population always exists. Criticizing the limits of Lenin's classic State and Revolution, *he argues that politics and political institutions have been neglected in socialist societies and that there can be no socialism without democracy, without the participation of the mass of the population in the political process.*

Gramsci had learnt from his experience in Turin that a revolutionary transformation had to be rooted in those elements in the mass movement which were not just corporative but tended toward a transformation of human potential. This is a theme which is developed in considerable detail in the last piece in this collection, Alberto Maria Cirese's analysis of Gramsci's notes on folklore.

Perhaps the most useful thing I can do is to try to assess the importance of what I believe to be Gramsci's major contribution to Marxism, his pioneer work on a Marxist political theory. Gramsci's theory is neither complete, nor immune to criticism. Nor has it, or ought it to have, the status of a classic text, to which we appeal in order to settle theoretical disputes. Some forty years after his death we honour a noble man, a leader of the communist movement, and an enormously original and fertile Marxist thinker. We congratulate ourselves on his growing influence. Nevertheless, I hope we shall all continue to read Gramsci as a thinker and a guide and not as a dogmatic authority. Let us follow his example and think for ourselves, even if this may lead us to disagree with him.

Marx did not develop a comprehensive theory of politics, comparable to his economic analysis, because in one sense the field of politics was analytically secondary for him. He did indeed begin his theoretical labours with a critique of political theory, namely that of Hegel's *Philosophy of Law* (1843), but he soon realized that it was political economy which was 'the anatomy of civil society' and therefore concentrated on its critique. Moreover, for polemical reasons it seemed important to him to stress above all that 'legal relations as well as forms of state could not be understood from themselves, but are rooted in the material conditions of life'. Therefore the materialist conception of history actually discouraged the study of politics and the state as autonomous subjects – except in the crucial field of the state and revolution. Perhaps, as Engels admitted in some of his late letters (to Mehring XXXIX, 96ff) Marx and he had gone too far in this direction. Though there is an enormous quantity of Marx's and Engels' writings about politics, much of which was unknown to Gramsci, there is no systematic analysis of the subject.

Nevertheless, in Marx's praxis, politics was absolutely primary. As he pointed out when criticizing Proudhon, in class society 'social evolutions' must be 'political revolutions', and indeed during Marx's lifetime the main criterion which distinguished Marxian socialists from all other socialists, communists and anarchists (except those deriving from the Jacobin tradition) and from trade union and cooperative movements of the working class, was precisely the belief in the essential role of politics before, during and after the revolution. A theory of politics is therefore implicit in Marx, as Gramsci recognized. There are historical reasons why it was not developed by him. I will mention merely two of them.

First, for most of Marx's life – at any rate after the defeat of the 1848 revolutions – the prospect of revolution was remote. The main task was to form the growing proletariat into a political class movement, but its prospects of gaining power or even of influencing government except by pressure from below, were remote. Second, neither Marx nor Engels were able actually to lead an organized movement or party after the end of the Communist League, and therefore were unfamiliar with the kind of organized socialist mass working class movement which developed in the 1880s and 1890s. It is important to remember that Gramsci wrote not only as a theorist and an active participant in politics, but as a leader of a communist party and one with the experience of an actual mass proletarian movement, that of Turin. In this respect he had an advantage even over Lenin, for such a mass proletarian movement had not been possible in Tsarist Russia. Before 1917 Lenin wrote as the leader of a small, illegal or barely legal cadre party. He could not have experience of a permanent and rooted but at the same time revolutionary mass working class movement playing a major part on the political scene of its country. Gramsci had this advantage.

Gramsci's political theory, however, is more than a mere process of making explicit what is implicit in Marx. It is not merely the recognition that politics is an autonomous activity, within the context, limits and determinations established by historical development. Politics, as Gramsci's English editors have rightly said (*PN* XXIII) is for him 'the central human activity, the means by which the single consciousness is brought into contact with the social and natural world in all its forms'. That is to say it is wider than the term as commonly used; wider even than what Gramsci himself, in a narrower sense, describes as 'the science and art of politics'. It goes beyond the field of 'the State' – even of the state in the broad form as conceived by Gramsci, namely, 'the entire complex of practical and theoretical activities with which the ruling class not only justifies and maintains its dominance, but manages to win the active consent of those over whom it rules'. (*SPN* 244) For 'every man, in as much as he is active, *i.e.* living, contributes to modifying the social environment in which he develops . . . in other words, he tends to establish "norms", rules of living and of behaviour'. (*SPN* 265) This contribution is 'politics'.

What is more novel, Gramsci insists that it must be analyzed as politics, not merely at the level usually recognized as such – as the level of state and party – but at all levels; in other words that sociological analysis must be reformulated as politics, *i.e.* in terms of action to change the world, and not merely to interpret it. Hence politics is not only instrumental. It is not simply a means for achieving ends distinct from it. It is both the winning of power and the core of the new society itself – of socialism. And indeed it is not, and cannot be, confined to the realm of the state, because socio-political relations between human beings in Gramsci's sense will survive even the disappearance of the state. This double aspect of politics, and this continuity between the movement to overcome the old society and the construction of the new, is well brought out in several recent articles. (*cf* Giuseppe Vacca) The point is that Gramsci realizes that Marx's own 'philosophy of praxis' requires the systematization and concretization of a science of political action. Machiavelli, or someone who thinks in terms of an autonomous politics, is a necessary complement to Marx.

This is not a matter of theory only but of practical importance, both for the strategy of transforming capitalism into socialism and for the development of socialist societies. Gramsci's writing is profoundly concerned with both, though many commentators, especially abroad, tend to stress only one aspect of it, namely the strategic. Moreover it is essential for socialists to develop such a theory today, and this is why Gramsci's thought is of particular importance. For our movement has been slow to develop adequate strategic thinking about the transformation of society, and even slower to develop adequate thought about the form and content of socialist societies. Let me say a few words about both.

For a long period of its history the socialist movement did not require – or thought it did not require – much strategic thinking about the politics of transforming capitalism into socialism. Both classical social-democracy in the period of the Second International and its opponents on the left tended, in different ways, to share the assumption that the transformation to socialism would, and indeed could, only begin on the day that the proletariat and its party acceded to power, whether by revolution or by winning the magical minimum of 51% of votes. What happened before that moment of power-transfer was significant only insofar as it prepared the transfer. Conversely, what happened from that day on – if it was a transfer of power – had no real connection with what went before. The movement before the power-transfer operated within the institutional system and the politics of the bourgeois state, but did not belong to it, and tried – though in practice this was impossible – to isolate itself from it. The social-democratic leaders themselves were passionately and systematically opposed to any participation in 'bourgeois' governments, sometimes even to any support for them. They could indeed be criticized by revolutionaries, because they did not even possess any strategy for winning power, since they relied on history to do this task for them. The proletariat, inevitably growing in numbers as capitalist concentration polarized society between a majority of workers and a diminishing minority of bourgeois, would eventually win electoral and therefore real power, because it would be the great majority of the people. The primary task of the parties was to mobilize and organize this growing army for a victory whose very date could sometimes be forecast by extrapolating the curve of the growth of socialist votes. However, though criticism from the left was easy, and justified, we must not forget that the revolutionaries themselves, if they were Marxists, also believed in an eventual polarization of society, and that they also considered the activities of the movement before the revolution simply as the preparation for the great moment of the revolution itself.

In the western countries – *i.e.* in the countries of mass

socialist and labour movements – the question of the political strategy of transformation was raised, paradoxically, only on the right of the movement. The critique of Revisionists and Fabians was rejected by both left and centre, since the revisionists seemed interested in strategy but no longer in socialism. Bernstein's famous phrase 'the movement means everything to me, the final aim of socialism nothing' allowed socialists to dismiss him. They were indeed right to reject revisionism. And yet the revisionists' critique raised three questions which required an answer, though not the revisionist one.

The first was: what were the implications for socialist strategy of the fact that the other classes and strata were not disappearing or being merged into the industrial and agricultural proletariat? Second: what would the movement do if by any chance the prospect of a single dramatic seizure of power – whether by insurrection or electoral triumph – proved unrealistic? Third, and more generally, could the movement assume that it stood entirely outside the politics of capitalist society, that the reforms it forced upon it were merely 'palliatives' and had no relation to the movement's prospects of power or to the socialism it intended to build subsequently? In the western movements these questions were not answered at all, and sometimes not even recognized. The social-democratic leaders therefore found themselves practising revisionism – reformism and opportunism – today while declaring that one day they would do something quite different. They were correctly criticized by the left, but most of that left, notably the anarchists and revolutionary syndicalists, had no alternative strategy except to reject politics altogether. They merely substituted a call for militant struggle, or an unrealistic leftism which demonstrated its bankruptcy in 1914 just as much as social democracy did.

In the non-industrial countries of Eastern Europe, and especially in Russia, a political strategy of transformation was indeed developed. However, for obvious reasons it was only partial, since two of the questions raised by the revisionists did not appear to require an answer. No alternative road to power except revolution was conceivable in practice, and was therefore seriously considered. (This is no longer so in all countries of the Third World today). The movement, even when not completely illegal, stood as an enemy outside state and society, and its integration into it through politics or reforms seemed negligible. On the other hand it was clear from the outset that revolution would have to be made not by the small proletarian minority alone, but by a broad front or alliance of the oppressed and discontented; and that even after the revolution the relations between the proletariat and other classes (notably the peasantry) would be crucial. To this extent Marxists in countries like Russia had to – and did – confront problems of political strategy which western social-democrats could hide from themselves; including the national question. In confronting such strategic problems they returned to Marx and Engels, who had paid considerable attention to such questions, especially in the period round 1848, and again in the period of the Paris Commune. In fact, the modern Marxist discussion of political strategy, including Gramsci's own, derives from the Russian strategic debates, as is clear when we consider the history of so characteristic a Gramscian term as 'hegemony'.

However, the very brilliance and profundity of Lenin's strategy and the success of the Bolsheviks in 1917 inhibited further development of theory. Strategy now aimed at the reproduction of October revolutions elsewhere. But from the early 1920s it became clear that October was a special case and not a general model. There were no other October revolutions, and even in other revolutionary countries – notably in China – defeat made a rethinking of strategy essential. At the same time – though communists did not pay much attention to it – the hopes of classical social-democracy also broke down. For 1914 had merely been a failure of social democracy in opposition. But in 1918–20 such parties actually found themselves in power in Germany and Austria, and failed even more dramatically. Most communists at the time dismissed this failure as simple treason, but it was more than this. Otto Bauer was not a Weimar Ebert or a Noske, but a genuine non-Bolshevik socialist. Yet Austrian Social Democracy also failed. It was at this historic moment that systematic Marxist thought about the political strategy of transformation became indispensable. It grew, not out of victory but out of defeat, not out of success but out of failure.

This failure became even more tragically evident in the west during the great crisis of the early 1930s and the triumph of fascism. It is significant that the bulk of Gramsci's writings in the *Notebooks* dates from these years of crisis. By this time it was not only clear that the movement could not regard itself as standing, in some sense, outside capitalist society, preparing for the single dramatic moment of its overthrow. It was also clear that the defeat of revolution (and of social-democratic hopes) did not leave the contestants in the class struggle unchanged, to prepare for a next battle like the last. Capitalism itself was changing, in part to meet the challenge of successful revolution in Russia, of unsuccessful revolutionary forces elsewhere: hence Gramsci's reflections on 'revolution/restoration' and 'passive revolution', which are attempts to give revolutionary and Marxist answers to the question of the dynamic relation between socialist movement and regime raised, in a wrong and uncritical form, during the revisionist controversy. They refer not only to fascism, which he saw as perhaps 'the form of passive revolution belonging to the twentieth century just as liberalism had been in the nineteenth', but also more generally to the changes in the structure of modern capitalism, which Gramsci noted in the USA. (*SPN* 279ff) (This initial passage of *Notebook 22* on Americanism and Fordism as Buci-Glucksmann shows is a particularly impressive example of Gramsci's genius.[1]) Finally, it became clear with the triumph of fascism that it was no longer possible to treat capitalist state power as an essentially homogeneous entity; to take a basically liberal democracy for granted as the framework for working class struggle, even in western countries.

It is the merit of the international communist movement that it pioneered new strategic thinking about the transformation. I cannot think of any equivalent within the socialist parties. Nevertheless, for obvious reasons, this development was limited and distorted until after 1956. That is why we are today not much further than Gramsci was 40 years ago. The situation itself is greatly changed, but our theory is not. Thus, while we are today considering the transition to socialism under conditions of a pluri-party democracy – which Gramsci did not – we have been slow to reflect, in the Gramscian way, on the historical experience of such a process (*e.g.* in the transition from pre-bourgeois to bourgeois society), and its implications for the future.

Let me make a few observations about Gramsci's own strategic thinking. I am not here interested in Gramsci's assessment of the Italian Communist Party's (PCI) strategy at any time in his life, or in the PCI's strategies, which have certainly been inspired by its leaders' interpretation of Gramsci. Our judgment of Gramsci does not depend on whether we think he was right in 1924 or 1930. I think that Marx's attitude towards the regime of Napoleon III was often wrong and unrealistic, but the *18th Brumaire* remains a profound and fundamental work. Similarly our judgment of the policy of the PCI should not depend on whether it has the textual authority of Gramsci or anyone else. There has been, especially in Italy, too much writing which judges Gramsci as a strategic thinker by whether the writer approves or disapproves of the policy of the PCI now or in the past. I would like to look at him in a more general perspective.

The most original characteristic of Gramsci's strategic thought is that, in spite of his fondness for military metaphors, he never became their prisoner. For the soldier, war is not peace, even if it is the continuation of politics by other means, and victory is, speaking professionally, an end in itself. Yet for Gramsci (as for Marx) the struggle to overthrow capitalism and build socialism is essentially a continuum, in which the actual transfer of power is only one moment.

This follows from the Gramscian view of bourgeois society as a system both of domination and hegemony, for it is only domination, the coercive power of the state, which can be transferred by the single victory of a successful seizure of power. It also follows from Gramsci's concept (which again recalls Marx) of the new society as the working class, *i.e.* the working class as a party, *becoming the state* and in doing so eventually absorbing the now unnecessary state into civil society. The bourgeoisie was unable to do this. (Q 937) The struggle to turn the working class and its party into a potential ruling class, the struggle for hegemony, is therefore *also* the process by which it constructs, even before the transfer of power, the elements of the new society which will develop after it. Gramsci's view of the party is therefore political rather than organizational. Like the later Marx he conceives the party as the organized class, but unlike Marx, who says little about the party, he devotes enormous attention to the nature of the organic leadership between leaders, party and masses. In this respect he also goes beyond Marx's successors, including Lenin. They, it seems to me, tended to see these relationships as posing organizational rather than political problems. I have noted elsewhere the limitations of the famous debate on *Done?* Thirdly, Gramsci's strategy follows from his concept – quite original in Marxism – of the working class as part of the *nation*. Indeed, I believe that he is so far the only Marxist thinker who provides us with a basis of integrating the nation as a historical and social reality into Marxist theory. He breaks with the habit of seeing it as 'the national question', something external to the working class movement, towards which we have to define our attitude.

That Gramsci conceives of the transformation to socialism as a continuum does not mean that he committed himself on principle to any particular strategy or forecast. He was not a 'euro-communist' *avant la lettre*, for him analysis was neither designed exclusively for developed 'western' countries – in the Italy of his time it could not be – nor is it exclusively applicable to them. It was natural that he opted for a strategy of protracted struggle – the 'war of position' – since the alternative of a new October was unrealistic. It is still unrealistic, including today in many countries of the Third World. But he did not commit himself to any particular outcome of this 'war of position'. It might lead directly, sooner or later, to a transition to socialism, or into another war of manoeuvre, or into some other strategic phase. What he insisted on was that the struggle could not *only* be one for power – whatever the nature of the campaigns and battles – and that the actual transfer of power, however it occurred, was merely one moment, though a crucial one, in the transformation. We need not defend him against the accusation of being a gradualist, or even of encouraging gradualism. He obviously did not believe, and neither do his followers, that the gradual accumulation of reforms and changes within capitalism, even structural reforms, will automatically and spontaneously transform capitalism into socialism. Indeed his theory of 'passive revolution' implies the opposite. Continuity of political transformation is not the same as continuity through evolution.

We must, in short, beware of a purely localized 'western' reading of Gramsci. Thus the struggle for hegemony *before* as well as during the transition to power is not merely an aspect of the war of position characteristic of western countries, but of all revolutionary strategy. It is naturally of special importance in countries where the core of ruling class power lies in the willing subalternity of the masses rather than in coercion, as in the west; in countries in which the ruling class, having to choose between the alternatives of hegemony and force, the velvet glove and the iron fist, have chosen hegemony – though, as always, keeping coercion in reserve. However, as we may see even in countries in which there has been a revolutionary overthrow of the old rulers, revolution may run into trouble because it has failed to develop a hegemonic force; as in Portugal. The revolution must still win enough consent and support from strata not yet detached from the old regimes. The basic problem of hegemony is not *how* revolutionaries come to power, though this is very important. It is how they come to be accepted, not only as the politically existing or irreplaceable rulers, but as guides and leaders. There are two aspects to this: how revolutionaries win assent and whether they are ready to exercise leadership.

There is also the concrete political situation, both national and international, which may make their task easier or more difficult. The Polish communists in 1945 established their power and were ready to exercise hegemony, but were probably not then accepted as a hegemonic force in that country. The German social-democrats in 1918 would probably have been accepted as a hegemonic force, but refused to accept that responsibility. Therein lies the tragedy of the German revolution. The Czech communists might have been accepted as a hegemonic force both in 1945 and in 1968, and were ready to play this role, but were not allowed to do so. The struggle for hegemony before, during and after the transition remains crucial in all circumstances. Power alone, even revolutionary power, cannot replace it.

Similarly, continuity is not only a problem affecting strategy in bourgeois-democratic countries. It is one of Gramsci's greatest merits to have discussed the dialectic of continuity and revolution; to have raised the question – seldom asked by Marxists – what exactly in the past is transformed by a revolution and what is conserved, and why, and how; of the way in which revolution is both the negation and the fulfilment of a people's past history. For cohesion and continuity belong to human societies. These are more than mechanisms of economic domination and political power. As Engels knew, they have a certain cohesion even when riven by class antagonisms – and indeed these very anatagonisms take their concrete form from them, and develop within the framework of specific countries and peoples. It is the identification of the society, the nation, the people past and present, with the state and civil society of the rulers which is the strongest element in their hegemony. Conversely, the struggle for hegemony, for victory in a revolution, and for the defence of a victorious revolution is so often, concretely, the struggle to represent and lead the entire people and nation – and in so doing to isolate the minority of exploiters and oppressors. That is what the communist movement tried to do during the period of anti-fascist unity, popular front and resistance; but let us not forget that even the Paris Commune was a rising of French patriotism – revolutionary patriotism. Gramsci recognized the enormous practical as well as theoretical significance of this relation between class and society, people or nation, between historic past, present and future more clearly than even Marx did, and we now know how important it is. And it is precisely because we can no longer rely on the simple growth of the manual proletariat until it becomes the overwhelming numerical majority of the nation, that the task of establishing the working-class movement as the leader of the nation is today more significant than ever.

Let me now turn, more briefly, to the other aspect of Gramsci's political theory: the nature of socialism. Like all Marxists, Gramsci was suspicious of speculations about the socialist future or utopian visions, and he was right. The weakness of utopianism, which is once again in fashion, lies not only in its a-historicity, but in its lack of organic contact with the social reality it wishes to transform. One of its most persistently surviving strands demonstrates this: architecture. Revolutionary architecture has always been given to designing, sometimes even to constructing, ideal cities and ideal environments for living. They have almost always – I am thinking of Le Corbusier but not only of him – either proved unrealizable or unattractive to those who are supposed to live in them. Indeed, architectural experience is one of the strongest arguments for

Gramsci's call for organic intellectuals. Nevertheless, from the 1920s on the discussion of socialist society was no longer a matter of speculation or utopian plans. And, as Gramsci saw with great clarity, its crux was the analysis of the politics and political organization of socialist states.

Here the socialist tradition was particularly weak. Lenin himself recognized the need for systematic thought on this subject on the eve of the October Revolution, but as we know he had not time to finish his *State and Revolution*. We cannot assume that it would have faced the actual problems which emerged in the course of the history of Soviet Russia, for the Marxist tradition of political thought had two major weaknesses. In spite of Marx's and Engels' more sophisticated approach, it tended to simplify the theory of the state into one of class power, the reversal of class power in the dictatorship of the proletariat, a withering away of the state, and a disappearance of politics. Yet it has become increasingly evident that communists must consider the political organization of socialist regimes, the process of political decision-making, and the relations between government and people in them. Indeed the necessity of this could be seen as early as 1921 when it became evident that even inner-party democracy in Soviet Russia was seriously undermined.

The systematic neglect of politics in socialist societies contrasts with the experience of bourgeois revolutions and bourgeois societies. For historical reasons which need not concern us here, such societies in the nineteenth century always paid primary attention to their political institutions and mechanisms. That is why political arrangements have become a powerful means for reinforcing bourgeois hegemony. Slogans such as 'the defence of the Republic', 'the defence of democracy' or the defence of civil rights and freedoms bind rulers and ruled together. This is no doubt for the primary benefit of the rulers, but this does not mean that they are irrelevant to the ruled. They are thus far more than mere cosmetics on the face of coercion, more even than simple political trickery.

Socialist societies, also for comprehensible historical reasons, have concentrated on other tasks – notably on planning economic growth. But they have hitherto also systematically neglected to pay attention to their actual institutional, political and legal processes; except perhaps in

multi-national states, those concerned with the relations between their national components. I shall not discuss the historic
reasons for this omission, but the result is that these processes
have been left to operate informally and in obscurity. The gap
between official laws and constitutions and political realities
always exists, but in socialist states up to the present it has
been particularly wide. This applies even to the constitutions
and statutes which were actually supposed to be effective, such
as those of the state parties. For long periods these were
systematically broken, *e.g.* by the failure to call regular con-
gresses and other assemblies. It is now clear that this neglect to
consider the political dimension of socialist states creates
critical problems for them and jeopardizes the future of socialism. How can we expect to transform human life, to create a
socialist *society,* as distinct from a socially owned and managed
economy, when the mass of the people, or even the mass of the
state party, are excluded from the political processes? Something is plainly very wrong when, as in China, major political
decisions, affecting the future of the country, appear suddenly
and in a manner reminiscent of palace intrigues in imperial
Rome and Byzantium. How can any socialist be satisfied even
by primitive, dangerous and inefficient mechanisms of politics
such as now appear to evolve here and there, in which absolutism is mitigated by periodic concessions to technically illegal
mass strikes? We now recognize that there are politics in a
socialist society and that it must provide a place, even an
institutional form, for them.

This, surely, lies behind our revaluation of political democracy. If I were to criticize the present discussions on 'euro-
communism' it would be for seeing this problem in eurocentric
terms, *i.e.* specifically in terms of countries which possess
certain political institutions and practices. It also exists in
countries lacking these institutions. Democracy requires institutions, formal or informal, everywhere – not necessarily those
of western constitutions and pluri-party institutions, though
in countries such as Italy and Britain these will be the general
framework and the basis for further democratic development.
But we should beware of a tendency to divide the world into
two parts, one in which political democracy is indispensable,
the other in which it is not. Democracy is indivisible. In one
form or another there can be no socialism without it.

How and why was such an unsatisfactory situation allowed to develop in socialist countries? Because the traditional Marxist conception of socialism and the transition to socialism lacked that systematic political conception which is at the heart of Gramsci's approach. Because it conceived the development of a new society and new human relations as a natural by-product of socialization in the economic sense, *i.e.* the socially owned and planned economy which is its necessary basis and framework, and not as *politics* which 'is permanent action and gives birth to permanent organizations precisely insofar as it is identical with economics'. (Q 1022) Gramsci does not deny the importance of the socialist economy, and certainly not the necessity to maximize production, but he denies the possibility of isolating production as a technical or economic problem. Consequently he also avoids the opposite error, found not only in Maoism, which counterposes economic and non-economic behaviour and incentives, or in its extreme form 'being red' and 'being expert'. For, as he recognizes in his critique of Bukharin, a voluntarist idealism is the other face of an economic determinism.

Secondly, the traditional Marxist conception, including the Bolshevik, assumed as solved the fundamental question to which Gramsci devoted so much attention: that of the relation between leaders, party and masses. What we criticize in so many of the socialist states derives precisely from the identification of leaders with party and masses. This problem to which Gramsci returns time and again is that of the genuine formation of a 'collective will' based on 'active and conscious co-participation' on 'socialization' in the sociological (or rather, in Gramsci's terms, political) sense of the word. But this is not only, as Badaloni puts it 'the formation of habits of the collective political man which themselves became automatic, making superfluous apparatuses which would impose them from the outside.'[2] It is also the school of a new consciousness, a fuller humanity for the socialist future. I cannot claim that Gramsci solved, or even completely confronted the difficulties he recognized. His observations on democratic centralism or on bureaucracy show not so much pessimism of the intelligence as optimism of will. Nevertheless, unlike other critics of 'substitutism' on the left, Gramsci knows that the problem is political even in the narrower sense of the term, for it deals with the relation between leaders and followers, between administrators and the administered, between organizations and the unorganized.

It is the active and conscious participation of the people which is the key to social transformation. I think Gramsci learned this from his experience in a genuine mass movement of the proletariat, that of the Turin workers. I return to this point, since revolutionary Marxists with such experience were rare in his time. Those who had this experience before 1917 were mainly reformists, and did not pay adequate attention to the elements in the mass movements of labour which were not merely instrumental and corporative, but which brought about a new consciousness, a transformation in human potential. In these movements men and women could be seen to make and remake themselves, and in doing so to begin the process of remaking humanity under socialism. That is why Gramsci's exploration of the way to socialism and of socialism itself is largely through a repeated, elaborate and microscopic analysis of the nature, structure and development of the political movement, the party. That is why he traces with such care the emergence of a permanent and organized movement – as distinct from a rapid 'explosion' – down to its smallest capillary and molecular elements. For the 'Modern Prince' the party 'is at one and the same time the organizer and the active, operative expression' of a 'national-popular collective will' and 'the proclaimer and organizer of an intellectual and moral reform, which also means creating the terrain for a subsequent development . . . towards the realization of a superior, total form of modern civilization'. (*SPN* 132-3)

Let me conclude with yet another quotation from Gramsci. Criticizing the distortion of Marx's tradition by Bukharin, he observed, correctly: 'The philosophy of praxis was born in the form of aphorisms and practical criteria for the purely accidental reason that its founder dedicated his intellectual forces to other problems, particularly economic (which he treated in systematic form); but in these practical criteria and these aphorisms is implicit an entire conception of the world, an entire philosophy.' (Q 426) It is this which Gramsci attempted to make explicit and to develop in the form of a theory of politics. He knew that it required making explicit and developing – even beyond Marx and Lenin. We are fortunate enough to be able to continue his labours. I hope we shall do so with as much independence as he did.

NOTES

1 See her article, 'State, transition and passive revolution,' in *Gramsci and Marxist Theory*, edited by Chantal Mouffe, London, 1979.
2 Nicola Badaloni, *Il marxismo di Gramsci*, Turin, 1975, p 165.

INTELLECTUALS AND THE MARXIST
THEORY OF THE STATE
Giuseppe Vacca

This article argues that the central thread running through Gramsci's writings is the theme of the intellectuals. It emphasizes the political nature of this question by taking as a definition Gramsci's own view that the intellectuals must be considered in terms of their organizational and directive functions, and in this wide sense seen as part of the government apparatus. It is the intellectuals who constitute a web of relations between the mass of the population and the state, between leaders and led. Gramsci's investigation of the role of the intellectuals in modern society is part of his attempt to understand what actually links the world of production and civil or private society with the political realm, given the increasing state intervention in the economy and society as a whole.

Because he sees the theme of the intellectuals as a connecting thread, Vacca's approach is wide ranging. He begins by examining changes in the status of the intellectuals as a result of the development of industrial society and traces the crisis of the intellectuals related to the First World War and its aftermath. He then considers the changed perspective for a proletarian revolution after the October 1917 Revolution in Russia and the consequences for revolutionary strategy. He goes on to consider Gramsci's contribution to a Marxist theory of the state; and his notes on totalitarianism which Vacca argues can be read in terms of the Soviet Union. Because Gramsci studies the actual forms, institutions, customs, conventions of real states, of concrete political systems, he sees the state not only as the instrument of a class, as Marx, Engels and Lenin had maintained, but as a complex web of relationships. Thus the proletariat must create a new complex of relations to establish a new kind of state. The question of creating organic intellectuals of the working class, that is, intellectuals who will provide the links between leaders and led in a socialist society, is not just a matter of substituting a new group for an old one but of creating a new organization of knowledge by the mass of the population.

Towards the end of 1931, Gramsci began drafting the ten notebooks that constitute the central core of the *Prison Notebooks*. Here, besides his new notes and comments, he further developed a great part of what was already contained in the first seven notebooks which date from the three-year period 1929-1931. The main themes of his prison research thus received fuller elaboration in monograph form, and as such were destined to remain definitive. In these ten central notebooks, the main monographic subjects – Croce, the study of philosophy, the history of the intellectuals, Machiavelli's politics – were all reworked. The monographic studies on the Risorgimento and on *Americanism and Fordism*, re-elaborated in 1934-35 and put in order in notebooks 19 and 22, complete the framework of the basic themes of his prison research.

Attention must be drawn to one fact. At the start of the eighth notebook, the first one of the second series, Gramsci, in putting together a summary index of all his subjects of study, presented his entire prison research under the title *Scattered notes and comments for a history of the Italian intellectuals*. (Q 935-6) The entire *Prison Notebooks*, then, are conceived of by Gramsci as an enquiry into the intellectuals. The crisis of the inter-war years, the analysis of fascism, the investigation of Italian history, the enquiries into American society, the reflections on political theory and the reformulation of Marxism: all these themes are gathered together under the single heading of an enquiry into the intellectuals.

Gramsci's whole thought thus emerges as an attempt to work out a theory of proletarian revolution after the October Revolution, in the presence of a defeated workers' movement in Europe, and a general reorganization of capitalism in Italy which has different historical characteristics from Russia; characteristics which in fact have been determined by the modern development of the whole of Western Europe.

If we wish to understand Gramsci's conception of the intellectuals in a concrete historical, and not an academic, fashion, we must begin here. We must then ask ourselves: why does the whole of Gramsci's thinking on the proletarian revolution take the form of a theory of the intellectuals?

The Inter-war Crisis and the Traditional Elite Intellectuals

Gramsci states:

> Since the State is the concrete form of a productive world and since the intellectuals are the social element from which the governing personnel is drawn, the intellectual who is not firmly anchored to a strong economic group will tend to present the State as an absolute; in this way the function of the intellectuals is itself conceived of as absolute and pre-eminent, and their historical existence and dignity are abstractly rationalised. This motive is fundamental for an historical understanding of modern philosophical idealism, and is connected with the mode of formation of the modern States of continental Europe. (*SPN* 117)

This is how Gramsci sums up relations between intellectuals and state as developed in European culture and above all in 'classical German philosophy' from Kant to Hegel.

With the transition to the age of imperialism, this type of intellectual-functionary went into crisis. At the ideological level, it was no longer possible for intellectual groups to conceive of themselves as 'absolute' élites. The growth of mass production and increasing state intervention gave rise to an age where science was progressively subsumed by capital and to a standardization of the intellectuals. Bourgeois culture reacted to the crisis which developed by elaborating a new status for the intellectuals' changed condition. It developed a theory which allowed for the separation between nature and history, science and philosophy, economics and politics, knowledge and values. The figure of the intellectual was transformed into an 'expert' and only as such relocated in the functions of the ruling classes.

The Working Class Movement and the Intellectuals

The working class movement, for its part, did not succeed in developing an answer to this crisis. The whole turn-of-the-century polemic on revisionism could be read as a great debate on the structural changes in capitalist societies, focussing on the question of the intellectuals[1]. But, Lenin aside, who in fact became involved with these themes only after 1905[2], there was an oscillation in the European workers' movement between a crudely anti-intellectual response, coming from the new anarcho-syndicalist currents including Sorel himself, and a capitulation before the new orientations of the bourgeois intelligentsia, as in the case of the social democrat Bernstein and the neo-Kantians. At the centre of all this was Kautsky, who in his writings on the intellectuals ineffectively extends the perspective of the proletarianization of society[3]. Only an isolated minority, which included the Austrian Marxist, Max Adler, placed the question of the intellectuals at the centre of the debate with Bernstein about revisionism, and argued that Marxism had to measure itself seriously against the new bourgeois culture. The main problem that faced the workers' movement in the period of imperialism was that of developing an ethical-political dimension to the struggle for socialism.

The war and the October Revolution intervened against this background and also threw the cadres of bourgeois culture into disarray. Max Weber's celebrated lecture to the young German officers is symbolic of the adjustment that European high culture had to make in the definition of its status. 'Specialization', 'research free from value conditioning', were the horizons now indicated by Weber for 'science as a vocation', separating it for ever from politics, the sphere of another 'specialization'[4]. Faced with the war and the eruption of the new political passions of the masses, the perspective followed in Italy by Croce, the intellectual leader of the nation, was no different.

The Ordine Nuovo and After

The line followed by the intellectual group that Gramsci inspired and in which he underwent his first political and theoretical test was quite different. The *Ordine Nuovo*'s entire emphasis was directed towards the definition of the historic transformations that emerged from the imperialist war and the October Revolution. It was an intellectual group of the highest rank: men such as Gramsci, Togliatti, Tasca, Terracini; and their review included what was best in the European intellectual debate. But above all they made their review the cultural instrument of a new political movement. Moved initially 'by a vague passion for a vague proletarian culture', they reacted very quickly to the crisis in Italian society by contributing to the construction of a new state. In so far as they were an intellectual group they set themselves the problem of the state. In so far as they were socialists, faced with the Russian Revolution, they asked themselves:

> Is there any working-class institution in Italy that can be compared to the Soviet, that shares some of its characteristics?.. Something that would allow us to say: the Soviet is a universal form, not a Russian, and only a Russian, institution; wherever there exist proletarians struggling to win for themselves industrial autonomy, the Soviet is the form in which the working class manifests this determination to emancipate itself; the Soviet is the form of self-government of the working masses. Is there any germ, a vague hope or hint of such Soviet-style government in Italy, in Turin? (*PWI* 291)

An answer was found to these questions in the factory committees known as internal commissions. What is relevant for our discussion is the perspective that such an attitude opened up for both analysis and redefinition of the status of the intellectuals.

The famous essay *Some Aspects of the Southern Question*, which Gramsci wrote a few months before his arrest in 1926, defines the main lines of the research that he was to develop in prison, re-elaborating at the theoretical level the revolutionary experiences of the tumultuous decade 1917-1926. In this essay, Gramsci already establishes the importance that the *Ordine Nuovo* movement had in changing some of the basic elements of the Italian intellectual tradition; and in posing the complex question of the intellectuals' relation to the working class.

The point of rupture lies in the group's refusing a whole tradition of thought in which intellectuals, sheltering behind the particular way in which the state had hitherto existed, conceived of themselves as the protagonists of historical development. The intellectuals of the *Ordine Nuovo* on the other hand concretely 'posed the urban proletariat as the modern protagonist of Italian history . . . translating into national historical language' the thought of Marx and the work of Lenin. The result was that 'having served as intermediaries between the proletariat and certain strata of left intellectuals, they succeeded in modifying – if not completely at least to a notable extent – their mental outlook'.

As proof of this, Gramsci points to the figure of the liberal intellectual, Piero Gobetti, a man destined to become central to post-fascist Italian culture. He 'was not a communist and probably would never have become one. But he had understood the social and historical position of the proletariat, and could no longer think in abstraction from this element.' This is the source of his anti-fascist influence on the new Italian intelligentsia.

Gramsci derived his understanding of the centrality of the intellectuals in the struggle for socialism from this experience. The essay on the Southern question concludes with a theoretical sketch which makes the question of the intellectuals the kernel of Marxist reflection on the state-revolution nexus.

> The proletariat, as a class, is poor in organising elements. It does not have its own stratum of intellectuals, and can only create one very slowly, very painfully, after the winning of state power. But it is important and useful for a break to occur in the mass of intellectuals: a break of an organic kind, historically charac-terised. For there to be formed, as a mass formation, a left tendency, in the modern sense of the word: *i.e.* one oriented towards the revolutionary proletariat. (*PWII* 460-462)

Revolution and War of Position

To turn to questions of strategy, the importance of Gramsci's note on the 'transition from the war of manoeuvre (frontal attack) to the war of position – in the political field as well' (*SPN* 238), lies in the way he translates the 'actuality of the revolution' into the conditions of the thirties. Gramsci is searching for new roads towards socialism in an historical context that has undergone profound change because of the October Revolution. He viewed the latter as the last episode of the 'war of movement' in the political field (*SPN* 235)[5]. The transition to the 'war of position' is now seen as 'the most important question of political theory that the post-war period has posed, and the most difficult to solve correctly'. This is the case because:

> The war of position demands enormous sacrifices by infinite masses of people. So an unprecedented concentration of hegemony is necessary, and hence a more 'interventionist' government, which will take the offensive more openly against the oppositionists and organize permanently the 'impossibility' of internal disintegration – with controls of every kind, political, administrative, etc., reinforcement of the hegemonic 'positions' of the dominant group, etc. (*SPN* 238-9)

This passage belongs to a note of 1930 or 1931, criticizing Trotsky's conception of 'permanent revolution'. Trotsky is regarded as 'the political theorist of frontal attack in a period in which it only leads to defeats'. The war of position implies a differentiated strategy. With regard to the USSR, it confirms Gramsci's support for the choice of 'socialism in one country', already clearly defined in 1926 at the time of his dramatic correspondence with Togliatti. (*PWII* 426-40) Further, in the passage we have quoted there are obvious echoes of Gramsci's confident support for the 'revolution from above' that Stalin was carrying out during the early thirties, after the first five year plan had been launched and forced industrialization had commenced.

At the general level, the transition to a 'war of position indicates that we have entered a culminating phase in the political-historical situation, since in politics the "war of position", once won, is decisive definitively'. (*SPN* 239) In fact, he dates this transition to the policy of the 'united front', launched by Lenin at the IIIrd Congress of the Communist International in 1921. Lenin 'understood that a change was necessary from the war of manoeuvre applied victoriously in the East in 1917, to a war of position which was the only form possible in the West'. (*SPN* 237)

In Western Europe, then, the 'war of position' constitutes the strategy for the transition to socialism. Defining the differences between East and West, Gramsci observes:

> In Russia the State was everything, civil society was primitive and gelatinous; in the West, there was a proper relation between

State and civil society, and when the State trembled a sturdy
structure of civil society was at once revealed. The State was
only an outer ditch, behind which there stood a powerful system
of fortresses and earthworks: more or less numerous from one
State to the next, it goes without saying – but this precisely
necessitated an accurate reconnaissance of each individual
country. (*SPN* 238)

The accurate reconnaissance of each individual country
constitutes the task of the various communist parties, not only
because Lenin 'did not have time to expand his formula', but
above all because 'he could only have expanded it theoretically'
and in broad outline. 'The fundamental task' on the other hand
'was a national one; that is to say it required a reconnaissance of
the terrain and identification of the elements of trench and
fortress represented by the elements of civil society'. (*SPN*
238) What, then, are these elements of civil society?

'The historical unity of the ruling classes', Gramsci asserts,
'is realized in the State, and their history is essentially the
history of States.' As such, that unity 'results from the organic
relations between State or political society and "civil society".'
(*SPN* 52) On the other hand, he maintains:

> In any given society nobody is disorganized and without party,
> provided that one takes organization and party in a broad and
> not a formal sense. In this multiplicity of private associations
> (which are of two kinds: natural, and contractual or voluntary)
> one or more predominates relatively or absolutely – constituting
> the *hegemonic apparatus of one social group over the rest of the
> population (or civil society)*: the basis for the State in the narrow
> sense of the governmental-coercive apparatus.(*SPN* 264-5. My
> emphasis)

The elements of civil society therefore define the real woof of
the relations between the rulers and the ruled, the molecular
fabric of dominion and consensus that underlays the different
types of state, in which the unity of the dominant groups and
the different way in which they exert their political leadership
is summarily expressed.

Hegemony, Rulers and Ruled

Thus the strategy of the 'war of position', in its concrete

operation as the recognition of the different relations between rulers and ruled, gives rise to the analysis of the forms and apparatuses of hegemony. Indeed, Gramsci states 'the war of position, in politics, is the concept of hegemony'. It 'can come into being only after certain premises have been established' ... and these are: the great popular organizations of a modern type, that represent the "ditches" and permanent fortifications of the war of position'. (Q 973) It is here that the particular relevance of the 'war of position' to the strategy of the battle for socialism in Western Europe becomes clear.

In the concrete relations between rulers and ruled 'the supremacy of a dominant group manifests itself in two ways, as "domination" and as "intellectual and moral leadership" '. The strategic centrality of the theory of hegemony recalls the analytic centrality of the question of the intellectuals. Gramsci's conception of hegemony and the struggle to win it, its central function in the government of the state, puts the problem of the relation between the working class and the 'educated classes' at the top of the agenda for the Communist Party. Lenin had already indicated that 'a social group dominates antagonistic groups, which it tends to "liquidate" or to subjugate even by armed force; it leads kindred and allied groups'. For Gramsci, the development of capacities for bringing these groups under its own leadership makes the problem of hegemony central to the working class. On a par with any other social group, the working class:

> can, and indeed must, already exercise 'leadership' before winning governmental power (this indeed is one of the principal conditions for the winning of such power); it subsequently becomes dominant when it exercises power, but even if it holds it firmly in its grasp, it must continue to 'lead' as well ... There can ... and indeed must be hegemonic activity even before the rise to power and ... one should not count only on the material force which power gives in order to exercise an effective leadership. (SPN 57-9)

That the organizers of the new fabric of consensus and of the relations between rulers and ruled, i.e. the intellectuals, are essential for this work is obvious. This leads to the need for a new development of Marxism as a theory of hegemony, capable of winning over the intellectual groups to the new tasks proposed by the advance of the working class on the terrain of the state. But the Gramscian theory of hegemony, which at the moment seems firmly anchored within the confines of Lenin's distinction between 'leadership' and 'domination', in reality goes beyond them. Intending to contribute to a development of Marxism as a theory of hegemony, Gramsci demonstrates that the limits and the non-expansive nature of the working class's first experience of State power are clear to him. This is evident in his ideas about the USSR of the 1930s.

The Soviet Union and the Failure to Develop a New Type of Intellectual

Gramsci's political theory serves to distinguish between the theory of social relations and the theory of political forms. His references to the USSR of the thirties are frequently part of a more general reflection on 'totalitarian' political forms or on 'Caesarism'; and his analysis very often proceeds through comparison between the USSR and the fascist regimes. Both are totalitarian political forms, differentiated, however, according to whether their political and economic forms are progressive or reactionary.

Thus, in a note of 1932, Gramsci defines 'Caesarism' as the expression of a situation in which the forces in conflict 'balance each other in a catastrophic manner; that is to say, they balance each other in such a way that a continuation of the conflict can only terminate in their reciprocal destruction'.

> There can be both progressive and reactionary forms of Caesarism; the exact significance of each form can, in the last analysis, be reconstructed only through concrete history, and not by means of any sociological rule of thumb. Caesarism is progressive when its intervention helps the progressive force to triumph, albeit with its victory tempered by certain compromises and limitations. It is reactionary when its intervention helps the reactionary force to triumph . . . Besides Caesarism is a polemical-ideological form, and not a canon of historical interpretation. A Caesarist solution can exist even without a Caesar, without any great 'heroic' and representative personality. (SPN 219-220)

The references to the contents of Caesarism – progressive or otherwise – , to the classes to which Caesarism offers a mode of leadership, to the fact that one can have 'Caesarism' even without a Caesar, and finally to the compromise between the classes in struggle and among allied classes, leave no doubts that Gramsci was thinking of the USSR as the expression of progressive Caesarism. The reference to Soviet reality is even more transparent in a reflection on the 'totalitarian' state and the function of the totalitarian party within it. (Q 1601-2)[6].

There can be no doubt that Gramsci looked at the developments of the first workers' state in a critical way. He saw parliamentary government as the classical political form of bourgeois hegemony precisely because it was based on the full development of civil society. Hegemony here was rooted in civil society and enlarged it.[7] The hegemony of the working class, no less than that of the bourgeoisie, must find its basis in civil society and direct its efforts towards the reabsorption of political society into civil society, that is, towards the withering away of the state.[8] He conceived of the working-class party as the modern prince (*SPN* 129), the collective intellectual (*SPN* 19), which, in a socialist or regulated society, 'does not merge organically with the government, but is the instrument for the transition from civil-political society to the "regulated society"'.(Q 734) As against this Gramsci notes that 'in the countries where there is a single totalitarian governing party . . . the functions of such a party are no longer directly political, but merely technical ones of propaganda and public order, and moral and cultural influence'. There does, of course, remain an indirect political function, 'for, even if no other legal parties exist, other parties in fact always do exist and other tendencies cannot be legally coerced; and, against these, polemics are unleashed and struggles are fought as in a game of blind man's buff'. (*SPN* 149). He concludes critically, 'it is certain that in such parties cultural functions predominate, which means that political language becomes jargon. In other words, political questions are disguised as cultural ones, and as such become insoluble'. (*SPN* 149)

The withering away of the party's political nature in those places where it is incorporated into the state and its governmental apparatus has serious consequences for the masses. In these regimes during the most recent period, Gramsci notes, the totalitarian party has been assuming mass dimensions, but the masses 'have no other political function than a generic loyalty, of a military kind, to a visible or invisible political centre'. From this it follows that the mass 'is simply for "manoeuvre", and is kept happy by means of moralising sermons, emotional stimuli, and messianic myths of an awaited golden age, in which all present contradictions and miseries will be automatically resolved and made well'. (*SPN* 150)

Certainly, Gramsci's views on totalitarianism were fuelled above all by the experience of the mass reactionary regimes. The phenomenon of Hitlerism was added in 1932-33 to Italian fascism but it is evident that where Gramsci speaks of the constant policing function of the totalitarian parties he is also thinking of the USSR. Why, otherwise, would he emphasize, that 'the policing function of a party can . . . be either progressive or regressive'? And that it is progressive when 'it tends to keep the dispossessed reactionary forces within the bounds of legality, and to raise the backward masses to the level of the new legality'? (*SPN* 155).

Furthermore Gramsci obviously has the USSR, its relations between party and state and party and masses in mind when he speaks critically of 'organic centralism'. For him 'democratic centralism' defines the peculiarity of the 'party of a new type' of the working class: here leaders have the capacity to promote the activity and conscious intervention of the masses on the basis of a dialectical relation between party and mass movements and a real harmony between them. (*SPN* 188-90) On the other hand 'organic' (or 'bureaucratic') centralism 'is based . . . on the presupposition – true only at exceptional moments, when popular passions are aflame – that the relationship between ruler and ruled is determined by the fact that the rulers satisfy the interests of the ruled and thus 'have their consent, i.e. the individual must identify with the whole – which (whatever the organism involved) is represented by the rulers'. (*SPN* 187n) If this can function well in the life of organisms like the Catholic Church, for other bodies, the vital question is, on the contrary,

> not that of indirect and passive, but of direct and active consent, the participation, therefore, of single individuals, even if this causes an appearance of disintegration and tumult. A collective

consciousness, in other words, a living organism is formed only after the multiplicity is unified through the attrition of its individual units: neither can one say that 'silence' is not multiplicity. (Q 1771)

There is no lack of explicit references to the USSR and to the relationship of leadership and masses there. Gramsci saw that it was impossible for the working class to construct the new economy simply on the bases of what Marx had written.

Once it had attained governmental position, the working class must be able to appropriate, albeit in a critical fashion, all the instruments economic science had developed for directing production and exchange. (Q 1261-2) The inability to do this revealed what by this time was prevalent among the Soviet *élite* and within Soviet culture: a bureaucratic practice in scientific and political life.

What is striking is this: how a critical point of view which requires the utmost intelligence, open-mindedness, mental freshness and scientific inventiveness has become monopolized by narrow-minded wretches who manage, due only to their dogmatic position, to maintain a position within the marginal bibliography of science rather than in science . . . An ossified form of thinking is the greatest danger in these questions: a certain chaotic disorder is preferable to the philistine defence of pre-constituted positions. (Q 1805-6)

These observations allow us to understand Gramsci's judgement on the USSR: 'socialism in one country' was the 'economic corporative phase' of the workers' state. This judgement forms part of his long critique of Bukharin's *Popular Manual* and is to be found among the notes drafted in 1931-32.

If it is true that all types of State must pass through a phase of economic-corporative primitivism, it may be deduced from this that the content of the political hegemony of the new social group which founded the new type of State must be predominantly of an economic order: the problem is that of the reorganization of the structure and real relations between men and the economic world or world of production. The superstructural elements cannot but be few in number and their character will be one of anticipation and struggle while still being insufficient in elements of a 'plan'. (Q 1053)

What is the problem the workers' State has not resolved and which prevents it from expanding its basis of support? Once again, Gramsci's analysis leads to the theme of the intellectuals. In Gramsci's opinion, the unity of theory and practice, which constitutes the central concept of historical materialism, poses 'the need for contact between intellectuals and "simple" . . . to construct an intellectual-moral bloc which can make politically possible the progress of the mass and not only of small intellectual groups'. That unity therefore 'is not . . . a matter of mechanical fact, but a part of the historical process'.

Taking Bukharin's *Manual* as the prototype of Soviet Marxism, Gramsci writes:

> In the most recent developments of the theory of praxis . . . people speak about theory as a 'complement' or an 'accessory' of practice, or as the handmaid of practice. It would seem right for this question too to be considered historically, as an aspect of the political question of the intellectuals. (*SPN* 332-4) . . .
>
> A human mass does not 'distinguish' itself, does not become independent without, in the widest sense, organising itself; and there is no organisation without intellectuals, that is without organisers and leaders (Q 1042) [or, in other words] without the theoretical aspect of the theory-practice nexus being distinguished concretely by the existence of a stratum of people 'specialised' in the conceptual and philosophical elaboration of ideas . . .
>
> Insistence on the practical element of the theory-practice nexus, after having not only distinguished but separated and split the two elements . . . means that one is going through a relatively primitive historical phase, one which is still economic-corporative, in which the general 'structural' framework is being quantitatively transformed and the appropriate quality-superstructure is in the process of emerging, but is not yet organically formed. (*SPN* 334-5)

The workers' state, in short, has not yet expanded its basis of consent. The formation of a new mass intellectuality, capable of changing the political relation between intellectuals and 'simple' in the construction of the new state, has not yet been initiated. For Gramsci, the question of the intellectuals comes to occupy an ever more central place in Marxist theory. It points the way beyond the economic-corporative limit of the first workers' state.

The State, Revolution and the New Intellectual

At this point, we may pause briefly to consider Gramsci's conception of the state. In Gramsci as in Lenin and in any serious theorist of socialism, the concept of the state is inseparable from the conception of revolution. The conception of the revolution determines and influences both the way of analysing the state and the way of conceiving the new state; the conception of the state, in turn, determines or influences the way of conceiving the revolutionary process.

A first example of this intertwining of themes may be noted in Gramsci by examining some definitions of the tasks of the state in general, in which his conception of the new state and therefore his view of socialist transformation obviously prevail. He speaks of an 'educative and formative role of the State. Its aim is always that of creating new and higher types of civilisation; of adapting the "civilisation" and the morality of the broadest popular masses to the necessities of the continuous development of the economic apparatus of production.' (*SPN* 242) He is evidently thinking of the organization of the State and its function, connected to the capitalist organization of production and still more to its most recent forms of development. So much is this the case that, a few pages later on, he speaks of the state as 'an instrument of "rationalisation", of acceleration and of Taylorisation' which 'operates according to a plan, urges, incites, solicits, and "punishes" '. (*SPN* 247)

In this outline 'every State is ethical in as much as one of its most important functions is to raise the great mass of the population to a particular cultural and moral level, a level (or type) which corresponds to the needs of the productive forces for development, and hence to the interests of the ruling classes'. (*SPN* 258)

It is impossible to detach this class conception of the state educator from a well-defined theoretical horizon, which at that time had its main reference point in the Soviet experience and was expressed theoretically in the view of socialism as a process of the development and rational organization of the productive forces under the direction of the state. Elsewhere, Gramsci himself asserts that 'for some social groups, which before their ascent to autonomous state life have not had a long independent period of cultural and moral development of their own' – and here the reference to the proletariat is obvious – 'a period of statolatry is necessary and indeed opportune'. This statolatry or state worship in Gramsci's view 'is nothing other than the normal form of "State life", or at least of initiation to autonomous State life and to the creation of a "civil society" which it was not historically possible to create before the ascent to independent State life'. (*SPN* 268) No great effort is needed to see in this quotation both political support for Stalin's 'revolution from above', and the USSR as a reference point for a theory of socialism which, in the short term, proceeds essentially from the political action of the state. It provides the concrete exemplification in a given territory of that unheard-of concentration of hegemony and that exceptional interventionism that are required of the working class in the era of the war of position.

From Statolatry to Self-government

But it is precisely at this point that Gramsci's thought is differentiated from Leninism. This is extremely important because it concerns the very concept of the state. At the very moment he emphasizes the necessity of a strong state interventionism so that 'the old "homo economicus" will disappear' and be 'buried with all honours', Gramsci refers to the state as an 'instrument for conforming civil society to the economic structure'. He thus distinguishes between state, economic structure and civil society, posing them in a reciprocal relation such that 'between the economic structure and the State with its legislation and its coercion stands civil society'. It is over civil society that, in reality, the state exercises its intervention, since it is that which 'must be radically transformed, in a concrete sense and not simply on the statute-book or in scientific books'. (*SPN* 208-9)

Statolatry, then, although constituting the normal form of state life in the phase in which the proletariat exercises greatest state intervention 'to conform civil society to the economic structure', carries with it a danger. A particular attitude towards government by functionaries or political society may become theoretical fanaticism and be conceived of as perpetual. What happens then is that the bureaucracy becomes commonly understood as the *whole* state.

On the contrary, Gramsci states, the identification of individuals with the form of state created by their own social group

> must serve to determine the will to construct within the husk of political society a complex and well-articulated civil society, in which the individual can govern himself without his self-government thereby entering into conflict with political society – but rather becoming its normal continuation, its organic complement.

Statolatry, then, 'must be criticized, precisely in order to develop and produce new forms of state life, in which the initiative of individuals and groups will have a "State" character, even if it is not due to the "government of the functionaries" '. This perspective is summarized by Gramsci in the expression 'make State life become "spontaneous" '. (*SPN* 268-9)

Stalin and the Strengthening of the State

One might, for a moment, compare these ideas with Stalin's contemporaneous ones. Drawing up the balance sheet of the first five year plan, Stalin launched the theory that the class struggle would sharpen within the proletarian state as socialist society developed. His celebrated Report to the Central Committee of 7 January 1933 came after a year of terrible crisis in the countryside. Here, while urging the party to intensify the struggle against the kulaks – who were represented to the peasant masses as responsible for the agricultural disasters – Stalin did not hesitate to assert the need for strengthening repressive apparatuses and state control in order to face up to the attacks of the internal and external enemies of the USSR. He did not fail to justify this at the theoretical level. This is the origin of the notion that 'the growth of the power of the Soviet State will intensify the resistance of the last remnants of the dying classes'. A more general thesis even claimed: *"The State will wither away not as a result of the weakening of State power, but as a result of its strengthening to the utmost."*[9] Some years later on, when Stalinism could be considered more or less fully developed, Stalin arrived at an open revision of the theses of Marx and Lenin. After having further reduced the Marxist conception of the state to the nature and function of the coercive apparatuses, he went as far as to assert the possibility of *communism* in a single country and he suggested the idea of a Communist State along with the thesis of the fully fledged survival of the state in communist society.

The Withering Away of the State

In contrast to this, the significance of Gramsci's sophisticated conception of the state is clear.

> By State should be understood not only the apparatus of government but also the 'private' apparatus of 'hegemony' or civil society . . . It should be remarked that the general notion of State includes elements which need to be referred back to the notion of civil society . . . One might say that State = political society + civil society, in other words hegemony protected by the armour of coercion. (*SPN* 261-3)[10]

Only this two-fold conception of the state in the conditions of a war of position keeps fixed the Marxist perspective of the withering away of the state. It was Gramsci himself who was to warn, immediately after the definition just quoted here, that 'in a doctrine of the State which conceives the latter as tendentially capable of withering away and of being subsumed into regulated society, the argument is a fundamental one'. On the basis of this definition of the state, 'it is possible to imagine the coercive element of the State withering away by degrees, as ever-more conspicuous elements of regulated society make their appearance'. Or again:

> One will have to pass from a phase in which 'State' will be equal to 'government', and 'State' will be identified with 'civil society', to a phase of the State as nightwatchman – i.e. of a coercive organization which will safeguard the development of the continually proliferating elements of regulated society, and

which will therefore progressively reduce its own authoritarian and forcible interventions. (*SPN* 263)

The Economic Sphere and the State

But Gramsci's distance from the Marxism-Leninism of the twenties and thirties on the theme of the state is not only political. It is, above all, theoretical. He does not limit himself to salvaging the perspective of the withering away of the state but, on the contrary, places the discussion on the level of the theory of the state. He warns that the distinction between state and civil society 'is purely one of method and not organic, and in concrete historical life political society and civil society are the same thing'. Thus, in countering the economism characteristic of liberal political theory, whose fundamental concept lies in the organic distinction between the state and civil society, (*SPN* 262-3) i.e. the State must not intervene in society, he observes: 'even liberalism has to be introduced by law, *i.e.* by intervention of the political power: it is a deliberate policy, not the spontaneous, automatic expression of economic facts.' (*Q* 460; also *SPN* 162) The distinction between state and civil society, the further distinction of this latter from the economic structure and, lastly, the conception of the state as the synthesis of civil society and political society allowed Gramsci to proceed beyond the Marxist conception of the state as the *instrument* of domination of the ruling class and its most recent crystallization in the simplified vision of the state as a *pure machine* or a *pure apparatus*. The definition of the state as 'hegemony protected by the armour of coercion' supposes a much more articulated conception of the class nature of the state; a complex and mediated re-linking of the state to the ruling class. It opens up the way for a differentiated analysis of the forms of the state since it allows us to climb from the *abstract* level of the concepts which define social relations to the *concrete* dimension of the actual forms which set the pattern for the relations between rulers and ruled.

Gramsci does not speak in a simplified manner of the class nature of the state; neither does he retrace the crude definitions of the Marxist tradition, which, reducing the theory of the state to the *expression* or reflection of ruling class interests, do not then allow a concrete analysis of different state forms. These are what count in practice. Gramsci analyzes the state according to the productive function of its classes and sketches out the following theory:

> Although it is certain that for the fundamental productive classes (capitalist bourgeoisie and modern proletariat) the State is only conceivable as the concrete form of a specific economic world, of a specific system of production, this does not mean that the relationship of means to end can be easily determined or takes the form of a simple schema, apparent at first sight. It is true that conquest of power and achievement of a new social world are inseparable, and that propaganda for one is also propaganda for the other, and that in reality it is solely in this coincidence that the unity of the dominant class – at once economic and political – resides. But the complex problem arises of the relation of internal forces in the country in question, of the relation of international forces, of the country's geo-political position. (*SPN* 116)

The state is related to but does not reflect the organization of the economy. From the abstract level of the mode of production to the concrete level of real society, there is a whole articulation of different theoretical fields, which Marxist analysis has to distinguish methodically in order to arrive at the particular elements that define actual state forms; or, in order to understand the specific nature of a specific state at a particular period in time. It is this concept of the Marxist theory of the state, already found in the 1926 Lyons Theses,[11] which is consciously elaborated right from the very first prison notebook. Here it is a matter of distinguishing between those concepts which define the mode of production and which allow us to establish the nature of the classes and their relationships in the abstract from the concepts which allow a concrete analysis of these classes. The latter proceeds from an investigation of the political history, forms of consciousness, and modes of organization of the classes. It is this dynamic which, by defining the forces in the field in concrete terms, allows the particular forms of the state to be determined.[12]

If, therefore, there is a basic historical correspondence between economic and political forms; if the state is composed of institutions which allow the dominant class to realize its unity; if the politically dominant class is always the one which dominates in the relations of production, all this is still insufficient to determine the concrete forms of the state. The particular features of the state derive, in fact, from the ways in which the rulers and ruled relate, relations in which the balance of power changes.

In Gramsci's view, what happens is that a determinate form of state acquires its particular characteristics because, while it comes into being on the basis of a determinate mode of production – so as to correspond to the interests of the fundamental productive classes – the initiative for its formation may, however, have come from particular sections of the possible dominant bloc, which do not correspond to the economically fundamental part of that bloc. In the formation of modern bourgeois states, the essential impetus, generally speaking, has come from the capitalist bourgeoisie which has taken the initiative and determined the form of the state. But there are cases, such as the Italian Risorgimento, where

> the impetus of progress is not tightly linked to a vast local economic development which is artificially limited and repressed, but is instead the reflection of international developments which transmit their ideological currents to the periphery – currents born on the basis of the productive development of the more advanced countries. Then the group which is the bearer of the new ideas is not the economic group but the intellectual stratum, and the conception of the State advocated by them changes aspect; it is conceived of as something in itself, as a rational absolute. (SPN 116-7)[13]

The relation between state and economically dominant class, then, is neither linear nor simple. Nothing concrete is said about the state if the dominant class is conceived of as a subject endowed with an organic consciousness and defined by its interests, abstracting it from the concrete form of the state. This is then conceived of as the instrument which will make these interests felt – an instrument which is always identical and on that account also a useful one for imposing the interests of another class, should the first one be eliminated or defeated. As against this, the concrete form of the state takes its shape from the way in which the fundamental classes succeed in organizing the whole fabric of relations between rulers and ruled; and it is this particular ensemble that constitutes the state in flesh and blood.

> It is true that the State is seen as the organ of one particular group, destined to create favourable conditions for the latter's maximum expansion. But the development and expansion of the particular group are conceived of, and presented, as being the motor force of a universal expansion, of a development of all the 'national' energies. In other words, the dominant group is co-ordinated concretely with the general interests of the subordinate groups, and the life of the State is conceived of as a continuous process of formation and superseding of unstable equilibria (on the juridical plane) between the interests of the fundamental group and those of the subordinate groups – equilibria in which the interests of the dominant group prevail, but only up to a certain point, i.e. stopping short of narrowly corporate economic interest. (*SPN* 182)

In short, there is no state without hegemony, or without compromises. And it is the concrete forms of hegemony which determine the different degrees and modes of coercion. The elaboration of hegemony, which allows the fundamental class to realize its historical goals by going beyond its narrow economic-corporative interest, connects the concrete forms assumed by the state with the particular kind of compromise established between rulers and ruled. Neither can the sacrifice of its economic-corporative interest, which the dominant class must make in order to assert its position as the leading or hegemonic class, be offset by political fraud and the ideological manipulation of the ruled. Ideologies, which define the terrain on which individuals and social groups become conscious of their own interests and enter into contradictory relations among themselves, are not 'mere illusions for the ruled, a deception they undergo' and 'a willed and conscious deception for the rulers'. (Q 1319-20) The elaboration of a complete culture and of hegemonic apparatuses by means of which a class, which is the fundamental one on the terrain of production, becomes the 'governing class' of the whole of society is, therefore, essential.

Intellectuals, Rulers and Ruled

We are thus led back by a new path to our basic theme, that of the intellectuals. Within the same social formation, the forms assumed by the state in fact vary according to the different social relations and functions of the intellectual groups. These are elaborated by the fundamental classes and define the relations between rulers and ruled. This social group is an extremely differentiated one, precisely because it is not in 'direct' relation with the world of production 'as it is with the fundamental social groups but is, in varying degrees "mediated" by the whole fabric of society and by the complex of superstructures, of which the intellectuals are, precisely, the "functionaries" '. The 'functions in question are precisely organizational and connective. The intellectuals are the dominant group's "deputies" exercising the subaltern functions of social hegemony and political government.'(*SPN* 12) They define the variegated woof of the fabric of relations between rulers and ruled, which constitutes political life as it exists in individuals and social groups and the element which differentiates the various forms of the state.

In thus enriching the conception of the state, we have the basis for going beyond the vision which the Third International had of the state and of revolution. If the relation between state and dominant class must always be specified by the concrete ways in which rulers and ruled are related, this means that political contradictions extend throughout the entire fabric of the institutions and the relations of hegemony. Political struggle cannot be reduced to the contradiction between bourgeois democracy and proletarian democracy as held by the Third International. There is no doubt that the working class must elaborate its own form of state. But this form of state is not given in the forms assumed by its antagonism to capital and the bourgeois state and which determine its political constitution as a class. The formation of the workers' state cannot but be a *differentiated process*, connected to the different ways in which the working class itself will produce a new overall organization of classes and social groups by taking apart the fabric of existing relations between rulers and ruled. Moreover:

It must be clearly understood . . . that the division between rulers and ruled – though in the last analysis it has its origin in a division between social groups – is in fact, things being as they are, also to be found within the group itself, even where it is a socially homogeneous one. In a certain sense, it may be said that this division is created by the division of labour. (*SPN* 144)

The elaboration, therefore, of the new state is a much more complex act than the *substitution* of the system of soviets for parliamentary democracy, which is where the Third Internationalist vision of the state-revolution nexus stopped.[14] Neither, on the basis of the war of position, could it be otherwise. In fact, the transition to the new strategy indicates precisely that the October Revolution and its conception of socialism as 'soviets + electrification' (Lenin's definition) were the last episode of the war of movement (assault on the bourgeois state in order to substitute for it the proletarian state. Reflecting on the Russian experience, if the entire capitalist reorganization of the state and the economy can be interpreted as a new type of passive revolution within whose shell elements of a planned economy continue to accumulate, then certainly the conceptions of socialism and the transition themselves need to be reformulated. It was Gramsci who laid the theoretical basis for this new formulation.

The Theory of the 'Organic Intellectual' and the Perspective of the 'New Intellectual'.

What then is the Gramscian theory of the intellectuals? Its novel core is found in the theory of the 'organic intellectual' developed in the *Notebooks*. Before proceeding to examine it, certain definitions of terms are useful, since the theme has been the object of much misunderstanding. And it must be understood in all its aspects if our examination of Gramsci's entire political theory as an attempt to answer the political question of the intellectuals is to conclude correctly.

The theme is crucial since, as we have seen, according to Gramsci, concrete political analysis is always an investigation of the relations of force and relations of hegemony. Within these, the way in which the element of consciousness and intellectual leadership defines the relations between rulers and ruled is determinant. On the other hand, in the era of 'mass politics', the analysis of situations is always political analysis, because it cannot be separated from the orientation and action of political parties and movements. The starting point of the analysis must be the development of a theory which allows the workers' party to transform the social relations and functions of the intellectual groups.

The first task that Gramsci indicates is a basically 'critical' one: to reveal the traditional behaviour of the intellectuals and to transform it. The new era opened up by the post-war crisis challenges their traditional view of their history.

> One of the characteristics of the intellectuals as a crystallised social group (as a social group which sees itself as continuing uninterruptedly through history and thus independent of the struggle of groups rather than as the expression of a dialectical process . . .) is precisely that of connecting itself, in the ideological sphere, with a preceding intellectual category by means of a common conceptual nomenclature. A new historical situation creates a new ideological superstructure, whose representatives (the intellectuals) can only be conceived as themselves being 'new intellectuals' who have come out of the new situation and are not a continuation of the preceding intellectual milieu. (Q 1043-4).

And here is how Gramsci defines the intellectual:

> By intellectual must be meant not only those strata commonly understood by this denomination, but in general the whole social stratum that exercises organizational functions in the broad sense, both in the field of production, and in the cultural one, and in the politico-administrative one. (*SPN* 97)

Their function is essential because it defines the fabric of hegemony. The exercise of specific directive or hegemonic functions, is, however, incorporated in their different technical specializations, which distinguishes them from the mass of other workers (the 'instrumental workers'), and underlies their very definition as intellectuals.

If such is the case then:

> In order to analyse the socio-political function of the intellectuals, it is necessary to recall and examine their psychological attitude towards the fundamental classes which

they put into contact in the various fields. Have they a 'paternalistic' attitude towards the instrumental classes? Or do they believe that they are their organic expression? Do they have a 'servile' attitude towards the ruling classes or do they think that they themselves are rulers, an integral part of the ruling classes? (*SPN* 97)

The way has thus been opened up for a differentiated analysis of the intellectual groups: analysis of the *intellectuals* can now be linked to the analysis of *classes*. To the question 'are the intellectuals an autonomous and independent social group, or does every social group have its own particular specialized category of intellectuals?' which opens the 'Comments and scattered notes for a group of essays on the history of the intellectuals', Gramsci replies:

> Every social group, coming into existence on the original terrain of an essential function in the world of economic production, creates together with itself, organically, one or more strata of intellectuals which give it homogeneity and an awareness of its own function not only in the economic but also in the social and political fields. (*SPN* 5)

The analysis of the intellectuals leads in this way to a new position, capable of taking account of 'the variety of forms assumed to date by the real historical process of formation of the different categories of intellectuals', through linking up their specific skills to the various functions which the fundamental classes perform in production and in the state. The organic nature of the relationship refers, first of all, to the functions of classes in the world of production. The various forms of the state stem from this. Secondly, it refers to the different technical functions that the intellectuals perform in the state. The examples quoted by Gramsci are most significant: 'the capitalist entrepreneur creates alongside himself the industrial technician, the specialist in political economy, the organizers of a new culture, of a new legal system, etc.' (*SPN* 16) The organic nature, then, of the bourgeoisie's intellectuals of a new type stems first of all from the technical aspects of the fundamental productive functions of the modern bourgeoisie. A further function is to help to elaborate and build consensus around a bourgeois model of society. The concept of organic intellectual makes sense if it refers to the relations of intellectual groups with the fundamental classes and to the development of their technical functions. The organic nature of the link is inherent in the very formation of their specialized skills, as well as in the development of the particular functions of organizing the masses and the economy.

The Gramscian theory of the organic intellectual therefore permits us to analyse capital society in a differentiated fashion, by examining its productive, social and political relations. To be an intellectual group organic to a class means to embody technical competencies and perform directive functions which are specific to a determinate mode of production; here, the capitalist mode of production. The concept of organic intellectual has a precise sense only from the point of view of the totality described by the socio-economic formation as a whole. And since modes of production are articulated in concrete terms in relations of dominance, the concept of organic intellectual specifically refers to the fact that the forms of direction or of social subordination must be understood, beginning with the technical functions that embody the social division of labour. The particular structure of this social division of labour offers the real basis for a materialist and class analysis of the intellectuals. By linking the social division of labour and the forms of the state the concept of organic intellectual allows us to go on to concrete political analysis.

The Organic Intellectuals of the Working Class

What then does the development of its own stratum of organic intellectuals mean for the working class? First and foremost it means the development of its own political leaders, its own organizers, who are indispensable to its political constitution as a class, since 'in the political party the elements of an economic social group get beyond that moment of their historical development and become agents of more general activities of a national and international character'. But this does not exhaust the problem. The elaboration of its own categories of organic intellectuals, for whatever class or social group, is interwoven with the formation of a new mode of production and the establishment of a new state. The formation of the organic intellectuals of the working class therefore makes sense and is possible only in connection with the *transition* to socialism, in the era in which, at the level of world history, the *transition to communism* is under way.

This applies firstly to the leaders and organizers of the party of the working class themselves, who are organic to the class only to the degree that the political constitution of the working class is on the agenda and the process of its becoming a state is actually or potentially under way. But how is the problem posed in the perspective of a socialist transformation?

> The problem of creating a new stratum of intellectuals consists therefore in the critical elaboration of the intellectual activity that exists in everyone at a certain degree of development, modifying its relationship with the muscular-nervous effort towards a new equilibrum, and ensuring that the muscular-nervous effort itself, insofar as it is an element of a general practical activity, which is perpetually innovating the physical and social world, becomes the foundation of a new and integral conception of the world. (*SPN* 9)

It is not then a question of substituting one stratum of intellectuals for another, communist entrepreneurs for capitalist ones, the hegemonic apparatuses of the workers' party for those of the bourgeois state, but of creating the conditions for a new social organization of knowledge to be elaborated from below: coming directly from the world of production and from a new relationship that the producers have with this social organization of knowledge. It is a question of the critical re-elaboration of the 'intellectual activity that exists in everybody at a certain degree of development' and which also exists on the basis of productive experience, so that it may constitute 'the foundation of a new and integral conception of the world'.

The development of the organic intellectuals of the working class thus describes the process of the formation of the 'regulated society' and the 'new state'. It is part and parcel of the process of transition. It expresses the most complex level of the process, peculiar to the advanced capitalist societies. Here the formation of the new state and the supplanting of the capitalist bases of production are firmly welded to overturning

the relationships between the masses and scientific understanding. This is expressed and measured by the degree to
which the masses appropriate scientific knowledge as new
technology is introduced into production.

It is by no means accidental that Gramsci refers in these
notes to the *Ordine Nuovo* as the place where a first definition
of this objective was given and the first laboratory for testing
the peculiar relation between revolution and production.[14] In
Gramsci's view, the new, socialist social formation, certainly a
much more unified one than capitalist society but one which is
characterized by a greater differentiation and diffusion of
productive processes than capitalism, is therefore marked by
an even more highly developed technical division of labour. In
such a society, however, integrated and organic as it may be,
one cannot expect everyone to possess the same levels of skills.
There will still be a differentiation between individuals and
groups, and intellectuals will still be characterized by their
directive functions. But these directive functions, the division
between leaders and led, will be determined on entirely new
bases. On the political plane, what is new is the way in which
the antagonistic relationship between leaders and led is overcome as the new directive functions are elaborated. This fact of
proceeding 'from below' is the organic expression of the need
to co-ordinate, organize, unify and develop the productive
forces. And such functions are no longer satisfied in an élitist
and authoritarian way: there is no economic isolation and
corporative fragmentation of the producers.

At the level of ideology, the form of consciousness that
comes to permeate the directive functions is Marxism,
understood as a 'humanistic conception of history'. It develops
along with the developments of the 'regulated society' and is
characterized by the tendency of unifying humanity now
divided into classes and corporate groups. Here then we have
Gramsci's definition of the 'new intellectual', the organic
intellectual of the working class, the synthesis of the
'specialized and political':

> The mode of being of the new intellectual can no longer consist
> in eloquence, which is an exterior and momentary mover of
> feelings and passions, but in active participation in practical life,
> as constructor, organiser, 'permanent persuader' and not just a

> simple orator (but superior at the same time to the abstract
> mathematical spirit); from technique-as-work one proceeds to
> technique-as-science and to the humanistic conception of
> history, without which one remains 'specialised' and does not
> become 'directive' (specialised plus political). (*SPN* 10)

The creation of the new intellectual category evidently has the
characteristic function of a process: the process, under the
impetus of the working class and the producers in general, of
separating scientific knowledge from capital and of re-
elaborating the social organization of knowledge on the basis
of a reappropriation of the productive forces by the producers.
This process designates the fullest and highest form of the
socialist transformation. At the concrete historical level, it is
expressed in the 'tendential' law of the political overturning of
the relations between rulers and ruled, as part of the transition
to a new society in which the existence of rulers and ruled is no
longer necessary or valid.

At the end of our investigation, the political question of the
intellectuals proves to have such a central position and to be so
rich in theoretical and strategic implications because, in the
concrete historical process, 'there really do exist rulers and
ruled, leaders and led. The entire science and art of politics are
based on this primordial, and (given certain general conditions)
irreducible fact.' Because of this in a certain way the whole of
contemporary political science is condensed into the
knowledge of the 'relations of force', which constitutes the
basis for the art of politics. At the concrete political level, 'it
will have to be considered how one can lead most effectively
(given certain ends); hence how the leaders may be best
prepared'.

But for the working class:

> in the formation of leaders, one premise is fundamental: is it the
> intention that there should always be rulers and ruled, or is the
> objective to create the conditions in which this division is no
> longer necessary? In other words, is the initial premise the
> perpetual division of the human race, or the belief that this
> division is only an historical fact, corresponding to certain
> conditions? (*SPN* 144)

The whole science and art of politics for the working class

therefore are based on a perspective of a *transition* to a new society, of a new concept of revolution. The nodal point of Gramsci's political reflection which culminates in the 'political question of the intellectuals' comes from that perspective. The central categories of his mature political reflection, the passive revolution, the war of position and hegemony allow the politics of the workers' movement to be retranslated in a phase in which the actuality of the revolution or revolutionary potential can no longer have the eruptive character of the imperialist war and of the post-World War I crisis. The theory of the intellectuals, by allowing us to analyse concrete reality, sheds light on the entire process of transition, of revolution.

NOTES

1   See for example L. Paggi, 'Intellettuali, teoria e partito nel marxismo della Seconda Internazionale. Aspetti e problemi,' introduction to M. Adler, *Il socialismo e gli intellettuali*, Bari, 1974.

2   These themes constituted the kernel both of *Materialism and Empirio-criticism* and of the *Philosophical Notebooks*.

3   K. Kautsky, *L'intelligenza e la social democrazia*, now published as an appendix to M. Adler, *Il socialismo e gli intellettuali*, op. cit. pp 331-360.

4   See 'Politics as a Vocation,' pp. 77-129 of *From Max Weber: Essays in Sociology*, edited by H.H. Gerth and C. Wright Mills, Galaxy Books, New York, 1958.

5   In actual fact, even before his imprisonment, it was clear to Gramsci that the transition to the 'war of position' was the fundamental strategic and theoretical question in the West, particularly after the October Revolution, because of the peculiarities that distinguish East from West See for example the passage in the famous report to the Italian Communist Party Central Committee of 3 and 4 August 1926. (*PWII* 408-9)

6   The first draft of this note, in Notebook IV, is less articulated and in place of the concept of the 'totalitarian state' there appears that of the 'dictatorial' state.

7   *SPN*. p. 80*n*: 'The "normal" exercise of hegemony on the now classical terrain of the parliamentary regime is characterized by the combination of force and consent, which balance each other reciprocally, without force predominating excessively over consent. Indeed, the attempt is

always made to ensure that force will appear to be based on the consent
of the majority, expressed by the so-called organs of public opinion –
newspapers and associations – which, therefore, in certain situations,
are artificially multiplied.'

8 See for example (*SPN* 252-3): 'The "Prince" could be a head of state,
a head of government, but also a political leader who wants to conquer
a state or found a new type of state: in this sense, "prince" could be
translated into modern language as "political party". In the reality of
some states, the "head of state", i.e. the balancing element of the various
interests in conflict with the interest that is predominant but not
exclusivist in the absolute sense, is, in fact, the "political party";
different, however, from traditional constitutional law, it neither
reigns nor governs juridically: it has *de facto* power, and, within "civil
society", exercises a hegemonic and therefore a balancing function
over the various interests. "Civil society" is, however, so interwoven in
actual fact with political society that all citizens feel, on the contrary,
that it does reign and govern. One cannot create a constitutional law
of the traditional type on this continually shifting reality, but only a
system of principles which assert, as the goal of the state, its end, its
disappearance, or in other words the reabsorption of political society
into civil society.'

9 J.V. Stalin, *Problems of Leninism*, Peking, 1976, pp. 626-7. My emphasis.
For the question in its historical setting see S.F. Cohen, *Bukharin and
the Bolshevik Revolution*, London, 1974, chapters IX and X.

10 It is true that Gramsci took over the concept of 'civil society' in the
sense understood by Hegel and not Marx, as he himself warns, 'One
must distinguish civil society as understood by Hegel and in the sense
that it is often used in these notes (i.e. in the sense of the political and
cultural hegemony of a social group over the whole of society, as the
ethical content of the state)', (Q 703); but the distinction between civil
and political society or between structure and superstructure is a
methodological and not an organic one, which, moreover, is obvious
given that Gramsci is a dialectical thinker.

11 cf. G. Vacca, *Saggio su Togliatti e la tradizione comunista*, Bari, 1974
chapter II, part VII.

12 These themes, although within a different and not yet fully
developed framework, are already found in Gramsci's pre-prison
reflections. From then on they play an essential role in the definition
of his thought.

13 cf. G. Vacca, *Vie e strategie del socialismo dall'ottobre a oggi*, in
Almanacco PCI 1977, pp 326-7.

14 On the relation between revolution and production in the Gramsci of

the *Ordine Nuovo*, see F. De Felice, *Serrati, Bordiga, Gramsci e il problema della rivoluzione in Italia*, Bari, 1971, pp. 292 et seq; and the article published in this volume.

THE THEORY OF MODERN BUREAUCRACY
Luis Razeto Migliaro
Pasquale Misuraca

A central question in current political debates in Britain, the rest of the advanced capitalist world and in the countries of 'really existing socialism' in Eastern Europe, is the growth of bureaucracy. In a number of liberal democratic states, the party systems and representative institutions are in crisis. Antonio Gramsci was one of the few thinkers on the left to study these aspects of what he considered a long-term crisis of capitalism, and his analysis remains extremely important.

Luis Razeto Migliaro and Pasquale Misuraca show how Gramsci's discussion of bureaucracy went beyond Hegel, Marx, and Weber. Marx, they argue, basically misunderstood Hegel's position on bureaucracy and failed to take adequate account of what was, for Hegel's day, a sophisticated view of the inter-relationship between the state bureaucracy and organizations in civil or private society. This led to a shortcoming in Marx's own view of the state as an instrument of a class. Thus Marx was unable to analyze the real connections between the state and the economy and society as a whole. Marx's theory of the state remained abstract, his discussion of politics inadequate, and the problem of the relationship between the economic structure and the political and ideological superstructure unresolved.

Gramsci's novelty, they say, lies in his historical, concrete analysis of the growth of bureaucracy and the way in which he relates the development of the liberal bourgeois state, based on consent and the separation of powers, to class conflict. Unlike Weber who considered bureaucracy to be the inevitable product of the development of industrial society and of the need for professional expertise, Gramsci rooted the ossification and entrenchment of bureaucracy and the crisis of representative government in the class struggle, and in the difficulty of the bourgeoisie to fulfill their promise of promoting the interests of the whole of society, their universalistic project.

Misuraca and Razeto Migliaro argue in the full version of this piece that as a theoretical advance on Marx and Lenin's ideas on the state, Gramsci's theory of the state is applicable not only to advanced capitalist countries, but also to less developed societies and to 'real socialism'. As the contrast between the British tradition of limited government and the more bureaucratic states of continental Europe grows less and less obvious with the enormous expansion in government activities and burgeoning of the Civil Service; and as the crisis of representative institutions becomes more accute, Gramsci's writing on bureaucracy seems strikingly relevant.

As political and economic forms develop historically, a new type of functionary is increasingly being produced — what could be described as a 'career' functionary, technically trained for bureaucratic work (civil and military). This is a fact of prime significance for political science and for any history of the forms taken by the State. (*SPN* 185-6)

Gramsci fully understood that any scientific analysis of the state must contain at its centre an analysis of bureaucracy. His view marks a fundamental change from the way the theory of the state has been set out in the Marxist tradition where the problem of the state has been examined by leaving the problem of bureaucracy virtually to one side.

The tendency to separate the two already exists in Marx. His analysis of the state establishes a clear distinction between the class 'content' of the state apparatus (which determines the essence, the 'character' of the state), and the institutional 'forms' (which make up the chance aspect, the 'appearance' of the state). (For evidence of this, see Marx's 'Critique of Hegel's Philosophy of Law' where he reduces bureaucracy to mere administration leaving out the police and judiciary.) Nor is the problem of bureaucracy the essential one in Lenin's analysis of the state. Lenin saw bureaucracy as a phenomenon of the deterioration of organization, and the bureaucrat as an official governed by 'routine' attitudes. But Gramsci recognized the centrality of the problem of bureaucracy and it forms part of his total re-elaboration of the theory of the state.

Gramsci's Conception of the State

We find Gramsci's most mature conception of the state in 'Machiavelli, Sociology and Political Science':

> . . . the State is the entire complex of practical and theoretical activities with which the ruling class not only justifies and maintains its dominance but manages to win the active consent of those over whom it rules . . . (*SPN* 244)

There are at least three novel elements in this conception of the state:

a)   The state is not described as an 'apparatus', a 'machine', or an 'instrument', but as the totality of the activities of the ruling class as rulers. This means that the state is no longer regarded as a fortress to be stormed, as a machine which can be operated differently by various political managements, or as an institutional apparatus which can be the property of a class. On the contrary, the state is regarded as the totality of actions performed by specific classes, specific social categories, specific ruling groups, and specific men.

b)   The activities which constitute the state are 'practical' and 'technical'. This means that the state is not reduced to administrative, judiciary and police activity — the practical exercise of power — but also involves elaborative activities: producing ideologies, information and knowledge. The state, then, ensures its own conservation by developing specific modes of feeling, understanding and action. The production, organization and diffusion of knowledge constitute one part of the state's activities, and hence intellectuals or some part of them, are also part of the state. Given this, it becomes clear why the problem of bureaucracy is central to the theory of the state.

c)   The state is not reduced to activities of domination (the use of coercion), but involves activities of leadership (the construction of consensus).

What is novel in Gramsci is that the state no longer appears as an entity separate from collective life, as a particular organism which dominates and controls society by placing itself above it. The state emerges as the complex of activities which organize and make the masses homogeneous, setting up the relations of the led with the leaders by means of representation, and eventually, actively involving the masses in the state itself. While the state is usually seen as the organism which dominates and leads from the outside (thus reproducing the condition of exteriority from it experienced by the dominated, the led), Gramsci grasped the fact that state activities are not carried on in order to separate leaders from the led. Rather they establish the integration of the led into the state. This does not mean that the led become leaders, but that they are integrated into the sum of state activities which tend to realize the plans of the ruling classes. The state is thus the organization of relations between leaders and led.

When the state is thus defined, the problem of bureaucracy becomes fundamental to the science of history and politics and especially to the theory of the state. But what exactly is the bureaucracy?

What is the Bureaucracy?

Hegel writes:

> The members of the government and the civil servants constitute the major part of the *middle estate*, in which is concentrated the developed intelligence of the mass of a people and its consciousness of what is lawful. That this section should not assume the isolated position of an aristocracy or use education and ability as a means to arbitrary domination depends on the institutions of sovereignty working from above and on the corporate institutions' rights exercised from below . . . In the middle estate, to which civil servants belong, there is consciousness of the state and the most pronounced degree of education. This estate therefore constitutes the pillar of the state in terms of uprightness and intelligence. . . The education of this middle estate is a principal interest of the state.[1]

As we see, Hegel locates the problem of bureaucracy at the level of relations between leaders and led. He also grasps the specific situation of bureaucrats as delegates of political power and as legitimated by technical competence. These two moments, political and technical, Hegel termed the subjective and the objective aspect.

The objective factor in (officials') appointment (to state office) is

knowledge and proof of ability. Such proof guarantees that the
state gets what it requires. . . . (The subjective factor is) the
selection of a *particular* individual for a post, his appointment,
and his authorisation to conduct public business; this linking of
the individual to the office, whose relation one to the other must
always be fortuitous, is the prerogative of the monarch as the
deciding and sovereign power in the state.[2]

In singling out these elements, Hegel did not make a critique of
them. Rather he justified a specific practice in positive terms.
Sociology, especially that of Weber, developed the analysis of
bureaucracy in similar terms, going little beyond the contribution made by Hegel. Weber restricted himself largely to
formalizing Hegel's analysis. Gramsci, on the other hand, re-
examined the Hegelian problematic of the bureaucracy,
critically reconstructed it, and thus went beyond Hegel,
beyond Weber, and also beyond Marx who had not successfully grasped the crucial nature of the problems posed by Hegel
in this instance.

Gramsci identifies the bureaucracy's function as *structuring
and stabilizing relations between the leaders and the led*. In
defining this connecting function he makes it clear that the
bureaucracy neither is, nor claims to be, representative of the
led. It is not elected and controlled from below. Nor is it an
intermediate social stratum performing a mediating function
as with Hegel. Rather the bureaucratic personnel of the state is
appointed from above by the political leaders of the state to
whom it answers for its activities. It is selected on the basis of
technical competence which is presented as a criterion of
legitimation. While the ruling classes require loyalty to the
state and to their policies from the bureaucrats, the subordinate classes can demand of them only technical efficiency
in the exercise of their functions. Thus, for Gramsci, the
bureaucracy is both political fact and technical fact. He makes
this clear when he examines the relations between leaders and
led.

The first element is that there really do exist rulers and ruled,
leaders and led. The entire science and art of politics are based on
this primordial, and (given certain general conditions) irreducible fact. . . Given this fact, it will have to be considered how one
can lead most effectively (given certain ends); hence how the

leaders may best be prepared (and it is more precisely in this that the first stage of the art and science of politics consists); and how, on the other hand, one can know the lines of least resistance, or the most rational lines along which to proceed if one wishes to secure the obedience of the led or ruled. . . Yet it must clearly be understood that the division between rulers and ruled — though in the last analysis it has its origin in a division between social groups — is in fact, things being as they are, also to be found within the group itself, even where it is a socially homogeneous one. (*SPN* 144)

The dual nature of bureaucracy, as at once technical and political, follows from the separation between leaders and led in any forms of collective life. By seeing that this is so, Gramsci was also able to see that even a 'classless' society, or a homogeneous social group, or a party which has a bureaucracy, has in it not merely a technical instrument, but also a political structure. Bureaucracy, says Gramsci, is not just a matter of the impersonal administration of *things*: 'Those who see everything purely in terms of "technique", "technical necessity" . . . avoid the fundamental problem.' (*SPN* 144)

The third element in Gramsci's theory of bureaucracy concerns the process of the formation of the bureaucracy and the problem of its social origin. Gramsci saw one historical basis for the bureaucracy in the political parties themselves: 'The principle once posed that there are leaders and led, rulers and ruled, it is true that parties have up till now been the most effective way of developing leaders and leadership.' (*SPN* 145) A second source lies in the dissolution of the former ruling classes during the formation of the new state. It is the intellectuals and cadres of those classes who became officials (administrators, technicians, organisers, etc.) of the new state power. Gramsci saw that this process was rooted in the

birth of the modern European states by successive small waves of reform rather than by revolutionary explosions like the original French one. . . The period of the 'Restoration' is the richest in developments of this kind; Restoration becomes the first policy whereby social struggles find sufficiently elastic frameworks to allow the bourgeoisie to gain power without dramatic upheavals, without the French machinery of terror. The old feudal classes are demoted from their dominant position to a 'governing' one, but are not eliminated, nor is there any attempt to liquidate them as an organic whole. Instead of a class they become a 'caste' with specific cultural and psychological characteristics, but no longer with predominant economic functions. (*SPN* 115)

Gramsci went on to ask if an analogous process could be discerned in the formation of a socialist state: 'Can this "model" for the creation of the modern states be repeated in other conditions? Can this be excluded absolutely, or could we say that at least partially there can be similar developments in the form of the appearance of planned economies?' (*SPN* 115)

This pattern of formation of the modern bureaucracy accounts in part for the fact that 'the State (represents) every attempt to crystallise permanently a particular stage of development, a particular situation'. It also helps to explain 'a certain unstable equilibrium between the classes, which is a result of the fact that certain categories of intellectuals (in the direct service of the state, especially the civil and military bureaucracy) are still too closely tied to the old dominant classes.'

These two converging processes in the creation of the bureaucracy reflect and extend the distinction Gramsci made between *organic* and *traditional* intellectuals. He defined the question thus:

> The problem of functionaries partly coincides with that of the intellectuals. However, though it is true that every new form of society and State has required a new type of functionary, it is also true that new ruling groups have never been able, at least initially, to ignore traditional or established interests – i.e. the categories of functionary (especially in the ecclesiastical and military spheres) who already existed and had been constituted before they came to power. (*SPN* 186)

However, the Gramscian analysis of the historical formation of modern bureaucracy also points out a third element:

> Does there exist, in a given country, a widespread social stratum in whose economic life and political self-assertion (effective participation in power, even though indirectly, by 'blackmail') the bureaucratic career, either civil or military, is a very important element? In modern Europe this stratum can be

identified in the medium and small rural bourgeoisie, which is more or less numerous from one country to another — depending on the development of industrial strength on the one hand, and of agrarian reform on the other. Of course the bureaucratic career (civil and military) is not the monopoly of this social stratum; however, it is particularly well suited to the social function which this stratum carries out; and to the psychological tendencies which such a function produces or encourages. These two elements impart to the entire social stratum a certain homogeneity and energy in its aims — and hence a political value, and an often decisive function within the entire social organism. The members of this stratum are accustomed to direct command over nuclei of men, however tiny, and to commanding 'politically', not 'economically'. In other words, their art of command implies no aptitude for ordering 'things', for ordering 'men and things' into an organic whole, as occurs in industrial production — since this stratum has no economic functions in the modern sense of the word. (*SPN* 212-213)

Through this analysis of the social origins and the channels which lead to the creation of the bureaucracy, Gramsci faced up to the problem of the state and its class structure at a level of concreteness different from that of Marx's analysis, and from its re-elaboration as developed by Lenin. For Marx and Lenin the problem was to define the 'character' of the state, which came to be determined in the correspondence between the specific mode of production (capitalist, socialist) and the dominant classes (bourgeoisie, proletariat). The conceptualization of the nature of the state in terms of 'bourgeois dictatorship' and 'dictatorship of the proletariat' derived from this. Gramsci's analysis, on the other hand, led to the identification of the concrete relations between the ruling classes and the subordinate classes, and the mediations (*i.e.* the activities undertaken to effect the subordination of the latter to the former) carried through by individual social categories (intellectuals, bureaucrats and technicians).

The fourth element of Gramsci's theory of bureaucracy involves the process by which a bureaucracy grows into a caste and conceives of itself as a 'body apart'. A crucial factor in understanding this process lay in Gramsci's remark about the partial overlapping of the problem of bureaucracy and the question of the intellectuals. In his analysis of the intellectuals, Gramsci pointed out both the reasons for their constitution as a social group as well as for their conception of themselves as distanced from the classes and their interests:-

> Since these various categories of traditional intellectuals experience through an *'esprit de corps'* their uninterrupted historical continuity and their special qualification, they thus put themselves forward as autonomous and independent of the dominant social group. This self-assessment is not without consequences in the ideological and political field, consequences of wide-ranging import. The whole of idealist philosophy can easily be connected with this position assumed by the social complex of intellectuals and it can be defined as the expression of that social utopia by which the intellectuals think of themselves as 'independent' autonomous, endowed with a character of their own, etc. (*SPN* 7-8)

More specifically on the bureaucracy:-

> . . . the group which is the bearer of the new ideas is not the economic group but the intellectual stratum, and the conception of the State advocated by them changes aspect; it is conceived of as something in itself, as a rational absolute. The problem can be formulated as follows: since the State is the concrete form of a productive world and since the intellectuals are the social element from which the governing personnel is drawn, the intellectual who is not firmly anchored to a strong economic group will tend to present the state as an absolute; in this way the function of the intellectuals themselves is conceived of as absolute and pre-eminent, and their historical existence and dignity are abstractly rationalised. This motive is fundamental for an historical understanding of modern philosophical idealism, and is connected with the mode of formation of the modern States of continental Europe as 'reaction-national transcendence'* of the French Revolution . . . (*SPN* 117)

In these two passages Gramsci points out the existence of a relation between the position of the bureaucracy as a separate

---

* Gramsci is referring to the attempt to avoid the experience of the French Revolution in other countries in Europe.

social category, and the conception of the state as an autonomous body distanced from the life of the classes. In these conditions, the 'spirit of the State', of which the bureaucracy is guardian, consists neither in a totality of ethical principles which the state sets before all citizens as a norm, nor in adopting points of view and criteria of a 'universal' kind (such as the common weal, patriotism, etc.) It consists instead in the ideological cement which makes the bureaucracy itself both homogeneous and compact. That is, there is a specific group ideology which rationalizes the position the bureaucrat occupies. In this way the 'state spirit' expressed by the bureaucracy consists not of the adoption of general ends by state officials (as Hegel argued), but in proposing their own group aims as general ends for the collectivity. That is why 'the governing power' appears as a separate body, and why

> the state was conceived of as something abstract by the collectivity of citizens, as an eternal father who was supposed to have thought of everything, foreseen everything, etc.: hence the absence of real democracy, of a real national collective will, and hence, as a result of the passivity of individuals, the need for a despotism of the bureaucracy, more or less disguised. (Q 750-1)

Hegel and Marx on Bureaucracy

This element of the theory of bureaucracy was constructed by Gramsci in direct reference to Hegel's analysis of the bureaucracy unmediated by Marx's interpretation since Marx's *Critique of Hegel's Philosophy of Law* was still unpublished. A brief look at Marx's ideas here will help explain how Gramsci went far beyond him.

Marx's interpretation and critique of Hegel's analysis are the key to understanding the whole of his theory of the state, and most specifically to limitations in his ideas. In one way Marx manages to transcend Hegel's conception of the state. He grasps the fact that the state does not represent general interests abstractly, but the particular interests of the ruling classes (recognizing a certain level of universality in the action of certain classes, at the moment they carry out a progressive, revolutionary function). In another way, Marx does not go as far as Hegel, in that he does not completely grasp the essential function of the bureaucracy in the state.

Marx did not see that for Hegel 'civil society' is not merely the sphere of *private, individual* interest, but also that of *common, particular* interests; and that consequently in Hegel's analysis 'civil society' is not only citizens as private, economic subjects, but organized in corporations.[3]

Given that Marx attributed to Hegel the exclusion of bureaucracy both from the sphere of civil society and from that of the state, he interpreted Hegel's conception of bureaucracy as though it were based on the separation of state and civil society:

> Hegel proceeds from the *separation* of the 'state' and 'civil' society, from 'particular interests' and the 'intrinsically and explicitly general'; and indeed bureaucracy is based on *this separation.*[4]

Because Marx did not perceive that Hegelian analysis distinguished two concrete levels of bureaucratic organization (in the sphere of civil society and that of the state), and that, for Hegel, the *relation* between state and civil society is the specific responsibility of these bureaucracies, he directed against Hegel the criticism that he had left the bureaucracy in mid-air, and given a speculative account of it.

This shortcoming in Marx's interpretation and critique of Hegel's work is in fact the basis of the way in which Marx frames and solves the problem of the relations between economy and state, and between 'structure' and 'super-structure', as he explains in the *Preface* to the *Contribution to the Critique of Political Economy*.

As soon as Marx reduced civil society – on the basis of this reading of Hegel – to economic relations, and removed the bureaucracy (and the intellectuals) from civil society and state, he lost the chance to individuate the concrete relations between economy and state, between 'structure' and 'super-structure'. These relations are in reality conducted by specific social categories (the bureaucracy, intellectuals), so that, if these categories are not defined according to their particular function, the concrete ways in which the economy and society actually relate to the state escape analysis and subsequently are seen abstractly, by means of speculative concepts, such as determination, correspondence, reflection, conditioning, etc.

In response to his reading of Hegel and Marx on the

problems of the state, Gramsci criticized the speculative character 'the superstitious "miracle"' (Q 1422) of the relations between 'structure' and 'superstructure', and between civil society and state. He had grasped the connecting function, discharged specifically by the intellectuals ('officials of the superstructure') and the bureaucracy. On this basis he defined the relations between 'structure' and 'superstructure' with the concept of *historic bloc* — a social bloc formed between the classes engaged in organizing the economy and the leading groups of the state, cemented by the activity of different intellectual categories. In addition, he defined relations between leaders and led on the basis of the concept of the state as civil society plus political society, relations organized by the bureaucracy.

Gramsci underlined the importance of the Hegelian analysis of civil society, which had allowed Hegel to see the state as a body which organizes and educates to create a consensus through political and corporative associations, as well as through its own resources. However, he simultaneously grasped the limitation of Hegel's ideas: limitations due to his lack of experience of mass parties. Marx faced a similar lack, but in comparison to Hegel he had more of 'a feeling for the masses', though less understanding of the complexity of life and of state organization. (*SPN* 259)

Where Hegel identified the creation of state spirit in the corporations,[5] Gramsci distinguished it in the political parties, (*SPN* 147) thus grasping the historical transition to more highly evolved forms of state organization. In addition, whereas for Hegel the corporative spirit could develop into the state spirit because the state guaranteed the realization of the objectives of the corporations and the rights of the citizen, Gramsci conceived of the development of the spirit of the party into a state spirit because it is in the party that people and social groups acquire a universal-national consciousness, thus transcending such ends as individualism and group economic-corporative interest. It is in the party that the leaders and the state officials are educated: through the parties, the classes become the state.

The Historical Nature of the Bureaucracy

The fifth element of Gramsci's theory of bureaucracy lies in his understanding of the historically determined character of bureaucracy. 'It can be said that every form of society has its approach or solution to the problem of bureaucracy. These must inevitably vary,' he wrote in examining the English case in relation to the French and German ones. 'Certainly every type of society and State has had its own problem of functionaries, which it has resolved and formulated in its own way; every society has had its own system of selection and its own type of functionary to be trained.' (*SPN* 186) When Gramsci maintained that the problem of bureaucracy is historically determined, it was not only a general methodological reminder, but an argument which he considered of fundamental importance. By emphasizing the historical specificity of bureaucracy, he intended to criticize all those theories such as Weber's which view bureaucracy as a typical feature of all modern societies, and give us a general and abstract 'sociological' analysis, not an historical one.[6]

The historical nature of the problem of bureaucracy led Gramsci to examine the institution of modern bureaucracies in the context of the 1929-30 world crisis, insofar as this marked a complete reorganization of relations between leaders and led. In the three responses to the crisis — the American, the fascist, and the Stalinist — he grasped that the expansion and predominance of the bureaucracy was a sign of the failure to overcome the crisis.

Gramsci started by characterizing the organization of the state developed by the bourgeoisie as having the specific task of making the led accept the bourgeois objective as universal.

> The previous ruling classes were essentially conservative in the sense that they did not tend to construct an organic passage from the other classes into their own, i.e., to enlarge their class sphere 'technically' and ideologically: their conception was that of a closed caste. The bourgeois class poses itself as an organism in continuous movement, capable of absorbing the entire society, assimilating it to its own cultural and economic level. The entire function of the State has been transformed; the State has become an 'educator', etc. (*SPN* 260)

The bourgeois project was to organize relations between

leaders and led on the basis of consent, that is, by shaping the led to the objectives of the leaders.

This project is made up of two elements. The first is the principle of representation (as delegation of power) expressed in the parliamentary system and the parties. The second is the principle of technical competence expressed in the bureaucratic system (in the division of the state's powers). Having identified the project, Gramsci examined the conditions for its realization and its structural limitations, and criticized the resulting state organization. He viewed the project of the bourgeois class not as the conceptualization of an abstract model of organization of state life and as the proposal of means to bring it into being; but as the result of real conflicts and conditions which ideologues then rationalize and make systematically consistent in theory.

> The separation of powers, together with all the discussion provoked by its realisation and the legal dogmas which its appearance brought into being, is a product of the struggle between civil society and political society in a given historical period. This period is characterised by a certain unstable equilibrium between the classes, which is a result of the fact that certain categories of intellectuals (in the direct service of the State, especially the civil and military bureaucracy) are still too closely tied to the old dominant classes. (*SPN* 245)

Gramsci's criticism of the bourgeois state does not consist in singling out abstract contradictions in the model of the state, nor in counterposing the abstract model to its concrete realization. Rather he undertakes an historico-critical analysis of the struggle between classes. From this struggle a state is shaped which exhibits the effects of an unstable equilibrium of relations between the classes, a 'contradictory' state inasmuch as it is the product of struggle.

To put it more precisely, the conflict between political representation and technical competence, between parliamentary and bureaucratic systems, demonstrates the fact that the categories of intellectuals in the direct service of the state, especially the civil and military bureaucracy, are too closely linked to the old ruling classes. This link is such that the bourgeois project of representing the interests of the whole society breaks down because of a bureaucracy transformed into a caste, which separates the state from civil society, and makes it absolute. The bourgeois class cannot produce enough of its own organic intellectuals, does not achieve full hegemony and must have recourse either to Jacobin violence or to the use, by compromise, of the traditional intellectuals. The result is that the bourgeois state cannot rely solely upon the representative system, given that the activity in educating towards consensus is insufficient and does not manage to organize a mass conformity. Consequently, the civil and military bureaucracy increasingly discharges political functions and occupies enlarging areas in the life of the state. Gramsci's critical conclusion follows:

> Essential importance of the separation of powers for political and economic liberalism; the entire liberal ideology, with its strengths and its weaknesses, can be encapsulated in the principle of the separation of powers, and the source of liberalism's weakness then becomes apparent: it is the bureaucracy — i.e. the crystallisation of the leading personnel — which exercises coercive power, and at a certain point it becomes a caste. Hence the popular demand for making all posts elective — a demand which is extreme liberalism, and at the same time its dissolution. . . (*SPN* 245-6)

Much further on, in the note 'Machiavelli. The State', Gramsci reconsidered the problem:-

> And what grounds are there for the accusations made against parliamentarianism and against the party system — which is inseparable from parliamentarianism? (Objective grounds, naturally — i.e. ones related to the fact that the existence of parliament, in itself, hinders and delays the *technical* actions of the government).
>
>   That the representative system may politically 'be a nuisance' for the career bureaucracy is understandable; but this is not the point. The point is to establish whether the representative and party system, instead of being a suitable system for choosing elected functionaries to integrate and balance the appointed civil servants and prevent them from becoming ossified, has become a hindrance and a mechanism which operates in the reverse direction — and, if so, for what reasons. (*SPN* 254)

The Crisis of Representative Government

The historical development of these 'contradictions' ends in a crisis of representation and the victory of the bureaucracy, processes which mean the historic crisis of the liberal state. This crisis shows the failure of the bourgeois class's state project, in that it has failed to become a general class which makes the other classes take its own form.

> How this process comes to a halt, and the conception of the State as pure force is returned to, etc. The bourgeois class is 'saturated': it not only does not expand — it starts to disintegrate; it not only does not assimilate new elements, it loses part of itself (or at least its losses are enormously more numerous than its assimilations). (*SPN* 260)

This is exactly what constitutes the *organic crisis* of capitalist society. Gramsci explains the relation between the crisis of the representative state organization and the bureaucracy's predominance (in the state organization) in 'Observations on certain aspects of the structure of political parties in periods of organic crisis':-

> At a certain point in their historical lives, social classes become detached from their political parties. In other words, the traditional parties in that particular organisational form, with the particular men who constitute, represent, and lead them, are no longer recognised by their class (or fraction of a class) as its expression. (*SPN* 210)

Gramsci noted the important fact that the crisis of the representative system is above all manifested as a crisis of the parties, of the channels through which representation is expressed and consensus organized. This concerns not only the fact that the subordinate classes do not recognize themselves in the given state leadership, but that the ruling classes themselves perceive their own party organs as inadequate for the tasks they assign to them in that given historical moment. This happens because, though the classes evolve, the parties crystallize, shutting themselves up in a process of bureaucratization.

> When such crises occur, the immediate situation becomes delicate and dangerous, because the field is open for violent

solutions, for the activities of unknown forces, represented by charismatic 'men of destiny'.

These situations of conflict between 'represented and representatives' reverberate out from the terrain of the parties (the party organisations properly speaking, the parliamentary-electoral field, newspaper organisation) throughout the State organism, reinforcing the relative power of the bureaucracy (civil and military), of high finance, of the Church, and generally of all bodies relatively independent of the fluctuations of public opinion. How are they created in the first place? In every country the process is different, although the content is the same. And the content is the crisis of the ruling class's hegemony, which occurs either because the ruling class has failed in some major political undertaking for which it has requested, or forcibly extracted, the consent of the broad masses (war, for example), or because huge masses (especially of peasants and petit-bourgeois intellectuals) have passed suddenly from a state of political passivity to a certain activity, and put forward demands which taken together, albeit not organically formulated, add up to a revolution. A 'crisis of authority' is spoken of: this is precisely the crisis of hegemony, or general crisis of the State. (*SPN* 210)

In this passage there is the fullest formulation of the process which involves the *failure of the project* of the bourgeois class to represent the interests of the whole of society as expressed in the loss of hegemony; the *development of ideological autonomy* of the subordinate classes expressed in the coming of the mass party; and the *reinforcement of the bureaucracy* as means of stabilizing the relations of power between classes.

Gramsci continued:-

The crisis creates situations which are dangerous in the short run, since the various strata of the population are not all capable of orienting themselves equally swiftly, or of reorganizing with the same rhythm. The traditional ruling class, which has numerous trained cadres, changes men and programmes and, with greater speed than is achieved by the subordinate classes, reabsorbs the control that was slipping from its grasp. Perhaps it may make sacrifices, and expose itself to an uncertain future by demagogic promises; but it retains power, reinforces it for the time being, and uses it to crush its adversary and disperse his leading cadres, who cannot be very numerous or highly trained. The passage of the troops of many different parties under the banner of a single party, which better represents and resumes the needs of the entire class, is an organic and normal phenomenon, even if its rhythm is very swift — indeed almost like lightning in comparison with periods of calm. It represents the fusion of an entire social class under a single leadership, which alone is held to be capable of solving an over-riding problem of its existence and of fending off a mortal danger. When the crisis does not find this organic solution, but that of the charismatic leader, it means that a static equilibrium exists (whose factors may be disparate, but in which the decisive one is the immaturity of the progressive forces); it means that no group, neither the conservatives nor the progressives, has the strength for victory, and that even the conservative group needs a master. (See *The Eighteenth Brumaire of Louis Bonaparte*). (*SPN* 210-11)

When a crisis of the representative system occurs, the immediate problem for the ruling class is that of avoiding its own break-up and of reorganizing itself as ruling class. It becomes aware of the crisis of hegemony, and is not in a condition to continue its project of making the other classes conform to its own project. The ruling class then no longer uses the representative system and the parties as organizations for the construction of consensus. It unifies and organizes itself around the bureaucracy (civil and military), which emerges as the 'single party', the only one capable of discharging the new tasks set by the ruling class. The organic dominance of the bureaucratic system is thus outlined.

This dominance, as Gramsci went on to explain, is made evident not only through the state (the party of the ruling class), but also involves social organizations, parties, and cultural institutions (including those of the subordinate classes, even where they have become the state).

This order of phenomena is connected to one of the most important questions concerning the political party — i.e. the party's capacity to react against force of habit, against the tendency to become mummified and anachronistic. Parties come into existence, and constitute themselves as organisations, in order to influence the situation at moments which are historically vital for their class; but they are not always capable of adapting themselves to new tasks and to new epochs, nor of evolving *pari passu* with the overall relations of force (and hence the relative position of their class) in the country in question, or in the international field. In analysing the development of parties, it is necessary to distinguish: their social group; their mass membership; their bureaucracy and General Staff. The bureaucracy is the most dangerously hidebound and conservative force; if it ends up by constituting a compact body, which stands on its own and feels itself independent of the mass of members, the party ends up by becoming anachronistic and at moments of acute crisis it is voided of its social content and left as though suspended in mid-air. (*SPN* 211)

For Gramsci this bureaucratization of the parties was rooted in the very definition of the tasks the classes set themselves in the course of their development. The parties are born to lead and organize the expansion of classes and accomplish their project of universalization. But once they fail to establish hegemony, or are forced into defensive positions, the party bureaucracy — which carries out the functions of internal dominance — becomes supreme. This results in the separation of the party from the class which in turn makes the party anachronistic, politically sectarian and dogmatic in its theory.

The dominance of bureaucracy is the common element of the American, fascist and Stalinist responses to the 1929-30 crisis. These responses did not resolve what was a long-term crisis. The very consolidation of the bureaucracy shows the extent to which the crisis had been stabilized and underlay the crystallization of relations between leaders and led.

However, as these responses to the organic crisis are developed, a change occurs in the internal structure of the bureaucracy. This change is due to the need to organize and control the processes which create the collective behaviour of the mass of the population and which are linked to new methods of production (e.g. assembly lines) and to the rationalization of labour. A technocratic bureaucracy emerges, which reflects technical criteria of administration more in conformity with the requirements of the process of rationalization of capitalist production. This bureaucracy first stands beside, and progressively thereafter replaces, the traditional bureaucracy. The new technocrats are no longer tied to the old ruling classes but are organic to the new.

Gramsci analysed this process in 'Observations and notes towards a collection of essays on the history of the intellectuals':-

> In the modern world, the category of intellectuals, understood in this sense, has undergone an unprecedented expansion. The democratic-bureaucratic system has given rise to a great mass of functions which are not at all justified by the social necessities of production, though they are justified by the political necessities of the dominant fundamental group. (*SPN* 13)

A little further on, he expanded this:

> In modern civilisation all practical activities have become so complex, and the sciences so interwoven with everyday life, that each practical activity tends to create a new type of school for its own executive and specialists and hence to create a body of specialist intellectuals at a higher level to teach in these schools ... The crisis of the curriculum and organisation of the schools, i.e. of the overall framework of a policy for forming modern intellectual cadres, is to a great extent an aspect and a ramification of the more comprehensive and general organic crisis... The development of an industrial base both in the cities and in the countryside meant a growing need for the new type of urban intellectual ... It may also be observed that deliberative bodies tend to an ever-increasing extent to distinguish their activity into two 'organic' aspects: into the deliberative activity which is their essence, and into technical-cultural activity in which the questions upon which they have to take decisions are first examined by experts and analysed scientifically. (*SPN* 26-7)

Gramsci passed from specifying the conditions from which technical intellectuality grows — that is, the practical needs of production and institutions which emerge in the process of modernization — to a more specific examination of the changes involving the bureaucracy.

> This latter activity has already created a whole bureaucratic body, with a new structure; for apart from the specialised departments of experts who prepare the technical material for the deliberative bodies, a second body of functionaries is created — more or less disinterested 'volunteers', selected variously

from industry, from the banks, from finance houses. This is one of the mechanisms by means of which the career bureaucracy eventually came to control the democratic regimes and parliaments; now the mechanism is being organically extended, and is absorbing into its sphere the great specialists of private enterprise, which thus come to control both regimes and bureaucracies. What is involved is a necessary, organic development which tends to integrate the personnel specialised in the technique of politics with personnel specialised in the concrete problems of administering the essential practical activities of the great and complex national societies of today. Hence every attempt to exorcise these tendencies from the outside produces no result other than moralistic sermons and rhetorical lamentations . . . The traditional type of political 'leader', prepared only for formal-juridical activities, is becoming anachronistic and represents a danger for the life of the State. (*SPN* 27-8)

This passage from traditional to technocratic bureaucracy — though in one sense derived from the needs of the rationalization of production and labour — constitutes a complex change in relations between leaders and led. It concerns the passage from the liberal model of organizing the representative-bureaucratic regime to the technocratic model of organizing a bureaucratic-representative regime. *Technical competence,* here, comes to dominate the process of representation and the creation of consent. The consequence is a draining of ideological content. No longer is consent constructed through rhetorical discussion, but through the introduction of behavioural stereotypes without obvious ideological content. The mass media, with their complex techniques, then replace the bureaucrat as the bearer of ideology.

Gramsci's theory of bureaucracy does not end with the general terms considered here. It is elaborated in his theory of the party where he examines the evolution of mass parties and the process of bureaucratization, particularly concentrating on the problem of bureaucratic centralism.

Parties as 'schools of state life' are models for the organization of the relationship between leaders and led. To the extent that they are bureaucratic, they help to reproduce the same kind of links between the state and society which exist in society as a whole. The question to be posed, according to Gramsci, is whether a different, more democratic solution to the problems of representation and bureaucracy can be developed as part of a socialist project. (Ed. note)

NOTES

1 From Karl Marx, 'Contribution to the critique of Hegel's Philosophy of Law' in Marx-Engels, *Collected Works,* III, Lawrence and Wishart, London, 1975. pp 43-4.

2 *Ibid.*

3 *Ibid* p 41.

4 *Ibid* p 45.

5 *Ibid* p 41.

6 Max Weber, *Economy and Society,* I, Bedminster Press, New York, 1968. p 217.

II
STATE AND POLITICAL STRATEGY

HEGEMONY, WAR OF POSITION AND POLITICAL INTERVENTION
Anne Showstack Sassoon

Hegemony is undoubtedly the key concept in Gramsci's thought. He uses it quite differently from the way it has been used in international affairs where the 'hegemonism' of a country indicates its will to dominate. A complete definition of Gramsci's concept of hegemony is impossible in a few words because of the controversy it has engendered; and because, as the foundation stone of Gramsci's work as a whole, it leads into a number of other concepts. A good working definition has been provided by Gwyn Williams:

> By 'hegemony' Gramsci seems to mean a sociopolitical situation, in his terminology a 'moment', in which the philosophy and practice of a society fuse or are in equilibrium; an order in which a certain way of life and thought is dominant, in which one concept of reality is diffused throughout society in all its institutional and private manifestations, informing with its spirit all taste, morality, customs, religious and political principles, and all social relations, particularly in their intellectual and moral connotation. An element of direction and control, not necessarily conscious, is implied. ('Gramsci's Concept of "Egemonia",' *Journal of the History of Ideas,* No. 4, 1960, p. 587)

Influence, leadership, culture, ideas, organization are all involved. But when Gramsci describes the state as force plus consent or hegemony armoured by coercion, does he underestimate the use of force by state institutions? Given his personal history, it would be surprising if he did, since so much of his work was done inside a fascist prison. This article argues that Gramsci saw force and consent as interdependent; that any state in the modern period of mass organizations depends on consent while its use of coercion is conditioned by this consent.

Did Gramsci overestimate the role of Parliament? Did he argue that the working class movement should copy the politics of the bourgeoisie? These are some of the questions addressed here.

Increasing references to Gramsci's concept of hegemony in a variety of contexts usually assume an understanding of the term without discussing it theoretically. In current debates within Marxism, particularly with regard to the attempt to develop a Marxist theory of politics and the state, Gramsci's ideas have provided a focus of attention. In France and Italy they have become necessary elements in a wide-ranging discussion, especially on the role of the revolutionary party, the question of democracy and socialism, the nature of revolutionary strategy in Western Europe, and the difficulties of building socialism in the USSR. Moreover, criticisms of common elements in the strategy of a number of communist parties, described as 'Eurocommunist', have been made by criticizing Gramsci's concept of the state which, it is assumed, underlies this strategy.

Taking account of the difficulties in understanding Gramsci and given the wide debate which exists about hegemony — undoubtedly the key concept in his thought — I would like to argue against certain misreadings by concentrating on three aspects central to a proper understanding of his ideas. First, it is important to realize that Gramsci develops the concept of hegemony in his attempt to analyze the state in a specific historical period. Thus his analysis of the modern state is part of the task he sets himself of examining the contradictory effects of changes in capitalism and the consequences of these changes for the creation of a revolutionary strategy appropriate to the transition to socialism, demarcated on the one hand by imperialism and the dominance of monopoly capital and on the other by the *concrete* problems presented by the Russian Revolution.

Furthermore, the *political* basis of hegemony is rooted in his study of the French Revolution and the Risorgimento and the political lessons to be drawn from these examples of bourgeois revolution. As we shall see, Gramsci's indications for a political strategy for the working class, which aims at establishing its hegemony and building an alternative historic bloc, are quite complex and do not simply suggest a symmetry between the bourgeois and proletarian revolutions. Finally, related to the above and relevant to eventual applications of Gramsci's theory to concrete political strategy and tactics is his discussion of hegemony as a relationship of compromises of a particular nature and within certain limits.

Taking these features into account, the inadequacies of certain interpretations become apparent. Probably the most common of these in the Anglo-Saxon literature sees hegemony as legitimization in the Weberian sense, or as 'false consciousness', a process of indoctrination.[1] Although Gramsci is determined to 'unmask' the nature of politics, he is quite outside a problematic which views the working class as a mere *object* of culture and ideas abstracted from the class struggle. Hegemony, here, is reduced merely to ideological and cultural activity. A result of this view has been to present hegemonic intervention by a political party as simply a fight for different ideas and a different culture. This obscures the complexity of determining the *content* of an alternative hegemony, a content which can only be created through a continuous analysis of the nature of the historic bloc maintaining the present social formation. It is this analysis which in turn determines a political strategy.

Another controversial aspect concerns the *site* of the struggle for hegemony. The difficulty of delineating civil and political society in Gramsci's works has been noted.[2] At the same time there has been a tendency to place the struggle for hegemony in civil society whereas politics, the state, or political society, is understood in a reductive way as the public area of coercion. A useful indication in this regard is provided by Togliatti's comment that in Gramsci's work there is a *methodological* rather than real or substantive difference between these two aspects of social formation.[3] It is the changing relationship between the state in the narrow sense and society as a whole which is the object of Gramsci's study. Moreover it must be stressed that he never separates force and consent but argues that they are always interrelated. The fact that different aspects of a single, complex, and contradictory phenomenon, the dominance of a class — which maintains its ability to reconstitute and reproduce itself and a dominant mode of production —, *cannot* be separated is related to precisely the new relationship between society and the state in the modern period.

The 'culturalist' or 'ideologistic' reading of Gramsci is at the root of a criticism of his notion of the state as a 'weak' concept which underestimates the effectiveness of the elements of coercion and the use of force. This view considers Gramsci's concept of the state and its strategic corollary, the war of position, as a product of a period in which the working class is forced to wage a defensive struggle. Gramsci's argument in fact is an attempt to go beyond the dichotomy of defensive or offensive strategies which was the hallmark of the II International and which remained the basis for the sudden zigzags of Comintern policy.

The Modern State

It is of crucial importance to understand that Gramsci developed his concept of hegemony (and the war of position) with regard to the state in a specific historical period: the state in the period of imperialism and the dominance of monopoly and finance capital. This is most obvious if his writings in the 1919-1920 period are related to a series of notes from prison. In the earlier writings he discusses the crisis of the liberal state and the difficulty for the bourgeoisie to guarantee production in this specific historical conjuncture. This is the basis of his argument that the working class has a special opportunity to replace the bourgeoisie in all its aspects as a ruling class.

Nor should it be forgotten that the concept of hegemony is developed in a period in which the problems of building a socialist state have become concrete after the Russian Revolution, problems which were the subject of wide debates in the Comintern and in the working class movement in general. It can be argued that it is his qualitatively original development of the concept of hegemony, when the word itself was fairly commonly used, which constitutes an attempt to suggest a theoretical basis for a new strategy in advanced capitalist countries as well as provide theoretical tools for the building of a socialist state. This is an historically new task which neither Marx, nor Engels, nor Lenin could have investigated fully.[4]

What is the period of the modern state, which Gramsci calls the integral or extended state, defined as hegemony armoured by coercion? (*SPN* 263) This state engages in a war of position, argues Gramsci, a strategy developed in the period beginning about 1870. In a passage rich in implications, which illustrates among other things his argument that the war of movement is reduced (but not eliminated) to a *tactical* instance *within* an overall strategy of the war of position, Gramsci discusses the

> political concept of *the so-called 'Permanent Revolution'*, which *emerged before 1848* as a scientifically evolved expression of the Jacobin experience from 1789 to Thermidor. The formula belongs to an historical period in which *the great mass political parties and the great economic trade unions did not yet exist*, and society was still, so to speak, in a state of fluidity from many points of view: greater backwardness of the countryside, and almost complete monopoly of political and State power by a few cities or even by a single one (Paris in the case of France); *a relatively rudimentary State apparatus, and greater autonomy of civil society from State activity;* a specific system of military forces and of national armed services; greater autonomy of the national economies from the economic relations of the world market, etc. *In the period after 1870, with the colonial expansion of Europe, all these elements change:* the internal and inter-national organisational relations of the State become more complex and massive, and the Forty-Eightist formula of the 'Permanent Revolution' is expanded and transcended in political science by the formula of 'civil hegemony'. The same thing happens in the art of politics as happens in military art: war of movement increasingly becomes war of position. . . The massive structures of the modern democracies, both as State organisations, and as complexes of associations in civil society, constitute for the art of politics as it were the 'trenches' and the permanent fortifications of the front in the war of position: they render merely 'partial' the element of movement which before used to be 'the whole' of war, etc. (*SPN* 242-3 My emphasis)

Thus the state is expanded and its relationship to civil society changes in the period of imperialism and the period of the greatest organization of the working class in trade unions and political parties, indeed the period of the growth of mass organizations in general. Moreover, the historical example of the potential of the working class to construct a new type of state, the Paris Commune, is the new 'spectre' haunting Europe. It is a period in which the masses are *in* politics, in which political parties with mass bases are represented in Parliaments, whatever the *content* of this participation, for the first time in history. The organization of the masses economically and politically is a necessary though not a sufficient condition of their fulfilling their role as political subjects. They now have a *potential* for political intervention understood in the sense of a potential for constructing a new society. This potential is hereafter a permanent feature of the concrete situation. (*SPN* 106) At the same time the bourgeois social formation no longer represents the advancement of the whole of society, is no longer 'progressive' as it had been in the period of ascendant capitalism.

The context of the new relationship between masses and politics is ignored when the war of position is reduced to a mere defensive strategy applicable to the post-1921 period and the downturn in the revolutionary fortunes of the working class movement. This reduction of Gramsci's theoretical and strategic indications is in turn related to a specific tactic or policy, in particular the 'United Front', and the promotion of NEP in Russia. This interpretation is usually based on a note in which Gramsci writes:

> It seems to me that Ilitch understood that a change was necessary from the war of manoeuvre applied victoriously in the East in 1917, to a war of position which was the only form possible in the West ... This is what the formula of the 'United Front' seems to me to mean ... Ilitch, however, did not have time to expand his formula — though it should be borne in mind that he could only have expanded it theoretically ... (*SPN* 237-8)

There follows the passage contrasting East and West, which I shall discuss below. The passage quoted here can be read in terms of the necessity of understanding the change of policy with regard to a fundamental analysis of the nature of advanced capitalist societies, rather than a temporary setback in the transition to socialism. In a series of notes, Gramsci argues that while it might have *seemed* as if there were the possibility of using the October model in Western Europe in the post-

World War I period, the state was at all times the modern extended state so that at no time in this period of history could the war of movement have been adequate as a *strategy*.[5] This in fact constitutes a self-criticism and a critique of all those on the left who thought of the post-World War I period as 'revolutionary' simply because there was a crisis in the political and economic systems. Thus, the theoretical basis for a change in strategy has to do with the nature of the modern state in a whole epoch, not with fluctuations in the stability of capitalism.

A related aspect of Gramsci's development of the concept of hegemony concerns Gramsci's attempt to analyze the new relationship between state and society in the period of the dominance of finance capital. Dealt with most directly in his articles in 1919-1920, Gramsci tries to analyze the contradictory consequences of the increased intervention by the state in society in the period of organization, real or potential, of the masses. In these articles, Gramsci discussed the dominance of monopoly capital, a dominance increased by the war, which diminished the role of the individual entrepreneur and of traditional sources of investment and consequently the social and economic role of whole groups of people. The following passage, for example, examines the decline of the economic (and ideological) role of the individual entrepreneur and changes in the role of the state.

> The factory is not an independent entity. It is not run by an owner-entrepreneur who possesses the commercial know-how (stimulated by the interest that is inherent in private ownership) to buy the raw materials wisely and sell the manufactured object at a profit. These functions have been displaced from the individual factory and transferred to the system of factories owned by the same firm. And it does not stop here: *they are concentrated in the hands of a bank or system of banks* . . . But during the war, and as a result of the war, was it not the State which supplied raw materials to industry, distributed them in accordance with a pre-established plan and became the sole purchaser of production? *So what has happened to the economic figure of the owner-entrepreneur, the captain of industry* . . . This figure has vanished, has been liquidated in the process of development of the instruments of labour, in the process of

development of the technical and economic relations that constitute the conditions in which production and work are carried on . . . he has placed his 'rights' squarely in the hands of the State, so that it will defend them ruthlessly. In this way the State has become the sole proprietor of the instruments of labour and has taken over all the traditional functions of the entrepreneur, . . . (*PWI* 165. My emphasis)

Without claiming that Gramsci provides a developed investigation of the role of finance capital, which remains quite rudimentary in these writings, the changes in society and politics, in particular the changed relationship between masses and the state rooted in changes in the economy, are from this early period a permanent feature of Gramsci's investigations.

Later in the *Notebooks*, in the context of his notes on Americanism and Fordism and the passive revolution, Gramsci comments on the fact that in countries in which finance capital dominates with different forms of political organization (e.g. Roosevelt's United States, Nazi Germany and fascist Italy), there is the introduction of elements of planning in an attempt to eliminate the anarchy of the economy. The state's relationship to the economy, along with its intervention in spheres of social organization (e.g. different types of welfare systems) and related to this, the need to organize masses of people who particularly in the period following the 1914-18 war begin to appear as political actors, constitute a substantial change in the traditional limited bourgeois state. Threatened by the very development of capital itself, expressed in a variety of political forms, was the traditional liberal notion of a state removed from the economy, limited to a 'night-watchman' function, overseeing conflicts which are presented ideologically as reconcilable.

The state which has this new role and new relationship to society can only be understood if the dominance of a class is analyzed in *all* its aspects, as force plus consent, and if the state is viewed not just as the instrument of force of a class (the classical definition provided by Marx, Engels and Lenin) but as the whole variety of activities in a whole range of sites which enable the social relations of production to be reproduced.[6] Thus not only the Church but institutions such as the courts and schools combine political and 'private' functions. Gramsci explains that

> ... every State is ethical in as much as one of its most important
> functions is *to raise the great mass of the population to a particular*
> *cultural and moral level, a level (or type) which corresponds to the*
> *needs of the productive forces for development, and hence to the*
> *interests of the ruling classes.* The school as a positive educative
> function, and the courts as a repressive and negative educative
> function, are the most important State activities in this sense:
> but, *in reality, a multitude of other so-called private initiatives*
> *and activities tend to the same end — initiatives and activities*
> *which form the apparatus of the political and cultural hegemony of*
> *the ruling classes.* (*SPN* 258. My emphasis)

At the same time, it must be emphasized that Gramsci's
analysis of the crisis of the classical, limited liberal state is
related to a key feature of his political theory: the potential
protagonism of the masses. In the modern age the state is
transformed because the contradictory effects of the development of capitalism produce the organization of the masses who
now have a potential for self-government for the first time in
history. Thus, when Gramsci writes with regard to the war of
position 'the siege is reciprocal', (*SPN* 239) he is trying to
explain the following: the working class cannot choose the
terrain on which to fight, *but* it must realize that the existence
of mass organizations have played a crucial part in the creation
of that terrain. That is, the working class movement is forced
to engage in a struggle with a specific state. But there are
historical reasons why the present extended state has the *form*
that it has — force plus hegemony — and engages in the war of
position, using various forms of the passive revolution. In the
period of imperialism, by organizing the masses economically,
the capitalist social formation necessarily provides the basis for
their potential political organization and, therefore, their
potential to transform society. Gramsci reaffirms Marx's
statement that capitalism must constantly revolutionize itself
and put old forms, old modes of organization and old ideas
into crisis. He notes the contradictory aspects of the necessity
to organize the mass of workers in 1924, when the fascist
regime has begun to eliminate autonomous trade union
activity:

Why, while the trade union has lost ground organisationally under the pressure of reaction, has the internal commission instead enlarged its organisational sphere? . . . Why do the capitalists and the fascists permit such a situation to be created and to persist? For capitalism and for fascism it is necessary that the working class be deprived of its historical function of leader of the other oppressed classes of the population . . . it is necessary, that is, to destroy that organisation which is external to the factory and is concentrated territorially (trade unions and parties), which exercises a revolutionary influence on all the oppressed and takes from the government its democratic basis of power. But the capitalists, for industrial reasons, cannot want every form of organisation destroyed: in the factory discipline and a good state of production is only possible if there exists at least a minimum of constitutionality, a minimum of consent on the part of the workers. (*CPC* 6)

At the political level masses must be organized to provide a social basis for the state. The *content* of the activities of the political organization of the masses may remain insufficient for the task of substituting the present social formation with another. They may be incapable of waging a hegemonic struggle. But the very presence of the masses in politics for the first time in history is a precondition for their autonomy.

Thus the extended state is a product of a situation in which the potential of the mass movement is a constant threat. At the same time, the ability of the capitalist social formation to represent the social, political and economic advancement of society as a whole is increasingly diminished in the period of monopoly capitalism. This is the basis of the crisis of hegemony in which the role of traditional political institutions, in particular Parliament and the traditional political parties (which for Gramsci included the Italian Socialist Party) see their roles challenged.

The various political modes of reconstitution of the *social base* which is required by the state in this historical period are considered by Gramsci when he discusses Caesarism and the passive revolution. References by Gramsci to such diverse phenomena as reformism and fascism as well as the Italian Risorgimento in the context of the passive revolution can be better understood if two common features are highlighted: the attempt to create, maintain or increase a political and social base for the state through satisfying at least some of the corporative demands of various social groups, while at the same time introducing qualitatively new elements in the economic organization of society.

It should be clear that this modern, extended state is *not* the state which existed in Russia in 1917. Gramsci specifies that

> This question (of a more complex civil society and hence the war of position) is posed for the modern States, but not for backward countries or for colonies, where forms which else-where have been superseded and have become anachronistic are still in vigour. (*SPN* 243)

The famous passage contrasting the state in Russia and the West (*SPN* 238) is *not* simply referring to a geographical difference, but must be placed within the context of the numerous specifications of the modern features of the extended state, particularly mass organizations. Moreover, Gramsci writes that under feudalism, for example, the cohesion of society was not based on hegemony.

> In the ancient and mediaeval State alike, centralisation, whether political-territorial or social . . . was minimal. The State was, in a certain sense, a mechanical bloc of social groups . . . within the circle of political-military compression, which was only exercised harshly at certain moments, the subaltern groups had a life of their own, institutions of their own, etc., and sometimes these institutions had State functions which made of the State a federation of social groups with disparate functions not subordinated in any way. . . The modern State substitutes for the mechanical bloc of social groups their subordination to the active hegemony of the directive and dominant group, hence abolishes certain autonomies, which nevertheless are reborn in other forms, as parties, trade unions, cultural associations. (*SPN* 54f)[7]

Moreover it can be argued that the state which Gramsci is analyzing is different in certain important respects from that of Marx, Engels, and Lenin. The classical Marxist and Leninist discussion is based on the analysis of a situation in which the masses are excluded almost entirely from even the potential of effective political intervention. Certainly the problem in

Russia in 1917 where the Duma reflected an attempt to adjust political institutions to the needs of historical and economic development though it existed without mass political or trade union organization — was to create and then maintain a new type of state in which the masses could intervene.

The difficulty, then, of delineating the boundaries between civil and political society is a product, not of any 'slippage' into bourgeois thought as Perry Anderson writes,[8] but of the attempt to grasp the complex reality of this modern state. This is not to say that there are no criticisms to be made in this regard of Gramsci's writings. Certainly in articles in the *Ordine Nuovo* there are problems with his suggestion that political forms correspond to changes in the economy. Gramsci tends, for example, to underestimate the ability of the bourgeoisie to reconstitute itself politically and economically through fascism, and he reduces various political expressions of sections of the bourgeoisie to a single phenomenon.[9] Some of these problems and inadequacies undoubtedly extend into the *Notebooks* and must be examined critically. But the starting point for such a critical examination must be Gramsci's project of investigating the modes of dominance of the bourgeoisie in this specific historical period and the consequences for a strategy for the working class in the transition to socialism.

Gramsci's Discussion of Bourgeois Revolution

Another controversial point concerns the extent to which Gramsci's concept of hegemony is derived from his study of bourgeois revolutions. When we consider Gramsci's study of the French Revolution and the Italian Risorgimento, it must be borne in mind that there is an important difference between seeking a model from historical examples and trying to understand what is similar and what is structurally different. Gramsci is quite clear, for instance, that while the technique of passive revolution may be used by the bourgeoisie, it is not appropriate for the proletariat.

The thesis of the 'passive revolution' as an interpretation of the Risorgimento period, and of every epoch characterised by complex historical upheavals. *Utility and dangers of this thesis . . .*

> *theory of the 'passive revolution' not as a programme, as it was for*
> *the Italian liberals of the Risorgimento, but as a criterion of*
> *interpretation . . . (SPN* 114. My emphasis)

Moreover he states quite clearly that models cannot simply be transplanted from one context to another. *(SPN* 65)

With regard to Gramsci's discussion of the Risorgimento, some preliminary points must be made. Gramsci is considering the following problem: why was the *form* of the bourgeois state in Italy the 'bastard' which it was? *(SPN* 90) That is, why did one mode of constitution of the political dominance of the bourgeoisie win out over the possibility of another, specifically a state with an extremely restricted social base, not recognized in a formal-legal sense by the Vatican or in a real sense by the popular masses? In posing these questions and in discussing the Risorgimento, Gramsci's notes contain a number of implicit assumptions.

First of all, it is assumed that hegemony can be achieved by social and political forces representing a part of a class as well as by classes. The two political groupings in the Risorgimento which he discusses, the moderates and the Partito d'Azione (Action Party), represent different sections of the bourgeoisie. Secondly, there is the assumption that any historical situation is the product of a field of contending social and political forces (not just classes) and that the outcome of the struggle between these forces depends on the political abilities (or failures) of all those in the field. (Q 961) This approach is very much influenced by Lenin's method in *Two Tactics of Social Democracy*. The possibility of various outcomes to any moment of the class struggle, depending on the political intervention of the various classes, is a crucial aspect of the argument put forward by Lenin and demarcates his concept of political intervention from that dominating the II International. This is echoed by Gramsci when he writes:

> . . . knowing how to find each time the point of progressive
> equilibrium (in the sense of one's own programme) is the art of
> the politician, not of the golden mean, but really of the politician
> who has a very precise line with a wide perspective of the future.
> (Q 1825)

Finally, there is the assumption that there are different modes of political dominance with greater or lesser degrees of hegemony, with wider or more restricted social bases, the particular mode in any one case being determined by, first, the type of relationship between leaders and led, between intellectuals and masses (*SPN* 97); and, secondly, by the ongoing political activities of the different contending forces.

Certain aspects of Gramsci's discussion of the role of the Jacobins in the French Revolution were certainly relevant to problems of the maintenance of power and the building of a socialist state in the USSR, and for revolutionary strategy in general. It should be noted that Gramsci's use of the term Jacobin changes in the course of his work and comes to stand for a political force which is able to create a strategy which corresponds to the needs of the mass of the population and to the requirements of preserving the gains of the revolution, these two dimensions of the struggle being interrelated. (*SPN* 65ff; 78) How was the revolution to be protected? Gramsci writes,

> The first necessity was to annihilate the enemy forces, or at least to reduce them to impotence in order to make a counter-revolution impossible. The second was to enlarge the cadres of the bourgeoisie as such, and to place the latter at the head of all the national forces; this meant identifying the interests and the requirements common to all the national forces, in order to set these forces in motion and lead them into the struggle, obtaining two results: (a) that of opposing a wider target to the blows of the enemy, i.e. of creating a politico-military relation favourable to the revolution; (b) that of depriving the enemy of every zone of passivity in which it would be possible to enrol Vendée-type armies. (*SPN* 78-9)

The destruction of the enemy or of its potential to make the counter-revolution depended on the ability of the political leadership of the progressive class to unite the mass of the population in order to create a permanent base for the new state. This unity could only be founded on a concrete political programme based on a correct understanding of the need to build a concrete historic bloc and of the nature of that bloc.

This brings us to Gramsci's comparison of the political intervention of the moderates with the failure of the Partito d'Azione in the Risorgimento and the *political* basis of the struggle for hegemony. A theme which runs through the *Notebooks* is Gramsci's criticism of what he calls a rationalistic, abstract, and schematic approach to concrete political problems. His aim is to criticize a style of politics going back to the Risorgimento and including the Italian Socialist Party and Bordiga's early leadership of the PCI. It is also one of the reasons he criticizes Trotsky. (*SPN* 84-5n)

The discussion which illustrates Gramsci's position most clearly has to do with the role of religion as the ideological cement binding the mass of the peasantry, preventing their adherence to a more progressive struggle and helping to preserve the political and economic role of the Vatican. The Church in Italy was an important organizer of the intellectuals providing a certain world outlook; as well as being a feudal landlord bound in a more direct sense to the preservation of certain socio-economic relations on the land. The Partito d'Azione, for example Mazzini and others, were certainly not short of anti-clerical arguments. But this ideological, cultural struggle was not based, according to Gramsci, on a clear political strategy and a concrete political programme of land reform adhering to the potential of the situation. Gramsci maintained that the religious question could not be solved by propaganda. The political effects of religion as an ideology could only be counteracted through a strategy based on an analysis of the social and economic underpinnings of the ideological and political role of the Vatican.

The only way for the Partito d'Azione to have become the leading political force in the establishment of an Italian nation-state was to have won over the bulk of the population through such a concrete programme. It would thus have been able to prevent the moderates from establishing an historic bloc based on historically conservative forces.

It is obvious that, in order to counterpose itself effectively to the Moderates, the Action Party ought to have allied itself with the rural masses, especially those in the South, and *ought to have been 'Jacobin' not only in external 'form' in temperament, but most particularly in socio-economic content.* The binding together of the various rural classes, which was accomplished in a reactionary bloc by means of the various legitimist-clerical intellectual strata, could be dissolved, so as to arrive at a new

liberal-national formation, only if support was won from two
directions: from the peasant masses, by accepting their
elementary demands and making these an integral part of the
new programme of government; and from the intellectuals of
the middle and lower strata, by concentrating them and
stressing the themes most capable of interesting them (and the
prospect of a new apparatus of government being formed, with
the possibilities of employment which it offered, would already
have been a formidable element of attraction for them — if that
prospect had appeared concrete, because based on the
aspirations of the peasantry.) (*SPN* 74 My emphasis)

The moderates, Gramsci writes, understood their own task
very well. (*SPN* 108) They were able to prevent a land reform
thus gaining support from landed interests and creating a
nation-state with a very restricted social base in a relatively
backward political form.

There are a number of consequences which can be drawn
from this discussion. First of all, Gramsci specifically suggests
that there are different modes of political intervention
appropriate to different social forces and different political
groups. For example, the Jacobins had indeed been successful
in creating mass support and their slogans of liberty, equality,
and fraternity corresponded to the needs of the situation.
(*SPN* 78) But these slogans remain utopian to the extent that
the bourgeois social formation remains based on forms of
exploitation. In the Risorgimento, the possible mode of
hegemony of the moderates, a mode which involved the
'absorption of the enemies' élites' and the ability to influence
intellectuals based on the membership of the moderates in the
economically dominant class, (*SPN* 59-60) was quite different
from that of the Partito d'Azione because of their different
positions in society. Gramsci explained that,

For the Action Party to have become an autonomous force and,
in the last analysis, for it to have succeeded at the very least in
stamping the movement of the Risorgimento with a more
markedly popular and democratic character (more than that
perhaps it could not have achieved, given the fundamental
premises of the movement itself), it would have had to
counterpose to the 'empirical' activity of the Moderates (which
was empirical only in a manner of speaking, since it

corresponded perfectly to the objective) an organic programme of government which would reflect the essential demands of the popular masses, and in the first place of the peasantry. To the 'spontaneous' attraction of the Moderates it would have had to counterpose a resistance and a counter-offensive 'organised' according to a plan. (*SPN* 61)

An implication is that they also needed a different form of organization.

Gramsci is also quite explicit about the particular difficulties which the working class faces in establishing its hegemony.

> . . . creating a group of independent intellectuals is not an easy thing; it requires a long process, with actions and reactions, coming together and drifting apart and the growth of very numerous and complex formations. It is the conception of a subaltern social group, deprived of historical initiative, in continuous but disorganic expansion, unable to go beyond a certain qualitative level, which still remains below the level of the possession of the State and of the real exercise of hegemony over the whole of society, which alone permits a certain organic equilibrium in the development of the intellectual group. (*SPN* 395-6)

Indeed, Marxism has the very difficult task, he writes, of having to reach the cultural level of the masses and fighting the more sophisticated philosophy of the ruling classes. This implies the need for a special kind of hegemonic relationship in the socialist revolution, a democratic, a representative relationship. (Q 1505-6)

Gramsci is also quite clear that hegemony before state power is always incomplete and relative. The ability to attain and maintain state power depends on a political force representing the *most* hegemonic element. The achievement of state power presents the possibility of a full development of hegemony so that a class can become truly autonomous and hegemonic. (*SPN* 397-398)

Referring specifically to the struggle of the working class, Gramsci writes that the *content* of the hegemony of the new state and the *forms* of the superstructure cannot be pre-determined. That is, this hegemony is not simply based on the existing culture of the subaltern classes nor are the super-structures simply to be adopted from the past. (This would constitute, after all, a form of passive revolution). The class struggle produces changes in both the forms and content of hegemony and in the institutions of the superstructure. Coupled with his polemic against empty, rhetorical stances, this argument suggests that the precise content of a struggle for hegemony would depend on the particular situation and specifically on an analysis of the historic bloc supporting the present social formation.

Hegemony as a Relationship of Compromises

This brings us to my final point. The hegemony of a class consists in its ability to represent the 'universal' interests of the whole of society and to unite to itself a group of allies. A hegemonic intervention is the only activity which Gramsci qualifies as truly political. In his analysis of the three moments of a relation of political forces, it becomes apparent that it is not the site of the struggle (or the institution) which qualifies an intervention as political or hegemonic, but the nature of the intervention itself. Thus, for example, participation in Parliament which involves representing the corporative interests of a class is not a truly political activity. (SPN 181) In the truly political phase the struggle is undertaken as a battle between alternative hegemonies, when

> . . . previously germinated ideologies . . . come into confrontation and conflict, until only one of them, or at least a single combination of them, tends to prevail, to gain the upper hand, to propagate itself throughout society — bringing about not only a unison of economic and political aims, but also intellectual and moral unity, *posing all the questions around which the struggle rages not on a corporate but on a 'universal' plane,* and thus creating the hegemony of a fundamental social group over a series of subordinate groups. (SPN 181-2. My emphasis)

Consequently it is not the site but the mode of political intervention which qualifies it as truly political. Gramsci continues,

It is true that the State is seen as the organ of one particular group, destined to create favourable conditions for the latter's maximum expansion. But the development and expansion of the particular group are conceived of, and presented, as being the motor force of a universal expansion, of a development of all the 'national' energies. In other words, the dominant group is co-ordinated concretely with the general interests of the sub-ordinate groups, and the life of the State is conceived of as a continuous process of formation and superseding of unstable equilibria (on the juridical plane) between the interests of the fundamental group and those of the subordinate groups — equilibria in which the interests of the dominant group prevail, but only up to a certain point, i.e. stopping short of narrowly corporate economic interest. (*SPN* 182)

Thus the state *is* an instrument of a class in its ability to create and reproduce social relations of production, but the *use* of this instrument is qualified by the constantly changing relation of political forces and the compromises which must always be made by the dominant group and a range of allies.[10]

In another note, Gramsci specifies more clearly the relationship of these compromises to the maintenance of a dominant mode of production. Hegemony, he explains, is not simply an ideological struggle unrelated to the sphere of economic relations nor does it imply just any kind of compromises.

Undoubtedly the fact of hegemony presupposes that account be taken of the interests and the tendencies of the groups over which hegemony is to be exercised, and that a certain compromise equilibrium should be formed — in other words, that the leading group should make sacrifices of an economic-corporate kind. But there is also no doubt that such sacrifices and such compromise cannot touch the essential; for though hegemony is ethical-political, it must also be economic, must necessarily be based on the decisive function exercised by the leading group in the decisive nucleus of economic activity. (*SPN* 161)

What however, is the nature of these compromises? How do they differ from the compromises (or reforms) instituted by a variety of modes of bourgeois rule which Gramsci describes with the concept of passive revolution?

Now if these passages are related to Gramsci's argument that the passive revolution is not a suitable mode of intervention by the proletariat, it becomes clear that the compromises implied in a hegemonic relationship between the working class and its allies are not simply the result of giving in to the corporative demands of various sectors of the population but of transcending them. This is the difference between the kinds of compromises made by the bourgeoisie, which are a hallmark of social democracy, and those involved in a strategy by the proletariat to transform society. The proletariat can represent the 'universal' expansion of society as a whole only if it is able to unite various sectors around an alternative project which attempts to resolve fundamental problems. The reformism of social democracy and the welfare state in a number of countries is indeed a response to the class struggle, but the increase in the burden of the state in assuming responsibility for a number of social and economic problems (and giving in to certain corporative demands), without attempting in any serious sense to restructure society in order to overcome the causes of these problems, is another aspect of the passive revolution.

This is related to the fact that the utopianism of the bourgeois slogan of 'fraternity' stems precisely from the way in which the capitalist mode of production and the social relations it engenders separates sections of the population. In his early writings Gramsci stated that the very wage slavery of the worker is expressed in terms of his particular skill and his competition with other workers and with other sections of the population. When Gramsci criticizes the trade unions and the PSI for remaining within bourgeois legality, he is not arguing abstractly in favour of breaking the law. He is criticizing the way in which the corporatism of those organizations implies acceptance of the definition of the worker as a wage slave, separated from other workers and other sections of the population. (*PWI* 104-5; 110-111) This corporatism prevents the creation of a strategy able to overcome the bourgeois formal-legal definition of individuals as citizens, unrelated to their social and economic positions. If the working class remains limited within this corporatism, the demands it puts forward and the compromises it makes (or in other words its relations with other classes and groups) cannot form the foundation for a new social bloc, a new type of society.

Thus, the presence of working class organizations *per se* in state institutions, whatever their rhetoric, does not constitute a political intervention by the working class in the full sense unless it is an intervention which is able to unite different social forces going beyond their corporate interests. This is the only way to begin creating an alternative historic bloc and a new state. At the same time the *potential* of a political intervention by the working class conditions the existence of the modern state. This state, to the extent that it must preserve a bloc of forces, can never be viewed simply as an instrument of a class but must be understood as an instrument whose form and use is a product of the compromises necessitated by the class struggle. Yet if these compromises remain on the corporate level, even if they are a product of a militant struggle, the working class remains within the limits of the passive revolution undertaken by the dominant class to perpetuate its rule and to enable it to reproduce the social relations of production. The bourgeoisie is thus able to 'revolutionize' society, as Marx had suggested, reorganizing and changing elements, according to its own plan. What Gramsci calls the 'organic' crisis of capitalism in the age of monopoly capitalism continues without either resolving fundamental problems or resulting in the breakdown of capitalism. This crisis (and the more dramatic 'conjunctural' crises) provide an ever-changing terrain for the intervention of the working class, an opportunity for a creative, hegemonic role. If the working class does not seize this opportunity, the dominance of the bourgeoisie can be reconstituted in new forms, implying a reorganization of the economy and the maintenance of an historic bloc supporting the existing state. A hegemonic, non-corporate response to the crisis of capitalism is the only way to provide a different type of solution to a crisis which itself is a product of the class struggle and involves all sections of society. This solution is part of the process of moving society in the direction of socialism in a period in which the very crisis of capitalism provides the concrete potential for the transition to socialism.

NOTES

1 Ralph Miliband's *State in Capitalist Society*, London, 1969 explicitly reduces hegemony to legitimization while Carl Boggs' *Gramsci's Marxism*, London, 1976 considers hegemony as the maintenance of false consciousness.

2 Perry Anderson discusses this at length. 'The Antinomies of Antonio Gramsci', *New Left Review* no. 100, 1977. See also the introduction to the section on 'State and Civil Society' in SPN, pp. 206-209.

3 See 'Leninism in the Thought and Action of A. Gramsci', by Togliatti in *On Gramsci and Other Writings*, London, 1979.

4 See Christine Buci-Glucksmann *Gramsci and the State*, London, 1980, for a comparison of the use of the term by Bukharin and Stalin and by Gramsci.

5 See the way he argues, for example, in *ibid*, pp. 234-235.

6 It should be noted that Gramsci uses both a narrow and an extended definition of the state. With regard to the former (the state as force or defined as government) he almost always prefaces his usage with adjectives such as 'common' or 'restricted' to indicate that he is referring to the most usual if inaccurate use of the word.

7 It is true that Gramsci does not discuss the absolutist state here, and our argument is not that the Tsarist State in 1917 is adequately described as feudal, but simply that Gramsci is quite aware of the differences between various historical forms of state.

8 See for example Anderson, *op. cit.*, p 25.

9 See Franco De Felice, *Serrati, Bordiga, Gramsci e il problema della rivoluzione in Italia, 1919-1920*, Bari, 1971. This extremely important book and other works by De Felice develop the theme of the new relationship between state and society in the modern period.

10 In a note which is rich in implications Gramsci discusses how a rigid aversion to compromises is rooted in economism. See *ibid*, p 168.

HEGEMONY AND CONSENT:
A POLITICAL STRATEGY
Christine Buci-Glucksmann

The question of consent is an important aspect of the study of sociology and politics, and the fact that a variety of states base their legitimacy on the argument that they enjoy the 'consent of the governed' in some form is an essential element of contemporary political life. Christine Buci-Glucksmann contrasts Gramsci's concept of hegemony with both the traditional idea of consent – as limiting the power of the state to a restricted area while protecting the rights of the individual, associated with John Locke and the liberal tradition – and consent as reinforcing the power of the state as argued by a number of other thinkers. Gramsci's novelty, she says, has often been missed because people have translated his ideas into pre-existing notions. In fact, his concept of hegemony goes beyond both an economistic Marxist position which views consent as false ideology blinding the mass of the population to the reality of state power and the conditions of exploitation, and the ideas associated with Talcott Parsons and Max Weber, which define consent or consensus as legitimizing a certain pre-existing social order. Gramsci investigates the variety of ways in which consent is established in different historical periods and by different classes in order to consider the possibility of the transformation of representative democracy and the creation of new forms of democratic control rooted in the productive process. He thus leads us to the question of whether the methods and the institutions of establishing consent are the same for the bourgeoisie and the proletariat or whether they are qualitatively different.

In an analysis which indicates how the forms of bourgeois consent have varied as representative institutions have been put into crisis by the growth of state intervention, Gramsci provides us tools, Buci-Glucksmann argues, for considering the new forms which are being used to organize consent, some of them coercive, in a period of the long-term crisis of capitalist society. This passive revolution has implications for developing a working class strategy in advanced capitalist countries today. Gramsci's concept of hegemony provides the basis for outlining the limits of liberal democracy and for undertaking a critique of Stalinism. The anti-statism of the concept and the way in which Gramsci defines a truly democratic relationship in terms of hegemony make his ideas relevant to the question of whether a 'third way' is possible which transforms society in a democratic direction, avoiding the pitfalls of both social democracy and 'real' socialism, both based on accentuating state power. It is in this way that she links Gramsci to current political debates and what could be called 'left' Eurocommunism.

In Western political thought consent is traditionally defined in two ways: either consent creates force and refers to a civil society made up of isolated and atomized individuals who 'give' their consent (mystifying the relations of exploitation and power in capitalist societies); or force creates consent by laws, norms, ideological values and forms of legitimation of power (leading to an underestimation of rights and liberties). In short, all possible approaches to consent or consensus seem to be limited to the famous Centaur of Machiavelli's *Prince*, a permanent dual struggle of 'laws' and force which haunts Gramsci.

In these conditions, we can understand the decisive importance of Gramsci for the Marxist analysis of societies and their transformation. Yet, because he posed the question of consent in a way new to Marxism starting from a *new* reflection on hegemony, the state, the crisis of capitalism and the 'Revolution in the West', his political or historical categories have often simply been reduced to pre-existing ones, and the novelty of his ideas has been lost. This is precisely the case with the notion of hegemony. The location of the Gramscian concept of hegemony within the more classical categories of consensus as legal-political, as ideology (in the sense of subjection or class-inculcation) or as legitimation, results in a breaking up of the unity of the Gramscian problematic of consensus and a loss of its specific relevance. In fact, hegemony is reducible neither to ideology, nor to the approach of different modes of socialization. It is primarily *a political principle and a form of strategic leadership*, that is, a guide to political action, enabling the reformulation of the question of *socialist* transformation in the West. The context is the one of capitalist crisis, the restructuring of capitalism in the thirties (fascism and the New Deal) and of the historical processes of the 'passive revolution'. As a new strategy (war of position), different from the strategy of 1917 (war of manoeuvre), it involves an analysis in new terms of power specific to the developed capitalist countries. It thus clarifies the critique of the political forms of the liberal state of the twenties and the Stalinist state of the thirties.

At the very moment when the question of a democratic road to socialism, distinct from social-democracy and from Stalinism, is being posed, Gramsci's concept becomes increasingly important. So too does the question of a different socialism, capable of linking two historically contradictory processes: the transformation of representative democracy and the creation of new forms of direct democracy (self-management). This requires a new approach to consent at the level both of political practices and of institutions.

The Different Bases of Consent

Contrary to all theories of consensus which emphasize a single form of consensus in order to conceptualize the reproduction of a social system — its 'acceptability' — the Gramscian approach is, from the beginning, complex. Consensus must be subjected to a fundamental and primary question: who consents, to what and how? More precisely, are the instruments and practices which produce consensus always the same? Is hegemony independent of the historical subjects (classes) of this hegemony?

Relating his reflection on hegemony to the analysis of the relations between leaders and led in the realm of politics, Gramsci notes that consent can be either *passive and indirect*, or *active and direct*. In the first case it excludes 'any intervention from the base': the state instrumentalizes consent and treats the masses as 'masses for manoeuvre'. On the other hand, any form of active-direct consent requires a real interchange between rulers and ruled. Hence, in his remarks on the Church, Gramsci emphasizes that 'any intervention from the base would in fact cause the disintegration of the Church'. Thinking about the working class movement, he goes on, 'But for other organizations it is a vital question to obtain not a passive and indirect consent but an active and direct consent, the participation of all, even if it provokes a disintegration or an apparent tumult.' (Q 1771)

This is a vital question. For the notion of active and direct consent is to be linked to another Gramscian notion: the *expansiveness* of consent, which excludes any bureaucratic repressive relation between leaders and led, any corporate integration of the led, also any reduction of democracy solely to its legal aspect. From 1924 on, differentiating the dictatorship of the proletariat from that of the bourgeoisie under fascism, Gramsci insists upon a decisive point: 'The dictatorship of the proletariat is *expansive*, not repressive. A continuous movement takes place from the base upwards, a continuous replacement through all the capillaries of society, a continuous circulation of men.' (*PWII* 212) In the *Prison Notebooks*, developing this historical and differentiated analysis of the way in which consent is produced, Gramsci, conscious of the loss of expansiveness in the Stalinist 'revolution from above', criticized the complex of channels which establish passive consent from above to below, in which politics is always identified purely with the statist and instrumental domain of domination (bureaucratic centralism, authoritarian paternalism, forms of Caesarism and totalitarianism, corporation, etc.).

In this sense, hegemony — as defining democracy, as providing an index of forms of democracy from below to above — relies on the notion of the 'democracy of producers', an aspect of the factory councils, and functions effectively as a critical anti-statist principle.[1] This is why it cannot be reduced to a simple doubling of state force. Hegemony is primarily a *strategy* for the gaining of the active consent of the masses through their self-organization, starting from civil society, and in all the hegemonic apparatuses: from the factory to the school and the family. And this has the aim of creating a collective political will, at once national and popular: a historic bloc of socialism capable of unifying economic base and superstructure.[2]

If the Marxist tradition has always primarily though not exclusively insisted on the forms of *domination*, Gramsci brings to the fore in a detailed way the new historical role specific to developed capitalist societies of the forms of class *leadership* in the whole of social life. We must not be trapped by words: hegemony is not force, and the more the element of force dominates, the less hegemony there will be. In the strict sense, the hegemony of a class is not imposed: it is conquered through a specific intellectual and moral dimension, through a politics of alliances which must open up a national perspective to the whole of society. In this context, Gramsci contrasts the hegemonic class to the corporate class which defends its own present material interests. The hegemonic class goes beyond any bourgeois economistic position, any narrow corporatist vision of its role. It 'universalises' its own interests and ensures that 'they can and must become the interests of the other subordinate groups'. (*SPN* 181) This unity of economic and political objectives together with 'intellectual and moral unity', characterizes a hegemonic class.

Aware of the differences in the relations between state and civil society in Russia and in the West, the extraordinary diffusion of hegemony specific to the 'sturdy structure of civil society in the West', the richness of the democratic past and the complexity of the diffusion of power in the different hegemonic apparatuses, Gramsci insists more than Lenin on the necessary and *prior* conquest of civil society and political and cultural leadership. As he writes in a well-known passage: 'The supremacy of a social group manifests itself in two ways, as "domination" and as "intellectual and moral leadership" ... A social group can and indeed must already exercise "leadership" before winning governmental power (this indeed is one of the principal conditions for the winning of such power).' (*SPN* 57)

But then if hegemony as a specific moment of intellectual, political and moral leadership does not simply reproduce relations of domination/subordination, do not differences in the forms of consent relate to the proportions, the respective degrees of force and consent, of domination and hegemonic leadership specific to different classes and to their place in history? Are not the forms and quality of consent engendered by the proletariat fundamentally different from that of the bourgeoisie?

In fact the complexity of the relations between hegemony and coercion assume their full importance only if the study of politics is rooted in history. The forms of passive and indirect consent relate to the historical process of 'passive revolution', revolution-restoration, which Gramsci approaches from the basis of a comparative analysis of the French and Italian bourgeois revolutions. Contrary to the French Jacobin strategy of 'war of movement' which gave the bourgeoisie 'a much more advanced position than it could have had spontaneously', (Q 50) thus enabling a popular revolution, the *Risorgimento* as 'passive revolution' relied upon the absence of real popular initiative even if certain popular demands were satisfied 'in small doses, legally, in a reformist way', from above and by means of the state (the Piedmont State in this case). The result: instead of resolving its historical tasks of *leadership* by developing the democratic initiative of the masses, a class relied primarily on the state, on domination. In this case of 'dictatorship without hegemony' the state is (stage by stage) substituted for the class. It creates its own administrative and bureaucratic, even police, apparatus: 'Leadership becomes an aspect of domination'. (*SPN* 104-6) The unity of the power bloc realized through these statist links between leaders and led remains of a bureaucratic-military type.

Such a process of the statist encompassing of society by a dominant party-state is relevant of course to Stalinism. But equally it clarifies the forms of authoritarian statism specific to the present monopolist bourgeoisie, analysed by Nicos Poulantzas in *State, Power, Socialism*.[3] Within this perspective we could say that we are witnessing, precisely within the current crisis of capitalism, a modification of the balance between domination and hegemony, consecutive with the nascent crisis of bourgeois hegemony. This is, in effect, a tendency towards 'passive revolution'.

This shows us that there can be no ahistorical, abstract approach to consensus *in general*: hegemony is differentiated according to classes and historical phases. The hegemonic strategy of the working class in the conquest of majority consent can only be an 'anti-passive revolution', based on active consent. This can be summarized in the following table:

PASSIVE CONSENT	ACTIVE CONSENT
Indirect (without popular initiative, without democracy at the base)	Direct (self-organization of the masses)
Primarily through statist domination	Primarily through hegemonic leadership
Repressive/bureaucratic	Expansive/democratic
Bourgeois domination	Working-class domination
Passive revolution	Popular and democratic revolution
Statist	Anti-statist

A difficult question remains. If Gramsci analyzes the forms of domination without hegemony, can we envisage the opposite: a hegemony without coercion?

State and Hegemony: parliamentary democracy and passive revolution

If hegemony is an anti-statist principle, indicative of a political strategy, we could equally note that in a great number of passages Gramsci uses the concept of hegemony in quite a different sense. Criticizing all economistic and instrumentalist conceptions of the state which reduce it to a simple instrument of domination or to a 'neutral' instrument of government, Gramsci opposes to this unilateral concept of the state, another concept which I have called the 'extended state'. In effect: 'In politics the error occurs as a result of an inaccurate understanding of what the State (in its integral meaning: dictatorship & hegemony) really is.' (SPN 239)[4]

From this formulation, this 'integral state' seems in effect to incorporate the two forms of consensus mentioned at the beginning: 'The State is the entire complex of practical and theoretical activities with which the ruling class not only justifies and maintains its domination, but manages to win the active consent of those over whom it rules'. (SPN 244) If we take up again this complex of distinctions in Gramsci we can arrive at a second table noticeably different from the first:

INTEGRAL STATE   HEGEMONY ARMOURED BY COERCION

State or political society	Civil Society
Dictatorship	Hegemony
Coercive apparatus	Hegemonic apparatuses
Government (State in the narrow sense)	State in the integral sense
State as apparatus of power	State as organizer of consensus
Domination	Leadership

Could the presence of this dual functioning of hegemony: anti-statist and statist, be the index of a contradiction, of an unresolved political antinomy as Perry Anderson argues? Is there a fundamental contradiction in Gramsci's ideas?[5]

Without concealing the specific difficulties relating to this point, it seems to me that this apparent contradiction relates to the most original aspect of Gramsci's political thought: hegemony indicates a new political strategy because of the very transformations of the state and its historical base. In this sense, the analysis of the transition from the 'classical' liberal state, with its limited functions, to the new forms of state linked to the New Deal or to fascism makes Gramsci the Marxist contemporary of Keynes, the theorist of state intervention in the economy, rather than of Weber, the theorist of politics as a profession, as a field beyond the control of the mass of the population. Gramsci is the theorist of consent as legitimization.

As distinct from all mechanistic and economistic forms of Marxism, Gramsci's Marxism confronts the full implications of the crisis of capitalism in the years 1929-30 and the responses of capitalism to that crisis. These responses had the effect of throwing into question all the previous models of the organization of hegemony, and more specifically, its liberal forms. Gramsci's enlarged view of the state therefore aims to take into consideration a series of well-known modifications in capitalism: a more intense interpenetration of the economic and the political by a finance bourgeoisie attempting to control the economic cycles, the extension of state activities into civil society, but also the penetration of civil society by the forms of mass organizations such as mass political parties and pressure groups. This long-term evolution (of which Gramsci saw only the premises) develops a potential contradiction between the classic parliamentary forms designed for limited state intervention, and the process of capitalist 'restructuring': of 'passive revolution'.

Starting from the crisis of the Italian Liberal State in the post-war period, Gramsci approaches the question of parliamentary democracy through an analysis of the different modes of operation and organization of hegemony. If he does not go beyond a critique of the limits of parliamentary democracy to consider its place in a socialist strategy, he perceives all of its fragility and his analysis is never reduced simply to the denunciation of its class character, according to the classical schema: representative democracy = bourgeois democracy. He is more concerned with the reasons for its permanence and its nascent crisis from the twenties onward. At this point we can see why the 'French case', where, in spite of periods of Bonapartist dictatorship, 'the normal exercise of hegemony operates on the classical terrain of the parliamentary regime', (Q 1638) is so important.

If force and consent balance each other in a just relation, if 'force appears to rest on the consent of the majority', power is exercised in a 'normal' way. But such an 'equilibrium' (cf. for Gramsci, the French Third Republic) requires precise conditions: a great development of 'private energies' in civil society, an ideological and economic individualism, an enlargement of the economic base which will not upset the country-side/town equilibrium, a phase of colonial expansion, and finally a more or less link between universal suffrage and 'national feeling organized around the concept of nationhood' — which cements consensus at the national level. (Q 1645) All these conditions relate in turn to one which is even more essential: the absence of a relation of forces favouring the popular forces. In these precise conditions of equilibrium, government can obtain 'permanent and organized consent' (role of the parties, of public opinion, of the press etc.).

We should note in passing that Gramsci does not isolate consent from force. The division of powers between the legislature, executive and judiciary is not simply 'the result of a struggle between civil society and political society' in a phase of unstable class equilibrium; but above all of liberalism concealing its other face: the bureaucratic crystallization of its leading personnel which exercises executive or coercive power, the fact that the three classical powers, (excutive, legislative, and judiciary), — organs of differentiated political hegemony — collaborate nonetheless in the unification of state power. (*SPN* 245) And what is more, numerical consent, which aims ideally at each vote being equal 'is systematically falsified by the inequality of wealth' and by the existence 'of an organized centre of formation and persuasion'.

But what concerns Gramsci is always the relations between force and consent. The fine balance 'of civil society and political society' is thrown sharply into question by the development of imperialism, of monopoly capitalism and by the effects of the October Revolution: 'Cracks opened up everywhere in the hegemonic apparatus and the exercise of hegemony became permanently difficult and aleatory'. (*SPN* 80f) This is why, in reformulating the concept of the crisis of capitalism, Gramsci insists upon the specific mechanisms of a crisis of consensus: crisis of authority, crisis of values, crisis of social bonds and finally, crisis of the state in the integral sense. Fundamentally, as *equilibrium* of force and consent, parliamentary democracy has entered into an irreversible historical crisis which we can observe today, in the devaluation of parliamentary forms and in the recourse to other bourgeois political forms for the creation of consensus: bureaucracy, technocracy, and indeed, authoritarian statism.

In this sense, hegemony as anti-passive revolution, far from being a totalitarian concept opposed to pluralism, is the very condition of pluralism. The extension of the state is thus not to be confused with a simple reinforcement of the state, since at the same time as the state is extended, the terrain of the struggle for hegemony is enlarged and thus a modification of the relation of forces is brought about in favour of a democratic and socialist transformation of society. Of course, in the search for a socialism capable of transforming representative democracy through the development of forms of self-management in the factory and in the whole of society, we have today gone beyond Gramsci in certain aspects. But in developing a new strategic concept of consent, in indicating its specific forms, in going beyond the dual liberal/sociological horizon, and in relating this new strategy (war of position) to the modifications in the power structure in the developed capitalist countries, Gramsci designates a point of no-return for political reflection: no democratic transition to socialism without an 'anti-passive revolution', the expansion of active consent. It is up to us to draw the implications and consequences for our present situation.

NOTES

1   For a fuller discussion of the way in which Gramsci's concept of hegemony is rooted in his experience with the factory council movement in Turin, see Christine Buci-Glucksmann, *Gramsci and the State*, London, Lawrence and Wishart, 1980, especially Part Two.

2   Reference is being made here to the argument that only through the kind of democratic control by the mass of the population implied in Gramsci's view of socialism is it impossible to overcome the traditional split between an economy dominated by the anarchy of market forces and the political and ideological superstructures, themselves beyond the democratic control of the mass of the population. (Ed. note)

3   Nicos Poulantzas, *State, Power, Socialism*, New Left Books, London 1978. Particularly Part 4, 'The Decline of Democracy; Authoritarian Statism'.

4   On this problematic of the state, I refer the reader to my book *Gramsci and the State, op. cit.*

5   Buci-Glucksmann is referring to Perry Anderson's discussion and criticism of Gramsci's theory of the state. 'The Antinomies of Antonio Gramsci', *New Left Review*, No. 100, November 1976-January 1977. (Ed. note)

PASSIVE REVOLUTION AND THE POLITICS OF REFORM
Anne Showstack Sassoon

One of the more obscure of Gramsci's ideas is the notion of passive revolution. This notion helps tackle a problem which has been at the centre of debate in the working class movement since the end of the last century: the relationship between the struggle for reforms and the making of a revolution. Were reforms the basis for an evolution of the present society in the direction of socialism as the social democratic tradition from Eduard Bernstein to Anthony Crosland argued? Or did they constitute an attempt to mask the class struggle by buying off the working class movement? Gramsci tried to analyze the nature of reforms in terms of the need for capitalism to transform itself constantly and to maintain the working class movement in a weak position. The difference between reforms which are an aspect of the reorganization of capitalism and those which can contribute to a revolutionary break-through, according to Gramsci, has to do with control over politics and economics. That is, a premise of capitalist social relations is that the political and economic spheres should be controlled by a few people and that any attempt at democratic control should remain at a formal level. Reforms that maintain this split between rulers and ruled, however much they change society (and an important aspect of Gramsci's argument is that society does change), simply re-produce capitalism. Although he does not discuss revolutionary reforms in any detail, he argues that their hallmark must be a new, democratic control by the mass of society over economic and political decisions.

While we do not have any detailed evidence about the state of Gramsci's knowledge of the Soviet Union while in prison, and although his notes are not explicit in this regard, his experiences and his writings while working for the Comintern and as a Communist leader in the 1920s would have given the problem of the degeneration of the Russian

Revolution an important place in his thoughts. The lack of expansion of democracy and of a positive adhesion to a new socialist project for Soviet society by the vast majority of the population can be analyzed, it is argued, in terms of a passive revolution in which the state instead of the mass of society is the protagonist for change. This means that the building of socialism remains incomplete, and the lesson to be drawn is that while passive revolution can constitute a strategy for survival by the bourgeoisie, the proletariat must develop a qualitatively different path to socialism.

Changes in the forms and the dimension of politics have constantly challenged political scientists from the end of the last century. The practice of politics has extended far beyond the framework of traditional institutions with the extension of the suffrage and the development of mass political parties, pressure groups and trade unions. From the 1920s and 1930s onward, in the period of organized capitalism, governments in a wide range of countries have bargained increasingly with a variety of powerful groups, often completely by-passing traditional channels of politics, or rather, creating new ones. The increasing organization of the economy has been related to a new organization of politics, and the vastly enlarged state intervention into the economy and into society as a whole has blurred the distinction between economics and politics.

Much more recently new forms of political participation have appeared which do not fit easily into old categories and which have not always been obviously political. More and more people are organizing themselves in groups of very disparate nature as a response to state intervention in all aspects of social life. This has produced a contradictory situation. An increase in apathy with regard to traditional politics, particularly notable in the Anglo-Saxon countries, has been accompanied by demands for greater democratic control and for a change in the relationship between the individual and the state. The women's movement in its different forms is a good example. While often denouncing the political arena, yet at the same time posing questions about the restructuring of people's lives and the development of new social relations, the women's movement moves in a terrain which inevitably relates to the political arena and which has wide implications for the relationship between the mass of the population to the state and to politics.

Yet, given the vast changes which have taken place in politics in this century, the question must be posed: will recent changes in modes of political participation and new demands for an increase in democracy simply be absorbed within the general outlines of the present socio-economic-political system or can they lead to a breakthrough in which real democratic control over the economy and politics is established?

Antonio Gramsci's work is particularly relevant to a discussion of new forms of politics and to the problem of what constitutes a revolutionary reform. A crucial concept in his work is the *passive revolution* which relates changes in politics, ideology and social relations to changes in the economy. Gramsci uses the term passive revolution to indicate the constant reorganization of state power and its relationship to society to preserve control by the few over the many, and maintain a traditional lack of real control by the mass of the population over the political and economic realms. The specific points of reference for this concept were the attempts by a variety of regimes to reorganize capitalism in the 1920s and 1930s and the difficulties faced by the Soviet Union in building socialism with very narrow popular support. These had a common characteristic: the incorporation of various reforms and in varying degrees the expansion of an element of planning in the economy on the basis of a passive relationship between the mass of the population and the state. The relationship was passive in the sense that the traditional split between leaders and led was re-articulated in new forms at the same time as substantial changes were being instituted in social, economic and political life.

Before examining in some detail Gramsci's concept of passive revolution, it is necessary to consider how it fits into the whole of his thought. Gramsci is concerned to analyze the *modern* state, the organization of politics or the various forms of political domination from the end of the last century. He roots the extended state, which he defines as 'Hegemony armoured by coercion' firmly in the period beginning roughly in 1870, a period of the organization of masses of people then in politics for the first time in history. (*SPN* 242-3; 234-5; 106) Related to new forms of organization in which demands for social and economic changes can be articulated in a new way, is the increase in the range of activities of the state and an increasing organization of the economy. As the 'night-watchman state' and the role of the individual entrepreneur become eclipsed, the class struggle according to Gramsci assumes the form of a war of position — the only strategic possibility, given the nature of politics and of state power in the modern period. Gramsci makes the point that this terrain is not chosen by the working class movement but that the creation of this terrain has in large part been the effect of its organization.

Both the bourgeoisie and the proletariat in modern society must engage in a war of position, but there is an asymmetry between the mode of struggle of the bourgeoisie whose aim is to maintain control over politics and economics as the domain of a few; and that of a proletariat who, if it is to go beyond the fundamental relations of capitalism, must socialize or democratize and therefore transform politics and economics. The passive revolution is a conceptual tool to differentiate between forms of politics which simply reproduce the traditional division between leaders and led and those which will lead to an expanded democracy, or, in Gramsci's terms, between reformist and revolutionary politics.

Gramsci develops the concept of passive revolution in order to take account of the phenomenon whereby a dominant class maintains its power by promoting its adversary's weakness. It is rooted in Gramsci's earlier writings in the *Ordine Nuovo* in 1919-20 where he analyzed the crisis of the liberal state stemming from the changed relationship between the state and the economy. (*PWI* 165; 297) The passive revolution is an attempt to explain the fact that

> a social form 'always' has marginal possibilities for further development and organisational improvement, and in particular can count on the relative weakness of the rival progressive force as a result of its specific character and way of life. It is necessary for the dominant social form to preserve this weakness. . . (*SPN* 222)

This is one of Gramsci's most complex as well as obscure ideas, not least because it must be related to a series of notes in which it is only indirectly the subject of analysis. Gramsci insists on the fact that while the passive revolution, (or, in another formulation, revolution-restoration) — that is, an attempt to promote change which is not based on a positive hegemony — can be a technique or a programme for the bourgeoisie, it can only be a 'criterion of interpretation' for the working class movement. (*SPN* 114) One of the least explicit of his ideas, it is at the same time one of the most important because it provides a further explanation of the margin for political survival which the bourgeoisie enjoys despite political and economic crises. It further indicates the *novel* nature of the building of a new state by the working class.

This concept functions at two levels as do so many others in the *Notebooks* — as a category of historical interpretation and as an analytical tool for a theoretical problem. From the very way in which Gramsci reads history, it is possible to derive key aspects of his political theory. Gramsci describes the Risorgimento and in fact a whole series of other historical phenomena in nineteenth century Europe as the product of a passive revolution. The French Revolution established a bourgeois state on the basis of popular support and its concomitant elimination of the old feudal classes both economically and politically. In the rest of Europe, the institution of political forms to suit the expansion of the capitalist mode of production took place in a different manner:

> ... the 'passive' aspect of the great revolution which started in France in 1789 and which spilled over into the rest of Europe with the republican and Napoleonic armies — giving the old régimes a powerful shove, and resulting not in their immediate collapse as in France but in the 'reformist' corrosion of them which lasted up to 1870 ... the demands which in France found a Jacobin-Napoleonic expression were satisfied by small doses, legally, in a reformist manner — in such a way that it was possible to preserve the political and economic position of the old feudal classes, to avoid agrarian reform, and, especially, to avoid the popular masses going through a period of political experience such as occurred in France in the years of Jacobinism. ... (*SPN* 119)

While Gramsci uses the French Revolution as a model of a bourgeois revolution he is careful to avoid schematisms. He warns that,

The conception of the State according to the productive function of the social classes cannot be applied mechanically to the interpretation of Italian and European history from the French Revolution throughout the nineteenth century. Although it is certain that for the fundamental productive classes (capitalist bourgeoisie and modern proletariat) the State is only conceivable as the concrete form of a specific economic world, of a specific system of production, this does not mean that the relationship of means to end can be easily determined or takes the form of a simple schema, apparent at first sight. (*SPN* 116)

It is precisely because the form of the state may represent a disjuncture between the economic and political levels of a social formation that the exact form of political rule with all its peculiarities must be studied in order to avoid oversimplifications. The state cannot be understood simply as the instrument of a class.

In this passive revolution, or revolution-restoration, the old feudal classes maintained a political role, gradually being transformed from an economically and politically dominant class into a governing group serving the dominance of another class, the bourgeoisie. Gramsci explains that

restoration becomes the *political form* whereby social struggles find sufficiently elastic frameworks to allow the bourgeoisie to gain power without dramatic upheavals, without the French machinery of terror. The old feudal classes are demoted from their *dominant position to a 'governing' one,* but are not eliminated, nor is there any attempt to liquidate them as an organic whole; *instead of a class they become a 'caste'* with specific cultural and psychological characteristics, *but no longer with predominant economic functions.* (*SPN* 115. My emphasis)

At the same time this type of revolution, in the sense of changing the political superstructure to take account of the needs of a new mode of production, occurred without the prerequisite for massive popular support, an agrarian reform which would have meant the destruction of the old feudal classes. In terms of the Italian Risorgimento this method of political change is represented by the success of Cavour and the moderates over the Partito d'Azione, (Action Party), the name Gramsci uses to indicate the groupings around Garibaldi,

Mazzini and other 'radicals'. The new Italian State is somewhat of a 'bastard' according to Gramsci because it is founded with an extremely restricted hegemonic base, the product of the compromise between agrarian and industrial interests. (*SPN* 90) Rather than the hegemony of a whole class over the rest of society, the moderates based in Piedmont represented the hegemony of only a *part* of a class over the rest of that class. (*SPN* 104-6)[1] A weak political unity is both a result and a cause of a weak economic transformation of society. (*SPN* 116)

The new state which is made in the first instance by part of the bourgeoisie against feudal conditions, (the lack of a nation state in Italy representing the survival of feudal cosmopolitanism) which does not, however, eliminate but gradually transforms the old feudal classes in building a new historic bloc, survives using the same strategy but now against a new adversary, the popular classes. The 'passive' aspect consists in preventing the development of a revolutionary adversary by 'decapitating' its revolutionary potential. In Italy the form of this is 'transformism' whereby the leadership of opposing parties, first individuals of the radical bourgeoisie, and after 1900, whole groups, such as sectors of the working class movement, are transformed into politically harmless elements — not threatening the fundamental social relations — by absorption into more traditional political organizations. (*SPN* 587; 97; 109) The Europe-wide dimension of this technique is reformism. The acceptance of certain demands from below, while at the same time encouraging the working class to restrict its struggle to the economic-corporative terrain, is part of this attempt to prevent the hegemony of the dominant class from being challenged while changes in the world of production are accommodated within the current social formation.

The passive revolution is in fact a technique which the bourgeoisie attempts to adopt when its hegemony is weakened in any way. Its hegemony may be weakened for a variety of reasons. The bourgeois state may never have enjoyed a strong hegemony, as in Italy. A previously strong hegemony, such as in France, might be weakened because the dominance of the bourgeoisie and the capitalist mode of production no longer corresponds to the full expansion of the productive forces.

Gramsci would argue this is the case in the epoch of imperialism. (Q 1636-8) In this situation the concrete basis for bourgeois hegemony, the fact that the bourgeoisie at a certain stage of history represents the advancement of the whole of society, no longer holds.[2] As masses of people become organized economically and politically, as capitalism reorganizes itself in the period of imperialism, there is the potential for the first time in history of masses becoming the protagonists of a social transformation. Therefore the foundation of bourgeois rule changes, and reforms which provide a concrete basis for the consent of the majority must be part of an attempt by the bourgeoisie to prevent its adversary, the working class, from developing an alternative hegemony. Further weakening of bourgeois hegemony can occur as a result of a great upheaval such as the First World War when the old apparatuses of hegemony (such as the traditional parties) (Q 1638-9) are themselves thrown into a crisis. Moreover, the gap between, on the one hand, the changes necessitated by a development of the economic base in the period of the dominance of monopoly capital, and, on the other, the ability of the traditional political structures to accommodate these changes represents an organic contradiction which can only be overcome without destroying the dominance of the traditional relations of production, through a passive revolution which can have a variety of forms. Thus it is a strategy which allows the bourgeoisie to reorganize its dominance politically and economically, an aspect of the extension of the state as 'force plus consent'.

In the 1930s the reorganization of capitalism took a variety of political forms from the New Deal to fascism in which state intervention in the economy and society increased dramatically and some element of planning was attempted to overcome the effects of anarchy in market relations. The form of passive revolution in Italy in this period was fascism.

> . . . there is a passive revolution involved in the fact that — through the legislative intervention of the State, and by means of the corporative organisation — relatively far-reaching modifications are being introduced into the country's economic structure in order to accentuate the 'plan of production' element; in other words, that socialisation and co-operation in

the sphere of production are being increased, without however touching (or at least not going beyond the regulation and control of) individual and group appropriation of profit. In the concrete framework of Italian social relations, this could be the only solution whereby to develop the productive forces of industry under the direction of the traditional ruling classes, in competition with the more advanced industrial formations of countries which monopolise raw materials and have accumulated massive capital sums. (*SPN* 119-20)

This attempt to provide for the expansion of the forces of production has as its political concomitant the strengthening of the historic bloc of social forces underpinning the state by an expansion of the relatively weak hegemony of the dominant class to include new popular elements. Fascism did not simply restore a status quo but it changed the way in which masses of people related to the state, a state which had never enjoyed a mass base.

Whether or not such a schema could be put into practice, and to what extent, is only of relative importance. What is important from the political and ideological point of view is that this schema of fascism is capable of creating — and indeed does create — a period of expectation and hope, especially in certain Italian social groups such as the great mass of urban and rural petits bourgeois. It thus reinforces the hegemonic system and the forces of military and civil coercion at the disposal of the traditional ruling classes. (*SPN* 120)

Gramsci's discussion of fascism in these terms is the key to the importance of the concept with regard to revolutionary politics and to a series of theoretical problems. Faced with the dilemma of the resiliency of capitalism's various political forms — a resiliency which exists despite the fundamental contradiction at a stage in history between the forces of production and the relations of production — Gramsci produces a concept at the political level to take account of this disjuncture between the superstructure and the structure. That this disjuncture is a central problem for Gramsci is evident from his notes on the different moments in the relations of forces and on economism. (*SPN* 177-185; 158-168) Both in these notes and the ones on the passive revolution he refers to a passage from

Marx's Preface to *A Contribution to the Critique of Political Economy* which he paraphrases:

> The concept of 'passive revolution' must be rigorously derived from the two fundamental principles of political science: 1. that no social formation disappears as long as the productive forces which have developed within it still find room for further forward movement; 2. that a society does not set itself tasks for whose solution the necessary conditions have not already been incubated, etc. It goes without saying that these principles must first be developed critically in all their implications, and purged of every residue of mechanicism and fatalism. (*SPN* 106-7)

The crucial phrase is 'still find room' because the ability of the bourgeoisie to manoeuvre in terms of the passive revolution depends on its adversary. This is amplified when Gramsci writes, as we noted above, that

> . . . a social form 'always' has marginal possibilities for further development and organisational improvement, and in particular can count on the relative weakness of the rival progressive force as a result of its specific character and way of life. It is necessary for the dominant social form to preserve this weakness . . . (*SPN* 222)

The failure of the proletariat to exert its alternative hegemony allows the bourgeoisie to continue its rule despite the weakening of its own hegemony. The bourgeoisie may be able to undertake the strategy of the passive revolution, using the channels of the war of position, the various ideological apparatuses, the trenches of civil society, to whatever extent possible to *pre-empt* the creation of an hegemony by the working class. The passive revolution has different forms. It 'decapitates' the working class movement through reformism so that these leaders remain on a non-hegemonic terrain defending the corporate interests of the working class, but not challenging the logic of capitalist social relations. Another method is fascism whereby the leadership and the organizational autonomy of the working class is eliminated.[3] This is certainly not done in a 'passive' way. Here passive refers rather to the nature of the attempt at 'revolution' or development of the productive forces through a degree of state intervention and the inclusion of new social groups under the hegemony of the political order without any expansion of real political control by the mass of the population over politics.

To summarize, when the bourgeoisie is ascendent, the 'passive' aspect of its political revolution has to do with the molecular transformation of the political role of old traditional classes and of any relatively more progressive ones.[4] The revolution consists in the establishment of a new state, or a political superstructure generally suited to the eventual dominance of the capitalist mode of production. Gramsci argues that in the Italian case this state was the precondition for the development of an economic base which was very backward. (*SPN* 117-8)[5] Once this state is established, whatever the nature of its foundation, the bourgeoisie will attempt a strategy of a passive revolution whenever its hegemony is threatened or whenever its political super-structure in the integral sense (force plus hegemony) cannot cope with the need to expand the forces of production. If *allowed* to do so, the dominant class may find new forms of political domination.

Yet, as Gramsci points out, any situation is a product of all the forces in the field, not just the dominant forces. He writes the following passage about the Risorgimento, but it could as well apply to any historical development.

> The Risorgimento is a complex and contradictory historical development, which is made an integral whole by all its antithetical elements, by its protagonists and its antagonists, by their struggles, by the reciprocal modifications which these very struggles determine and also by the function of passive and latent forces like the great agricultural masses, as well as, naturally, the function stemming from international relations. (Q 961)

Indeed the form of the outcome of a clash of forces is dependent on the activity of all the antagonists. It is in this connection that the development of the concept of passive revolution is of vital importance for the politics of a revolutionary movement. If we go back to Gramsci's discussion of the Risorgimento — a discussion which he says is more of political than historical interest (Q 1815) — he argues that the backwardness of the outcome, the narrow base of the new state, not recognized legally by the Vatican or in a real sense by the mass of the population, arose not simply because of the attributes of Cavour and the moderates but also, dialectically, because of the deficiencies of Mazzini and the Partito d'Azione.

> . . . the absence among the radical-popular forces of any awareness of the role of the other side prevented them from being fully aware of their own role either; hence from weighing in the final balance of forces in proportion to their effective power of intervention; and hence from determining a more advanced result, on more progressive and modern lines. (*SPN* 113)

Cavour knew his own task, building an historic bloc based on an alliance between a section of the bourgeoisie and the old feudal classes. Gramsci writes, using a metaphor, that this was so because he understood the task of his 'dialectical' opponent, Mazzini, and therefore could pre-empt him from being effective. Mazzini would have needed a programme of agrarian reform to create a popular base and to eliminate the economic and political power of the old feudal classes in order to build an alternative historic bloc. Cavour was faced, however, by an adversary who represented a weak 'antithesis' because Mazzini would have been able to understand the nature of his own task in building an historic bloc only if he had understood that of Cavour. (*SPN* 109; Q 1782) In other words, the need for an alternative rooted in the popular masses, an historic bloc based on an agrarian reform, the content of a concrete political line, which would have prevented the formation of the historic bloc built by Cavour, could only have been understood, according to Gramsci, as the dialectical opposite of the historic bloc being established by the moderates.

Gramsci explains this in the following passage:

> The binding together of the various rural classes, which was accomplished in a reactionary bloc by means of the various legitimist-clerical intellectual strata, could be dissolved, so as to arrive at a new liberal-national formation, only if support was won from two directions: from the peasant masses, by accepting their elementary demands and making these an integral part of the new programme of government; and from the intellectuals of the middle and lower strata, by concentrating them and

stressing the themes most capable of interesting them (and the prospect of a new apparatus of government being formed, with the possibilities of employment which it offered, would already have been a formidable element of attraction for them — if that prospect had appeared concrete, because based on the aspirations of the peasantry). (*SPN* 74)

A political lesson can be derived for the revolutionary party. Its analysis must be centred on the specific configuration of class forces confronting it in order to be able to know the nature of the alternative historic bloc which it must build. It can only provide this kind of analysis by a non-schematic application of Marxist theory to the specific national context, not by 'intellectual and rational schemas'. (*SPN* 118) This is an argument for the national perspective to be the point of departure; revolutionary demands can only derive from a knowledge of the specific articulation of social forces. When only one of the opponents in the field 'knows' its task, there is, according to Gramsci, a kind of asymmetry at the theoretical level, a misconception of the dialectic whereby one element attempts to assert itself not by a dialectical overcoming of the adversary but by an absorption of certain elements of the antithesis.[6] The result is not as advanced as it would have been had the antithesis been fully asserted. Thus, by posing the question in this way, the result of a clash of different forces, of a conflict which is not simply one dramatic instance but the ongoing class struggle, is not presented as a simple victory or defeat but as a result of the political ability of the different forces in the field. The question is always present for the revolutionary party whether its strategy is producing the optimal results. The difficulties it faces or the achievements of the enemy are seen to be in part a result of its own efforts or rather failures.

The lesson for the working class is that the strategy of passive revolution will be attempted by the bourgeoisie. In order to counteract this, to prevent this kind of margin for political survival developing, the working class must exert its hegemony in the war of position. It is by exerting itself fully in this sense that it can push each moment of historical development forward so that it will be relatively more to the advantage of the working class than otherwise. A failure by the proletariat will allow the result of a clash of forces to be more to the advantage of the adversary. Moreover, an effective intervention by the proletariat depends on a precise comprehension of the political strategy of its enemy.

Gramsci's discussion of the dialectic thus has to do with the difference between reformist and revolutionary politics. Arguing that, from the point of view of the dominant class, reformism is a version of passive revolution, he notes that one aspect of the strategy is to break up the struggle into finite moments. It is based on an ideology which 'tends to weaken the antithesis, to break it up into a series of moments, that is, to reduce the dialectic to a process of reformist evolution, of "revolution-restoration", in which only the second term is valid.' (Q 1328)[7] On the theoretical level, Bernstein argued that a qualitative change would come about through a series of small, partial changes which, one added to the other, would result in a qualitative change.[8] Gramsci affirms that in the real world the dialectic presents itself, or appears, as separate moments, or, we would suggest, in more concrete terms as a struggle for reforms; but the relation between these reforms and a qualitative change has to do with the way in which they reflect a shift in the balance of forces as part of a concrete political strategy, as the result of political intervention in a particular concrete reality. As Gramsci writes '. . . knowing how to find each time the point of progressive equilibrium (in the sense of one's own programme) is the art of the politician, not of the golden mean, but really of the politician who has a very precise line with a wide perspective of the future.' (Q 1825)[9] Outside this context, if these partial moments are elevated to a theoretical principle of historical change, reforms can become a question of 'empirical opportunism'. (Q 1825)

Reformism or any other version of the passive revolution cannot be a suitable strategy for the proletariat. In a note entitled, significantly, 'First Epilogue', Gramsci summarizes the main points which he wants to make in his writings on the passive revolution. It is not, he writes, a '. . . *theory of the "passive revolution"* . . . as a programme, as it was for the Italian liberals of the Risorgimento, but as a criterion of interpretation . . .' (*SPN* 114) When Gramsci writes that it must not be a programme for the working class movement, an argument which must be related to his general critique of reformism as not going beyond an economic-corporative struggle, his reasoning is based on the idea of a fundamental asymmetry between the revolution made by the working class and that of the bourgeoisie. Since the bourgeoisie could transform the old feudal classes into political allies, converting traditional intellectuals to perform an organic function serving the new bourgeois dominance as they take over the existing state machinery, they can found a new state on the basis of the passive revolution. They can do without massive popular consent as long as they can continue a passive revolution in one form or another against any new adversaries. Thus the bourgeoisie can simply adapt the existing state to its own use, maintaining politics as a sphere of activity by a few, without transforming the mode of existence of the intellectuals, their relationship to the masses.

The proletariat cannot found a state on the same basis as the bourgeoisie for several reasons. First of all, the proletariat is founding a state to do away with all exploitation in the Marxist sense, whereas the bourgeoisie were replacing one form of exploitation with another. From his earliest work, Gramsci argues that the working class has as its historical project the creation of a new *type* of state, in which the very concept of politics is transformed as the masses intervene and control politics and economics.[10] Gramsci defines the socialist revolution in terms of a revolution made by the masses which expands the forces of production and which institutes a democratic control over politics and the economy, thus transforming politics itself.[11]

Furthermore, Gramsci argues throughout his work that an integral state can only be founded if a class enjoys hegemony before it achieves state power; and in terms of the struggle in an advanced capitalist country, if the war of position has been waged successfully. All of this implies widespread popular consent. This is also demonstrated if we reverse the argument. Since the proletariat cannot bring about its transformation of society through the passive revolution, it can only do so on the basis of a concrete programme which engenders widespread consent and a system of alliances under its hegemony. This hegemony is based on compromises and on a struggle to achieve reforms, but reforms qualitatively different from those conceded by the bourgeoisie in the passive revolution. For if the proletariat is to weld together an alternative historical bloc, it must promote changes which go beyond the corporate interests of the groups concerned and challenge the traditional mode of political control. Its historical project involves asserting a real control over politics by society, that is, the establishment of a new relationship between leaders and led.

Without going into this fully here, it is important to note that the notion of passive revolution is related to Gramsci's discussion of the intellectuals. Gramsci reflected on his activities with the Factory Council movement in Turin and the nature of the cohesion of the Italian social formation.[12] He tried to take account of the fact that the growth in size of the intellectuals as a social stratum and the changes in the relationship between intellectual work and the world of production had made the intellectuals less of an élite. Taking up the Hegelian theme of the political role of the intellectuals in the state, discussed in more contemporary terms by Weber in relation to a view of politics as a specialized activity which can only be undertaken by an expert few, Gramsci argues that changes in the productive sphere as capitalism develops are in fact undermining old divisions between intellectual and manual labour. Thus it is now possible to conceptualize a new organization of knowledge which is based on the acquisition of intellectual tools by masses of people. This change in knowledge is a prerequisite for an expansion of democracy. The mode of existence of intellectuals and their relation to the world of work and to the mass of the population — who themselves for the first time in history can conceivably acquire intellectual skills and hence political power — must be transformed. Whereas the bourgeoisie could simply absorb elements of intellectuals who once performed services organic to the maintenance of a previous social formation, feudalism, and allow them to maintain a traditional mode of existence separate from the mass of the population, the working class must win over to its side intellectuals who now help to reproduce capitalism, by fundamentally transforming their view of their own work and the relation of this work to the expansion of knowledge and political power by the vast majority of the population. The proletariat thus cannot simply take over the existing state and a pre-existing mode of intellectual activity in which all the old divisions are maintained, but must transform the state and its relationship with the mass of the population. The very nature of the consent it maintains must be qualitatively different.

Thus the project of the working class in founding a new type of state is fundamentally different from that of the bourgeoisie. It must unify groups of people on a basis which goes beyond the corporative interests which kept them separate under capitalism. It must break through the limitations of capitalist social relations and thereby bring the expansion of real democratic control. Any party or movement whose politics were not posed in these terms would simply contribute to social changes which could be incorporated within the present system as it reorganized itself. The basis for revolutionary change, according to Gramsci, was given by capitalist development, because capitalism, as Marx had argued, had to 'revolutionize' itself constantly and to challenge old relationships. But Gramsci maintained that reforms which were limited to the corporate demands of different groups and which did not go beyond the concept of politics as the privileged territory of a few could simply be absorbed as capitalism reconstituted itself through crises. The usefulness of the concept of the passive revolution as an interpretative device thus consists in measuring the adequacy of a political strategy and helping to explain the durability of bourgeois rule despite economic and political crises.

The way in which Gramsci views the contradictory effects of the various forms of capitalist development is illustrated by his analysis of fascism as a passive revolution. Any unilateral interpretation of fascism as a reaction or as a restoration, he argues, must be avoided. When Gramsci writes that there are never restorations *in toto* in a note on Caesarism[13] where the parallel with fascism is quite clear, he is suggesting that the full significance of the phenomenon of fascism or any other form of passive revolution will never be comprehended unless that aspect which represents the 'revolution' side of the binomial is analyzed. The 'progressive' element, or the fundamental change, which the passive revolution effects in the reorganization of bourgeois rule and in the capitalist economy must not be ignored. Thus in analyzing fascism, its real political support among sections of the population which considered fascism to be able to provide the solutions to their problems, in particular sections of the urban and rural petty bourgeoisie, must be given full weight in understanding how this kind of passive revolution could serve to maintain and transform the state — both as a hegemonic system and in terms of the instruments of coercion, which provided the conditions for the continued dominance of the 'traditional' social forces and the capitalist mode of production.

In this regard it had also to be recognized that fascism attempted to provide the conditions for the expansion of the productive forces in a period in which some kind of planning was necessary because of the dominance of monopoly capital (*SPN* 119-120) Indeed, in his notes on 'Americanism and Fordism' and in those on the concept of the falling rate of profit Gramsci studies the way in which state intervention in the economy in the period of 'organized capitalism' represented an attempt to overcome the tendency for profits to fall and to reorganize the masses both economically and politically. Because of the increasing contradictions in the period of imperialism, a new form of state is both required by and provides for a development of the economic base. Gramsci once more indicates the extremely complex nature of the relationship between base and superstructure, at the same time insisting on the multitude of essential features of any political phenomenon. Fascism may represent a form of bourgeois rule, but it or any other type of state cannot be reduced to a single feature without failing to understand its real significance. Moreover, the dynamic of the historical process during a passive revolution is something which cannot be controlled to suit the wishes of those who promote this form of political rule, and the contradictory consequences of the reorganization of capitalism in its different forms must be fully appreciated. Indeed, in developing the concept of the passive revolution, Gramsci is trying to purge Marx's argument that capitalism is forced to revolutionize itself of the mechanistic interpretation of the Second International which considered the development of the forces of production as leading in a unilinear manner to the downfall of capitalism. By insisting that capitalism must reorganize itself, Gramsci emphasizes that the changes introduced always represent a challenge to the working class movement which must be able to intervene in a qualitatively different situation; a situation with new dangers, but also new possibilities. Its politics must represent an 'anti-passive revolution'[14] in which the changes taking place within capitalism are developed as the basis for creating new social and political relations which overcome divisions between individuals and between groups and between individuals and the realms of politics and economics. Any given development must be viewed in its contradictions as having the potential to serve as the basis of an advance toward a new organization of society and human relations or as an aspect of the reorganization of capitalism.[15]

There is one last aspect of the conditions under which a passive revolution may take place which is of importance. In several passages Gramsci relates it to the relative economic backwardness of the progressive forces. He is very clear, however, that the level of economic development is only one factor in the possibility of a class establishing a state. The success of a class may be more related to a particular international conjuncture, for example, than to its innate strength as an internal, subjective force. In what is a description of uneven development, he suggests a particular danger which exists when a state is founded in a situation where the concrete conditions for a new social formation do exist, but more as potential than as reality.

One can see how, when the impetus of progress is not tightly linked to a vast local economic development which is artificially limited and repressed, but is instead the reflection of international developments which transmit their ideological currents to the periphery — currents born on the basis of the productive development of the more advanced countries — then the group which is the bearer of the new ideas is not the economic group but the intellectual stratum, and the conception of the State advocated by them changes aspect; it is conceived of as something in itself, as a rational absolute. The problem can be formulated as follows: since the State is the concrete form of a productive world and since the intellectuals are the social element from which the governing personnel is drawn, the intellectual who is not firmly anchored to a strong economic group will tend to present the State as an absolute; in this way the function of the intellectuals is itself conceived of as absolute and pre-eminent, and their historical existence and dignity are abstractly rationalised. (*SPN* 116-117)

In this passage he is specifically referring to the attitude to the state held by intellectuals of the modern idealist school, such as Croce, but we would argue that he is also thinking of the type of pitfall which a socialist revolution might face if it is not made and continued on the basis of widespread consent; if it does not create a new relationship between the masses and politics. Gramsci certainly is not maintaining that a political revolution must wait upon the development of economic factors, but rather he is insisting on the importance of the *form* of the revolution given the existence, at least in potential, of certain concrete conditions. We thus arrive at the possibility of a socialist state maintaining itself through a passive revolution and thus remaining the expression of an economic-corporative change. Here the development of an extended hegemony is stunted, and the working class is unable to represent the universal interests of the whole of society. Gramsci in fact offers a powerful analytic tool with which to examine the first concrete example of the establishment of a workers' state. To the extent that a separation is preserved between the realm of politics and the mass of the population and a traditional mode of existence of the intellectuals as an élite is reproduced, the historical task of the proletariat — of extending democratic control over the political and economic spheres — has still to be accomplished.

Gramsci's concept of passive revolution is thus relevant to the current debate over whether the transition to socialism in advanced capitalist countries must establish a 'third way' following neither the path of Social Democracy nor that of Bolshevism. This debate involves the question of the possibility of new forms of democracy in which the relationship of the individual to the state and politics is transformed, and goes beyond the formal limitations of liberal democracy. The question of the nature of state power and the kind of reforms which break through the logic of capitalist social relations is central to any analysis of the politics of any movement or party which maintains that it seeks to transform society. At the same time, it must be recognized that reforms are constantly being instituted by political groups and parties with all kinds of labels as a response to popular demands within the context of the reorganization of capitalism, a reorganization which implies a challenge to old modes of politics but which can take place on the terrain of a renewal of capitalism if the various forces in the field allow it to do so.

NOTES

1 Gramsci writes: 'The important thing is to analyze more profoundly the significance of a "Piedmont"-type function in passive revolutions — i.e. the fact that a state replaces the local social groups in leading a struggle of renewal. It is one of the cases in which these groups have the function of "domination" without that of "leadership": *dictatorship without hegemony*. The hegemony will be exercised by a part of the social group over the entire group, and not by the latter over other forces in order to give power to the movement, radicalize it, etc. on the "Jacobin" model.' (*SPN* 105-6) My emphasis.

2 With regards to the French example, Gramsci writes: 'The Jacobins, consequently, were the only party of the revolution in progress, in as much as they not only represented the immediate needs and aspirations of the actual physical individuals who constituted the French bourgeoisie, but they also represented the revolutionary movement as a whole, as an integral historical development. For they represented future needs as well, and, once again, not only the needs of these particular physical individuals, but also of all the national groups which had to be assimilated to the existing fundamental group.' (*SPN* 78)

3 Gramsci describes this in the following way: 'Between consent and force can be found corruption and fraud . . . that is the debilitation and the paralysis incurred to the antagonist or to the antagonists by cornering the leaders . . . in order to throw utter confusion and disorder in the *antagonists' ranks*. (*Q* 1638)

4 This, of course, does not mean that there is no conflict but that the bourgeoisie avoids a head-on clash with the feudal classes doing without the equivalent of a Terror.

5 He writes that the reasons that the Italian bourgeois revolution took the form it did are to be found '. . . in the economic field, that is to say in the relative weakness of the Italian bourgeoisie and in the different historical climate in Europe after 1815'. (*SPN* 80)

6 Gramsci refers to Marx's argument against Proudhon in *The Poverty of Philosophy, SPN*, 109, *Q*, 1220-1, and to Croce, *Q*. 1326-7.

7 Gramsci is specifically discussing Croce here but it is clear that he

considers Croce's work as part of the revision of Marxism in the tradition of the Second International. See Q, 1325.

8   This was part of Bernstein's rejection of the dialectic as he understood it.

9   There is a parallel in this argument with Lenin's *Two Tactics of Social Democracy* where he argues the case for the proletariat in Russia to lead the bourgeois democratic revolution.

10 See Franco De Felice, *Serrati, Bordiga, Gramsci e il problema della rivoluzione in Italia 1919-1920*, De Donato, Bari, 1971, especially 'La "conquista dello stato" come creazione di un nuovo tipo di stato', pp. 275-290, and the essay in this volume.

11 In Gramsci's view, therefore, politics does not disappear but is rather transformed. He thus goes a good deal of the way to answering those critics of Marxism who maintain that the negation of politics altogether is impossible.

12 See in particular 'Some Aspects of the Southern Question' in *Selections from Political Writings 1921-1926*, Lawrence and Wishart, London, 1978.

13 Gramsci writes, 'The problem is to see whether in the dialectic "revolution/restoration" it is revolution or restoration which predominates; for it is certain that in the movement of history there is never any turning back, and that restorations *in toto* do not exist'. *SNP*, 219-220. In the same note Gramsci explains that it is the organization of masses of people in the modern period which characterizes Caesarism and differentiates it as a political phenomenon from the coups d'état and military interventions of traditional Bonapartism.

14 This is Christine Buci-Glucksmann's phrase in 'State transition and passive revolution' in *Gramsci and Marxist Theory*, edited by Chantal Mouffe, London, 1979.

15 An example would be the vastly improved productivity through technical change which at the moment is producing pools of the permanently unemployed instead of resulting in a dramatic decrease in the working week which is a pre-requisite for an expansion of democratic control and for overcoming the present sexual division of labour.

III
GRAMSCI

SARDINIA 1891–1911

Antonio Gramsci was born on 22 January, 1891 in Sardinia, an impoverished island oppressed for centuries by foreign invaders. Its already backward agriculture was severely harmed by reforms instituted by a newly united Italy which favoured the industrial North. Gramsci's father, of Greek-Albanian origin, was a government clerk, later arrested for administrative irregularities. The family lived in considerable hardship. Antonio's mother, who had to support seven children by working as a seamstress, came from a lower middle-class Sardinian family and was unusually well-educated, reading, writing and speaking Italian.

At the age of four Antonio fell from the arms of a maid and suffered spinal injuries. These led to him becoming a hunchback as well as to constant bad health. In a superstitious, cruel and fatalistic society, his handicap made him the object of fear and persecution.

Gramsci's determination to study led eventually to his winning a scholarship to the University of Turin. In Sardinia his first political awareness was expressed in rebellion against the rich and in regionalist pride. He was introduced to the socialist movement by his brother, Gennaro. Gramsci's lifelong conviction of the centrality of the 'Southern question' in Italian politics, as well as of the importance of understanding a backward, subordinate folk culture, can be traced to his Sardinian childhood and youth.

TURIN 1911–1920

In 1911 Gramsci began to study at the University of Turin. He lived in poor conditions, was dogged by bad health, and was destined never to complete his degree in linguistics. At the university he made friends with Palmiro Togliatti, Angelo Tasca and others who would later found the socialist newspaper, the *Ordine Nuovo*. He first made contact with the socialist movement in Turin in 1913, which is probably when he joined the Italian Socialist Party (PSI).

His journalistic activity began in 1914 when he wrote a controversial article for the Turinese socialist paper, *Il Grido del Popolo*, challenging the passive socialist attitude to WWI. In addition to giving talks on such topics as the French Revolution, the Paris Commune and Marx to workers' cultural clubs, he began a period of intense activity as a theatre critic. He was also active with the socialist youth section. His articles in this period expressed a demand for creative socialist politics. In April and then in July 1917, he wrote pieces exalting the Russian Revolution and Lenin.

The working class in Turin — the most highly industrialized area of Italy — had opposed Italy's entry into WWI. The Turinese workers — with their history of militancy — impressed Gramsci. He saw in them a potential for running society differently. Discontent with the war and the lack of bread led to riots in August 1917 which ushered in a period of militancy to last until 1920.

When a number of socialist leaders were arrested, Gramsci assumed the editorship of *Il Grido del Popolo*. After the October Revolution, he hailed the Bolsheviks as having disproved any mechanical interpretation of Marx which assumed that revolutionaries had to wait until historical conditions were ripe before intervening in history.

In April 1919, the weekly, *Ordine Nuovo*, was founded and Gramsci and a group of friends undertook to work with the Factory Council movement which had burgeoned out of earlier forms of factory organization. The Councils, they thought, could translate the experience of the Soviets into the Italian context and provide the basis for uniting the working class which had joined the trade unions and the PSI *en masse* in these years and had engaged in many militant struggles. The Piedmont General Strike of April 1920 was followed in September of that year by the occupation of the factories throughout Northern Italy. As elsewhere in Europe, this ended in the defeat of the working class movement.

154

FASCISM AND THE PCI 1921–1926

The inadequacy of the PSI leadership during the general strike and the occupation of the factories convinced Gramsci that a definitive break with reformism and a separate communist party were necessary. In January 1921, the Italian Communist Party (PCI) was created and Gramsci was elected to the central committee. The politics of the new party reflected the sectarian ideas of its leader, Amadeo Bordiga.

Gramsci continued as editor of the *Ordine Nuovo* which became one of the daily papers of the PCI. In a series of articles he undertook an anlysis of the Italian fascist movement which had moved onto the offensive after the defeat of the occupation of the factories. Gramsci analysed the crisis of Italian liberal democracy and the mass base of the fascist movement, specifying how it differed from other reactionary political movements. Bordiga and other socialists and

communists tended to reduce fascism to simply another manifestation of bourgeois oppression.

In May 1922 Gramsci went to Moscow to work for the Comintern (Communist Third International). He was there when Mussolini seized power after the March on Rome in October 1922. Almost immediately upon his arrival in Moscow, Gramsci's ill health caused him to enter a sanatorium. There he met his future wife, Julia Schucht, daughter of an old Bolshevik family. In the next few years they were to have two sons, Delio and Giuliano. Imprisoned by Mussolini in 1926, Gramsci was never to see his second son, born in Moscow in that year.

The period in which Gramsci was in Moscow and then later in Vienna in the employ of the Comintern was one of great debate about the way to build socialism in the USSR and the correct strategy for communist parties elsewhere. The Bordiga leadership of the PCI was on bad terms with the leadership of the Third International because of differences concerning unity with the socialists. After Bordiga's arrest, convinced of the need for a change in the politics of the PCI, Gramsci initiated a correspondence from Vienna with Togliatti and other old *Ordine Nuovo* friends, in order to plan a new orientation.

Having been elected an MP and therefore enjoying parliamentary immunity, Gramsci returned to Italy in May 1924. He undertook to transform the PCI into an effective weapon against fascism. Mussolini's regime

had been shaken by the crisis ensuing from the murder of the socialist MP, Giacomo Matteotti in June 1924. But the opposition was divided and confused about the tactics to follow. Soon fascism consolidated itself, uniting different sections of the bourgeoisie. At its congress in exile in Lyons in January 1926, after almost two years of debate in clandestine conditions, the PCI overwhelmingly endorsed Gramsci's policy aimed at uniting various anti-fascist forces and rooting the PCI in the working class.

Meanwhile, in the Soviet Union the struggle between Stalin and Trotsky had become dramatic. In letters to the Central Committee of the Soviet Union and to Togliatti, then in Moscow, Gramsci criticized the nature of the attacks on Trotsky, although he did not share his position. He claimed that the standing of the Central Committee, ten years after the Revolution, had to be based on its record of building socialism. He also wrote a long essay on the Southern question which provided a complex analysis of Italian history and society and indicated a framework for its revolutionary politics. This essay would only be published in France several years later: Gramsci and many other top communist leaders were arrested in November 1926 despite their parliamentary immunity.

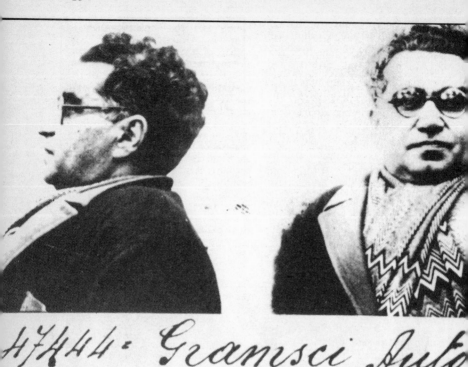

47444 · Gramsci Auto

PRISON 1926–1937

After his arrest Gramsci was transferred from prison to prison. Piero Sraffa, a friend from Turin, who was working at King's College, Cambridge, began sending him books. He and Gramsci's sister-in-law, Tatiana Schucht, who devoted a decade of her life to him, were Gramsci's main links to the outside world throughout his imprisonment.

Although he would not be granted permission to write for almost two years, in March 1927 Gramsci set down a plan of study in which the question of the intellectuals' role was central. In a letter to Tatiana, he emphasized that he wanted to create something which would last.

At the end of May 1928 the 'great trial' against Gramsci and other PCI leaders began. Gramsci was sentenced to twenty years, four months and five days. A public functionary declared: 'We must prevent this brain from functioning for twenty years.' He was sent to the special prison at Turi near Bari in Southern Italy. From December 1928 on, he was seriously ill, his condition aggravated by prison life.

Gramsci was in touch with the outside world through visits and each new wave of arrests brought political prisoners to Turi with news of the latest developments. Regularly scheduled lessons and political discussions were part of prison life. These came to an abrupt end for Gramsci at the end of 1930: the new 'social fascist' line of the Comintern declared that socialists were to be considered on a par with fascists. Gramsci was thus in *de facto* disagreement with the party line and hence found himself isolated from other prisoners.

His struggle to survive physically and morally despite appalling conditions focussed on his notebooks. Often unable to get required material, receiving only what was allowed by the prison authorities, controlled in what he wrote by a prison censor, Gramsci yet created what would become a classic of political thought. Between February 1929 and August 1931 he filled seven notebooks, only to be interrupted by a physical collapse. Another ten notebooks were to follow before a new and more serious crisis in March 1933. At the end of 1933 he was transferred to the first of several clinics, though still in detention. In a weakened physical state, he nonetheless managed to fill another twelve notebooks.

There had been campaigns abroad for his release: in 1928 at the time of his trial, again in May-June 1933 when Romain Rolland, Henri Barbusse and others participated, and rallies were held in various countries. In October 1934 Gramsci finally obtained a conditional release. Still under strict surveillance, his physical condition was so bad he was destined never to

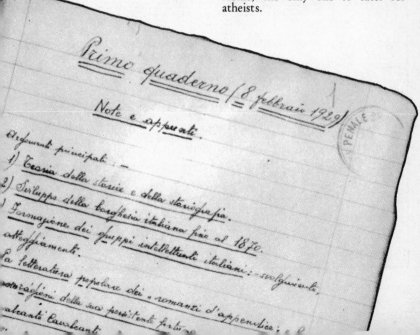

leave hospital. Transferred to the clinic 'Quisana' in Rome in August 1935, his work on the notebooks was at an end. Death came on 27 April 1937 when he was struck by a cerebral haemorrhage just days after he had been granted full freedom. Only a small paragraph in the Italian press announced his death. He was buried quietly in the Protestant cemetery in Rome, the only one to cater for atheists.

Tatiana Schucht who had attended Gramsci throughout his ten-year calvary, sent a telegram to Piero Sraffa and made sure the notebooks were safe. Only recently has it been revealed that they were deposited in the vaults of the Banca Commerciale in Rome which was headed by the anti-fascist Mattioli. They were then sent on to Moscow.

The first edition of Gramsci's *Letters from Prison* appeared in 1947. Substantially censored, they were only published without cuts in 1965. Between 1948 and 1951, six volumes were published of his prison notes to be followed by four volumes of his pre-prison writings. A definitive version of the notebooks appeared in 1975 with all versions of all notes. Gramsci's work has now been translated into many languages. A Gramsci bibliography today is itself the size of a small book.

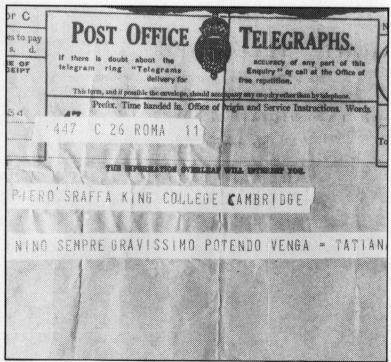

ANTONU SU GOBBU
Tom Nairn

Tom Nairn's article acts as a counterpoint to other interpretations of Gramsci in this book. Nairn argues that too often the specifically Italian context of Gramsci's ideas is ignored by those who wish to use him to support Euro-communist alternatives to the left. This raises a general problem. Any political theory is written in a specific historical context; and with writers like Machiavelli, Lenin and Gramsci who focus on a national reality in order to change it, this context becomes particularly important. Gramsci, referring to the experiences of the Bolsheviks and the Russian Revolution, maintained that any political theory developed in one set of circumstances had to be 'translated' for a new situation. It could never simply be applied. Can this be done with Gramsci's work? Does he have ideas which help us to understand our present situation better? Most of the articles in this book would say yes.

Nairn feels lessons from Gramsci can be learned only if he is placed firmly in his historical context. In a piece which appeared originally as a review, he provides an analysis of the specific characteristics of Italian history which must be taken into account when reading Gramsci. He argues that Gramsci's ideas are shaped by the peculiarities of Sardinian and Italian development. In so doing, he provides a stimulating interpretation of the history of Italian unification, the problem of the South, and Machiavelli.

As a child he was almost always alone. A tiny coffin and shroud stood in the house in Sardinia until he was twenty-three, mute and awesome memorials to the time he almost bled to death, at the age of four. However, the frightful injury which had caused the haemorrhage left him a permanent dwarf hunchback, in spite of repeated iodine rubs, and much familial pleading with the Holy Virgin.

Later on, when the father was jailed for petty embezzlement, the Gramscis slid downhill into humiliating poverty. Antonu attended a village school in the remote hinterland, alongside the children of the most direly exploited, miserable and little-known peasantry in Europe. They kept *su gobbu* (the hunchback) out of their games and threw stones at him, 'with the evilness which is found among children and the weak', as he was to recall later. This continued until he mustered enough rage to turn and hurl them back, in a paroxysm of rebellion.

This was the island impulse that saved him, and allowed him eventually to struggle out of 'the sewer of my past'. Yet the darkness always remained with him, both affliction and nourishment. 'The whole society of the Campidano was riddled with witch-craft, spell-casting and belief in the super-natural,' writes one biographer. The Gramsci children were reared to a knowledge of were-wolves, blood-sucking demons and other terrors of night-time. By day as well they learned the legendary Sard landscape and its archaic tongue, from older relatives or the itinerant story-tellers who passed through Sorgono and Ghilarza. Antonu's first adult ambition before he became the Italian revolutionary, Antonio Gramsci, was to rediscover this fabulous world, and justify it through scholarship.

A passion for reading developed out of his solitude and deformity. This counted in a countryside where few people knew Italian properly, and bore him up to the indispensable threshold of civilization and a career, knowing all 84 Articles of the Constitution of the Kingdom of Italy by heart. From here he got to a better school, and finally to university in Turin. In an essay written at the age of twenty, world history is still viewed very much as the Sard tragedy on a bigger scale. The truth of all times and places has been 'an insatiable greed shared by all men to fleece their fellows, to take from them what little they have been able to put aside through privations'. Garibaldi, the liberator of the South, is given a good word; but generally, 'Men possess nothing more than a veneer of civilization — one has only to scratch them to lay bare the wolf-skin underneath,' and the best solution would be a universal bloodbath, after which the oppressors will find it is a bit late to be sorry 'they left the hordes in that state of ignorance and savagery they enjoy today . . . '

Sardism gave way to the more positive and universal creed of socialism, in the ambience of a lively urban culture devoted to progress and industry. Yet the change was slow. Five years after the essay, in 1916, he wrote that he still felt and lived like a touchy bear in a cave. And two years after that the Liberal intellectual Piero Gobetti found him still seething with resentment, and diagnosed that 'his socialism was first of all a reply to the offences of society against a lonely Sard emigrant'. The emerging political and intellectual leader put this ferocious nationalism behind him; but not the wry, pessimistic sense of fate associated with it, or the knowledge that reality was such as to demand unfathomable power of will against impossible odds.

Euro-Gramscism

It is always important to recall this early phase of Gramsci's astonishing biography. He is the greatest of western Marxists. But it cannot be without some significance that he was also a product of the West's most remote periphery, and of conditions which, half a century later, it became fashionable to call 'Third World'. No comparable western intellectual came from such a background. He was a barbed gift of the backwoods to the metropolis, and some aspects of his originality always reflected this distance.

A second more particular reason for underlining that side of the man lies in the latest wave of Gramscian interpretation, which is actually in search of a new revolutionary ideology for the European left as a whole. The searchers are convinced that its underpinnings can be excogitated from the writings of Gramsci, above all the *Prison Notebooks*. A left-wing Euro-communism is seeking for its legitimation; and this Euro-Gramscism is its basis. Some years ago the American Marxist Paul Piccone predicted that if Marxism was to become a meaningful political force in the West, 'it will have to follow a Gramscian path', and that because Gramsci provides 'a formulation of Marxism free from all the traditional trappings of orthodox versions' he would become the inspiration of left opposition to the main Communist Parties as well as an object for ritual obeisances by their leaderships. The prediction is certainly being fulfilled.

However, its fulfilment brings new problems. A new prophet has been discovered. The tiny man's giant shadow is projected as a possible future for Europe. He becomes the key to a new, decent, revolutionary philosophy free from the tares of 'really existing socialism', and valid everywhere. Everything is re-cast in a heroic mould chiselled out from the dense, tortured seams of the *Notebooks*. The Sardinian, and even the Italian, disappears in its glow. Island bristles and peninsular warts have been smoothed away, to produce a curiously cosmopolitan and abstract figure. An Althusserian halo has been bestowed upon the country boy, as if he had retrospectively passed the *agrégation* and shed all merely human attributes.

Can the transformation be justified? Doubt on this score is not necessarily sentimentality. It is not a question of impiety, in the sense of wilful indifference to Gramsci's personality or sufferings. The point concerns, rather, the intellectual substance of Gramsci's writings. Can that really be disengaged and extolled as new political revelation, as a gospel for the 1980s? Or was it irremediably bound into certain Sard and Italianate dilemmas, and charged (therefore) with persistent ambiguities which must qualify all efforts at broad philosophical interpretation? Is it not the case that, as Alastair Davidson wrote in his 1977 intellectual biography, studying Gramsci makes one grasp 'how much each individual can only be explained by his position in a particular historical and social structure, which is *his* . . . The social and economic structure which "produced" him . . . can only be grasped structurally if it is grasped historically'?

Gramsci and Politics

At the same time, an escalating debate about Gramsci's ideas has been taking place, mainly in Italy and France. The problem of accessibility is central to this debate. Though a permanent dilemma of any democratic or mass politics, it has become impossibly aggravated for the left by the consolidation of academic Marxism since the later 1960s. That is, by the existence of a distinct social stratum now numerous and established enough to possess its own idiolect. This speech-mode is regulated around the key concept of *rigour*, a notion suitably combining professional strictness with quasi-Leninist disciplinarianism. Rigour in the new tribal sense is counter-posed for its justification to what one might call numbskull populism, an item never in short supply on the left.

Rigourists believe that Marxism is a science, in an exciting new sense, demanding new terminology and conceptual technicians for its development. Populists stick to the conviction that anything *worth* saying must be accessible to the humblest IQ in the land, and translatable into *Daily Mirror* rhetoric. Typically fixated by methodology and language, rigourism perceives departure from its own discourse-categories as mere slobbering humanism or (in the political version) 'reformism' and 'revisionism'. Populism answers, naturally enough, with impatient dismissal of the new priest-hood. Ever suspicious of élites, socialists could hardly avoid paranoia over such a blatantly hermetic we-group.

From one angle, Gramsci's life and writings were a final demolition of this preposterous polarity. His arduous scholarly background made him intensely aware of cultural differentiations, and of the impossibility of populist short-circuits: 'intellectuals' are a definite though variegated social stratum, of crucial political significance, and with irreducible functions. Innovation is one such task, and is rarely com-prehensible to everyone; culture spreads in phases, through the by-ways and reflections pondered on so carefully in his *Letteratura e vita nazionale* notes. Yet at the same time — the second unique aspect of Gramsci's life, after his upbringing — he was involved in organizing and leading a genuine, mass revolutionary movement. No other intellectual in his or the following generation of Western Marxists was to enjoy such an experience directly.

It immunised him completely against that scepticism of or even contempt for the masses which, later, infected the Marxist intelligentsia. Nobody had fewer illusions about 'ordinary people' than Gramsci. But the Turin experiences of 1919-20 guaranteed him against the supreme illusion: that of believing in their inevitable servitude and myopia. As a result all his writing from that period forward embraces a wider register, perhaps, than any other political figure of our century.

He wrestles constantly with the most difficult or out-of-the-way ideas; yet there is never anything at all arcane about his argument or attitude. Rather he was haunted by the sense that the most abstract phenomena — like the Crocean spirit-world which dominated the Italian universities at that time — always have a desperately practical significance, if only one can get them into the right focus. Conversely, the most 'concrete' things — a popular saying, street names, modes of address, talk of the weather — will betray a highly dialectical meaning, when interrogated with sufficient insight.

Marxism should, and can, know everything. But — in sharp contrast to the neo-Marxist academy — it is never for people 'in the know'. He pointed out of a great predecessor that 'Machiavelli had in mind "those who are not in the know", and it was they whom he intended to educate politically . . . ' Who is not 'in the know', in the relevant sense? 'The revolutionary class of the time, the Italian "people" or "nation", the citizen democracy which gave birth to men like Savonarola and Pier Soderini.' To keep open the doors is not easy, and not all will pass through them; there are many mansions in Marxism's house, which only windbag philistines pretend is one entity. Yet if openness is abandoned, the entire political aim of the project is enfeebled. Esoterism is a form of division spelling defeat. If Marxism becomes a structuralist algebra on one level, it is bound to remain cloddish orthodoxy among those 'not in the know'.

The new wave conceives Gramsci as the founder (with or without Lenin) of Marxist political theory in a sense transcending the sordid and the merely national. The political realm is autonomous, and Gramsci is something like its Galileo. Its adherents say of him roughly what he said of Machiavelli: 'The first question . . . in a study of Machiavelli is the question of politics as an autonomous science, of the place that political science occupies or should occupy in a systematic conception of the world.' This is why (incidentally) the new trend must appear strange to any Rip Van Winkles still convinced that Marxism is an economic-determinist creed. They will find the mode of production, the declining rate of profit and other old acquaintances held sternly at arm's length, when they are noticed at all.

The Second Machiavel

Is Gramsci the Machiavelli of Communist political thought? He himself devoted much time to the great Florentine, and conceived the Marxist revolutionary party as *il moderno Principe*, a contemporary equivalent to Machiavelli's Prince-saviour. It is newly fashionable to subscribe to this view, and to maintain that the 'modern Prince', properly understood, will furnish a 'possible' Euro-communism which avoids both the perils of Stalinism and of social-democracy.

The alternative interpretation goes something like this: Gramsci is indeed a modern version of Machiavelli, and a transposition of certain Machiavellian themes and impulses on to the stage of 20th century social movements. However, far from underwriting him as a prophetic figure, this truth does exactly the opposite. It circumscribes his thought, by demonstrating the persistence of certain problems of peninsular development from the 16th to the 20th century. 'Peninsular' is the correct term, not 'Italian'. For the crux of the persistent dilemma Machiavelli and Gramsci stand at opposite ends of has been a failure to constitute one Italian nation, as distinct from the Italianate state of the Risorgimento and after.

In Machiavelli's day the Italian lands were succumbing to foreign conquest by the embryonic nation-states beyond the Alps. There, great unifying dynasties had constructed bureaucratic and military machines dwarfing the resources of the city-states and princedoms. From the end of the 15th century onwards they turned avidly upon the fabulous and almost defenceless peninsula, where Renaissance treasure-houses were protected by dime-a-dozen *condottieri*. Though himself a staunch republican, Machiavelli saw that the only hope of repelling the tide lay in the formation of a central-Italian Kingdom able to compete. Without its own absolutism, its own equivalent of the Valois, Tudor or Hapsburg monarchies, Italy would decline into a collection of colonized provinces. Thus, he was forced to hope that the career of the papal bastard Cesare Borgia (idealized in *Il Principe*) would, miraculously, inspire some other Princeling to the task.

It was too late. Italian feudality was too fragmented and set in its ways to accomplish the transformation. It decomposed into three centuries of enforced quietism. The political retardation Machiavelli's formula was meant to cure became permanent. There arose a petty universe of chronic dependency and corruption, in which 'politics', divorced from the mainstream of European state-formation, assumed the form of purely personal or familial intrigue and advancement. Reflecting bitterly upon the country's economic history in the new Einaudi *Storia d'Italia*, Ruggiero Romano points out how, more than anywhere else, political power became the means to economic success: 'With only rare exceptions, politics have for centuries of our history been the springboard of economic progress. . . In short, is not that history the story of one colossal theft, perpetrated with assiduity across the centuries?'

However, endemic retardation at one level may promote advance at another. This has been strikingly the case as regards Italian political thought and initiative. That specific backwardness rendered 'politics' all-important, both in the Machiavellian sense of a search for alternatives and in the sense indicated by Romano, of *sottogoverno*, duplicity, self-interested manipulation, and so on. The Italianate legend of Machiavellianism conflates the two things into one sinister image: 'politics' *may* accomplish miracles if sufficient *virtù* is put into it (cunning and will-power); if not a new world, then at least the minor miracle of next year's contract or Uncle Gino's pension.

The intractable political problems of the peninsula, in other words, have fostered a dramatic search for answers, and an unusually intense preoccupation with 'the political' as a quasi-autonomous source of both verities and opportunities. Italian periods of crisis, above all, have invariably opened this fertile womb. Her offspring have been now marvellous, now disastrous; but always prodigies, in some way superior to the timid contrivances of those more stable societies which the Italians (for the most part) wished to resemble. The foundering of city-state Italy issued in Machiavelli, still the most important figure in the history of political thought. The renovation of Italy after the French revolutionary interlude brought, in Mazzinian nationalism, the archetype of the new 'age of nationalities'. After World War I, the crisis of the new and precarious national state engendered fascism, an invention which, less than two decades later, threatened to take over the world. The collapse of fascism produced in turn the larger-than-life heroism of the Resistance movements. As the post-war state has stumbled into debility and recession, the inheritor of these movements, Italian Communism, has contrived yet another epochal philosophy to clothe its designs: Euro-communism.

Revolutions from Above

It is generally conceded that Gramsci was no mere philosopher and that one must begin, at least, from the actual context of his political life. Some of the recent work on that context concentrates on the influence of De Leon and the English Shop Steward movement, his relationship to Leninism and the Third International, the arguments against Amadeo Bordiga and the Socialist leader Serrati — and so on. Important as this is, there is a characteristic left-wing weakness attached to it. The determining context of Gramsci's life and thought was not provided by these good causes and persons. It was furnished by the unprecedented defeat of all of them at the hands of the fascists.

It is still not easy to grasp the dimensions of that defeat, because of our post-1945 wisdom. We know that the Lion's day endured only a few years and petered out in the self-devouring farce of Salò. But saving foresight was not granted to Gramsci or his comrades in Turi prison and the other dungeons. They felt themselves hurled like stones into the sea, darkness so utter the only hope was to feel, one day, that the bottom might have been reached. Though Gramsci faced this trajectory with his customary toughness, it meant recognizing that one had been turned from a would-be ploughman of the historical field into manure. 'You don't live as a lion even for a minute, far from it: you live like something far lower than a sheep for years and years and know that you have to live like that. Image of Prometheus who, instead of being attacked by the eagle, is devoured by parasites. . . '

As a leader of the Torinese uprising of 1919-20, he felt the landslide more acutely than anyone else. It was he who, at its high point, had written a report to the Executive Committee of the Third International proudly describing how 'The proletarian army fell like an avalanche on the centre of the city, sweeping the nationalist and militarist rabble off the streets before it . . . ' Yet only two years later the wolves had returned, to revenge themselves on a thoroughly demoralized working class. After a blood-stained summer and autumn, and the surrender of the state to Mussolini in October 1922, Turin had still to be taught a lesson. One of the new order's academic spaniels, G.A. Chiurco, ended his panting chronicle with *i fatti di Torino*: 'Fascist bands speedily accomplished reprisals, awakening a great deal of terror among the communists. Conflicts broke out, leading to a number of deaths. At two in the morning the *Camera del Lavoro* was set alight; then what was left was turned over to the authorities, and the body itself dissolved. The local Fascist High Command took possession of the Karl Marx centre. After that the Railwaymen's Club in Via Risalta was occupied, and the editorial and printing premises of the communist organ *L'Ordine Nuovo* (Gramsci's paper) were set fire to and destroyed.' The Turin industrialists themselves were appalled by the violence, and sent off a delegation of protest to Rome the following day.

This reversal of fortune had taken place — it is certainly not irrelevant to recall — under the ideological banner of anti-statism. The subsequent evolution of fascist corporatism, with its new and extensive modes of state control, was to cancel out the fact from most memories. However, from early 1920 until he got into power, Mussolini sought to ingratiate his movement with the property-owning classes. His address to the second Fascist Congress was an invocation of the verities so prized today by Keith Joseph and other members of Mrs Thatcher's government. A year later, his first parliamentary speech sounded the same note. The Sardinian socialist Emilio Lussu wrote a famous memoir of the event: 'He had taken up his seat at the back, on the extreme right; high up and separated from the rest of his deputies, he seemed like a vulture, crouching upon a rock. "I must declare at once", he began, "that my speech will be reactionary in character. It will be reactionary because I am anti-Parliamentarian, anti-Democratic and anti-Socialist." ' What was the gist of this reaction? A return to simple-minded Manchesterism. It was time to 'deprive the State of all the functions which render it dropsical and vulnerable', he asserted. 'Let the State provide a police-force to protect decent people against villains, properly

organized courts, an army ready for anything, and a foreign
policy in tune with real national needs. Everything else — even
the secondary school system — ought to be left to private
enterprise. To save the State, we must first abolish the
collectivist state . . . ' Evidently, Lussu concludes with due
sarcasm, the Corporative State was not yet worked out in
sufficient detail.

Long before Professor Friedman, in fact, this kind of fool's
gold was employed to rot the civic sense and replace it with a
more atomized, manipulable climate of resentment. The
citizen gave way to a mythical, ill-done-by 'small man',
repository of the betrayed national virtues; causes and arguments were submerged by scape-goats (first at home, then
foreign ogres), chiromantic 'radicalism' and editorial frothing.
Though anti-parliamentary in Italy, where secular cynicism
had been transferred to all the institutions of the new
bourgeois state, the virus is perfectly compatible with voting
democracy. Provided the latter be addled and incompetent
enough, that is. Then when the patient is laid out it is
discovered — inevitably — that the crisis demands more state
operation, not less. The only real problem is how much more,
and how painful.

Whereas in Great Britain such convulsions produced merely
a parodic form of parliamentary rule, the National Government, in Italy the state gave way. The weakness in political
formation diagnosed by Machiavelli remained. The national
unification of Risorgimental times had been (in Gramsci's
phrase) 'a passive revolution', a change stage-managed and co-
opted from above, and not a re-making of society from below.
The semblance and impulse of revolt had been transformed
into counter-revolution, protecting the vitals of the old
system. Now, after the war's disappointments and the left-
wing threat of 1919-20, it was happening again. With far
greater violence and ingenuity, a soured middle class was
discarding the state-form of Piedmontese Liberalism and half-
blindly forging another. The form of hegemony was drastically
remade; and yet, it would only be to redeem the old interests
and lend new life to the ancient, festering ailments of the
country.

Revolution from above had again defeated the left's
revolution from below. It had done so by welding together

underlying socio-economic conservatism with the highest, most ruthless political intelligence — by exploiting to the limit the autonomy of the 'political', understood as a self-acting motor of historical change. Festooned with stolen liberal and socialist trappings, the chariot of counter-revolution rolled over the labour movement, the Catholic left, the Freemasons and all other organized resistance. Through Barnum & Bailey patriotism, its principal weakness, the absence of a homogeneous national reality, was converted into short-term advantage.

The defeat seemed endless. Seven years after the March on Rome, and three after Gramsci's imprisonment, Lussu escaped from the Lipari island prison with two other opponents of the regime. As dawn came up land was sighted from their small boat, at last. But even this prospect could not lift their spirits, he recalls. ' "Is Fascism going to last for ever?", asked some one, suddenly despondent. "It looks like it . . . " said another, and we fell into a pessimistic discussion on the general state of Europe. "Reaction is gaining ground everywhere", the first speaker went on, "The world is going to the right." ' The only consolation (they agreed) was that the tides and solar system seemed immune to the trend, so far.

The problematic conditioning all Gramsci's themes and researches was essentially one of Italian catastrophe; not Stalinism, workers' control, the nature of the Party, Leninism's Seventh Seal or the other preoccupations of the Euro-communists. The source of his long journey into night was this social explosion contradicting almost every rational expectation, and posing the most fundamental questions. What historical pathology had allowed two such 'passive revolutions' to succeed and sweep everything (politically speaking) before them? The relationship between state and civil society had been abnormal, clearly. Yet the very existence of this abnormality showed something was amiss with the habitual models, Marxist and other, and the deficiency was not confined to the level of political tactics or organization. The chronically broken and deformed crystal of Italian history had become a standing accusation of the wider philosophy of the Left, of its stereotyped world-view. And, within that world-view, above all of its political ideas and theories.

The Non-existent 'Prince'

Turning to the question of a 'possible' Euro-communism, the perspective of the new Gramscists itself is questionable. Without objecting for a moment to the 'new conception of socialism' which is its over-riding aim one can still discern a large question-mark over its method and assumptions; and consequently (to some extent) over the final presentation of that conception. By the end of this century Gramsci may well have replaced Machiavelli in the political Pantheon. But Gramscism will probably be as dubious a phenomenon as Machiavellianism has always been. Machiavelli's ideas were, after all, kept in a sort of irrepressible life by the diabolical legend woven by generations of *bien-pensant* enemies. Gramsci has not been so lucky. He has too many friends, falling over one another to exalt him. Euro-mummification might be as deadly as the peninsular variety practised for so long by the PCI.

The new vision of socialism depends upon an equally new idea of the party or movement that will take us there.

Machiavelli's original 'Prince' was a principled fantasy. He entertained no illusions about Borgia himself. On a legation to Rome he had witnessed the great man's decline and fall, and vented his disappointment in no uncertain terms. Cesare's father, Pope Alexander VI, had died. That and the withdrawal of French support left him a pricked bladder of indecision and conceit. Every trace of *virtù* drained out of it, the celebrated handsome countenance which had dazzled so many courts was now permanently contorted with self-doubt and drink, and able to contemplate little more than flight (which before long he did resort to, deserting the stage of Italian politics for good).

Machiavelli chose to extol him in *Il Principe*, none the less, because some facets of his career of conquest remained exemplary for anyone trying to establish a serious dynastic state. With better luck, a more perfect and unflinching embodiment of *virtù* might do the trick. He retained a general faith in what — in modern terminology — would be called the subjective factor, the ability of conscious will-power to shape the course of historical events in a more than small-scale way. 'Optimism of the will' was not disqualified by 'pessimism of the intelligence'. How often this motto of Gramsci's is nowadays quoted! But its specific Italianate resonance is rarely grasped: a world of objective difficulties so huge, that only superhuman amplification of the subjective forces can push things forward. 'Politics' is the concentration at fever pitch of both the leonine and vulpine traits of human nature, and their sapient manipulation to get the maximum leverage in each historical situation. Marxist Machiavellianism translates this into the collective mode.

The party and its effective practice is then seen as the aim of all Gramsci's reflection. With the perfect Party (thanks to Gramsci) democratic centralism can be made to prevail over the other sort, and a real social majority can be won over to the cause: 'hegemony' rather than the ballot-box arithmetic social-democrats deal in. That victory in turn — with its implication of having brought the public mind to reason — will enable a new form of socialist state to be made, free from the bigoted repression of most 'actually existing socialism'. The actually existing Communist and Socialist parties correspond in this scenario (one must suppose) to the concrete, raddled, nail-biting presence of Borgia, which Machiavelli contemplated with such distaste. Though something can be learned from their disasters — above all from the still commanding PCI — they would be eclipsed by the rise of the authentic modern Prince Gramsci strove to construct and then, when exiled from active politics, to plan in his prison notebooks.

Gramsci's analysis of the French Jacobins is brought in to prove that this is no idealist stance. He saw Jacobinism as the prototype of modern revolutionary movements, and the embodiment of that popular, active revolutionism absent from Italy's Risorgimento. But Gramsci also showed how the Jacobins were 'realists of the Machiavelli stamp and not abstract dreamers', because they understood so lucidly just how the collective will should be wielded.

Could anything underline more cruelly the snare in this kind of theorizing? Machiavelli was splendidly realistic in his exposure of the motives and doings of rulers, to the point of never being forgiven for it. But his vision of the Prince-Saviour was a doomed cry for help. There was regrettably no chance of such a Superman emerging from among the Italian tyrants, with or without the assistance of a peasant militia (the

Florentine's equivalent to the soviets or factory-councils which are always invoked in the contemporary version). The 'organic crisis' under way was not such as to favour or even permit that solution, however assertive the subjective forces chose to make themselves. Why? Alas, for drearily economic causes of the sort once associated with Marxist thought: the dry-rot of feudalism provoked by the very ascendancy and wealth of the trading city-states, and that kind of thing.

Is there any greater possibility of present-day conditions in Western Europe and North America fostering the rise of a 'Modern Prince'? Perhaps there is. But the hard-fought scientific triumphs of theory have no cashable relationships to such accumulations of contingency as 'the Basque Country', Monsieur Marchais' betrayal of the *Programme commun*, or the place of Europe between the super-powers.

Thus, how to defend Gramsci's view of Jacobinism against the obvious objection: as well as healthful-sounding things like the creation of widespread popular consent, the Jacobins are known for having wiped out the opposition? The 'new collective will' employed the guillotine, and attempted to terrorize the remains of the old state-formation out of existence. Why should any future hegemonically-based power be different, or better? What is to protect pluralism? If there are good answers to such questions, they involve reference to pimply particularities such as the history of Yugoslavia, the Czech reform movement, Cambodia, Rudolf Bahro's analysis of Eastern Socialism, and so forth.

The Southern Roots

Gramsci was arrested in November 1926, and freed only when on his death-bed, ten and a half years later. A colleague went through his belongings in the flat in Rome, and discovered an essay, 'already finished, written on small parliamentary notepaper' (he had been a deputy in the token parliament permitted by the fascists for the previous two years). Its title was 'La Questione meridionale'. It was not in fact completed, as Camilla Ravera thought, and did not appear in print until four years later, in an obscure exile journal published in Paris. Yet in the long run this fragment was to become possibly the most influential Italian writing of modern times.

Its cardinal significance was quickly understood after World War II, and is reflected in the judgement made by Giuseppe Fiori's *Life* of Gramsci (published in translation in 1971). 'Gramsci's *Notebooks* in prison', he says simply, 'are essentially the continuation and development of the essay on "The Southern Question" '. This view has of course become the obverse of the new 'European' one. For the latter, the essay appears as just one phase (admittedly important) in the elaboration of a political philosophy originated in 1919-20, in the pages of *L'Ordine Nuovo*, then deepened in the *Notebooks*. It loses its focal position, to become one more example of how promising the 'earlier writings' were.

What was this 'Southern Question'? It was the crucial failure of peninsular historical development which had ruined the new Italian state, and made fascism possible. And — at the same time — it was Gramsci himself. The old Southern intelligentsia came under a special and bitter arraignment in his analysis, as a stratum which had sold out to the Piedmontese-Italian state apparatus. They had betrayed the Southern masses into a permanent internal colonialism, and made all-Italian unity possible only at the cost of festering internal corruption and chronically uneven development. 'Politicking, corrupt and faithless', they had not been content with bleeding the peasants dry and turning Vittorio Emmanuele's new Kingdom into a Mafia; through Croce's flatulent Neapolitan philosophy, they had also won a kind of spiritual stranglehold over the new era. *La filosofia dello spirito* cast a cloak of polite European liberalism over what was, in truth, 'a monstrous agrarian bloc' functioning as the overseer for Northern capitalism, and within which there existed 'no intellectual light, no programme, no drive towards improvement or progress'.

Gramsci himself, of course, was a deviant by-product of this group. His father Francesco was a minor state functionary, caught with his hand in the till by a rival clique of *intellettuali*. That and his accident had obscured Antonu's own career-prospects. Yet had it not been for the war and post-war upheavals in Turin, he would almost certainly have found a new niche somewhere in the academic branch of this deplorable machinery of hegemony. Saved from it by his communism, Gramsci retained an intense hatred for *Mezzogiorno* decadence and its effects. Southern Italy — which in this use means 'backward Italy', including areas of the unredeemed Centre and North — 'represents a great social disintegration', the decay and re-subjection of the old, pre-unification societies by another alien state. Only surface remedies had been provided for Machiavelli's chronic ailment. It had survived the centuries to become the main problem for Italian Communism. And its viruses constituted the very intellectual personality, the innermost drama of the founding father of the new revolutionary movement.

The 'Southern Question' notes are read in the left-wing political perspective as a plea for social revolution. This they certainly were: Gramsci's strategic point was that only a new kind of alliance between the Northern working class and the Southern peasantry would ever furnish a basis for a genuine revolution. However, the Southern Question was also the National Question. It was — in effect — the task of this novel hegemonic bloc to constitute an Italian nation and state. The proletariat had to accomplish, by revolution, what the bourgeoisie of the Risorgimento had — as his essay showed so powerfully — failed to do. On its home ground, the spirit of Mazzinian nationalism had been utterly betrayed by Cavour and the *Moderati*. Everything had been done from above. A rigid, centralized French state-model had been imposed upon peoples who, because of the failure of peninsular absolutism, had never enjoyed any period of slow maturation towards civil homogeneity.

Secular Italian problems are crucial for understanding Gramsci the Sardinian-Italian man, and Gramsci the theorist. Neither the post-war PCI totemization nor the more recent theoreticist and 'European' readings have really coped with this, and sometimes they have positively fled from the issue. However, closer historical appreciation is a prerequisite for any endeavour to disentangle a theoretical kernel out of the *Prison Notebooks*.

All Gramsci's key notions, like 'hegemony', 'passive revolution', 'the intellectuals' (and so on) were valiant efforts to wrestle Italian dilemmas into some kind of theoretical sense. Though brilliantly inventive (and indeed shaming to most of what passes for Marxism) these struggles were only partially successful. Methodologically, their exploratory and uncertain character led to persistent conceptual 'slippage', or over-extension, whereby too much was crammed under one or the other heading. Commentators have always underlined the obvious causes of the gnomic aspects of the *Notebooks*: arduous prison conditions, censorship, and Gramsci's desperate physical state and personal problems. However, these factors may also have served to amplify certain quite inherent difficulties of the Gramscian intellectual project. The national realities sketched in 'The Southern Question' were imperfectly understood; the Marxist theory brought to these realities was still primitive and defective; it is not surprising that even a theoretical genius, striving to remake both things at once, occasionally tied himself in knots.

Theory must, of course, proceed through such moments of indeterminacy in order to advance. But Gramsci's own progress was halted by his death. The resultant legacy of a decade of 'notes' inevitably poses excruciating problems for anybody anxious to disengage a more finished message or theory.

Gramsci and History

Does the refusal of Gramsci's prophetic status condemn him to a merely historical and national importance? Those vexed by the thought should turn to John Davis's collection of historical essays, *Gramsci and Italy's Passive Revolution* (London, 1979). It is concerned with aspects of Italy's failed revolution, in both the 19th and the 20th centuries. Mr Davis's lucid introduction emphasizes how essential this context remains for reading Gramsci. A propos the Southern Question, above all, 'Gramsci the historian cannot be separated from, or contrasted to, Gramsci the political theorist or Gramsci the revolutionary'. Here lay the primary nexus of 'hegemony', in the new domestic colonialism of a weak, belated state anxious to establish its place in the European sun. Lay nationalism and forced anti-clericalism were ideological compensations for weak industrial development. 'It was', as Davis points out, 'the sons of the Southern gentry who filled the law courts, the schools, the universities and the political institutions of the liberal state, and it was they who provided the most effective evangelists of the ideology of that state', under Croce's grandisonant guidance. Through this bourgeois 'cultural revolution' the real one was contained, and the 'Cities of Silence' (or pre-capitalist cities) obtained a historical revenge over the forces disturbing them.

In his own contribution to the volume, Davis carries this analysis farther by criticizing Gramsci's famous essay. It is not really accurate to state that the South-North polarity was comparable to the relationship between countryside and city, he argues. This was a post-unification retrospect which even Gramsci had become the victim of. In reality there had been two 'different and divergent' economies, the Southern one far less related to the North than is now remembered. Great Britain had been its main trading partner, not Piedmont and Lombardy. During the first half of the 19th century the Bourbon state pursued its own fitful programme of modernization, like the Hapsburgs and Romanoffs but with less success. The resultant crisis discredited that state with devastating completeness, and made the Southern gentry willing to contemplate union. However, this meant that 'the economic unification of the two regions was the product of a political rather than an economic process'. There was no complementarity between South and North, as apologists of post-1960 Italy pretended.

Once again, politico-cultural will prevailed over socio-economic realities. The Southern ruling groups abandoned their own society *en masse*, and attached themselves greedily to the new state apparatus. Hence (concludes Mr Davis) 'the problems of the South were transposed into an economic and political context in which the need to find solutions was outweighed by the advantages of preserving and exploiting those very weaknesses'. Without autonomy, deserted by its ruling class, the South was helpless before the predatory capitalism of the North. It became 'backward', in short, while at the same time the toxins produced by the disintegration of its ancient regime permeated the new order, in the form of the *intellettuali* above all.

What alternative vision of Gramsci's significance is suggested by Davis's approach, and other work of a similar kind? Only theoretical puppeteers will sniff reductionism or historicism at work here. In fact another theory is present, one which locates both Gramsci and politics differently to the mainstream of historical materialism. According to the latter, while certain economic factors or trends are indeed common and generalizable in capitalist history, their political correlates remain far more diverse and *sui generis*. This is not to be ascribed to anything mysterious about 'politics' imagined as an autonomous realm. It is the crassly uneven eruption of modern capitalist societies which is to blame. Modernization has attacked societies as they were, with utterly divergent pasts, customs and languages; hence it has precipitated state-forms which can only be 'irrational' fusions of old and new. The national-particular element, as Hobsbawm says, has remained internal to all subsequent general social development, and crucial to politics. Nineteenth century liberals and 20th century socialists pretended that it was some sort of excrescence, always on the way out. In truth — as the last few years have demonstrated conclusively — it will remain intrinsic to all foreseeable socialist development, as well as the better-known capitalist sort.

In this perspective, Gramsci's location within the Italian dilemma *is* his universal significance. It is his marvellous exploration of that particular antagonistic reality which provides the model for socialists elsewhere — not what can be distilled out of it as abstract political theory or revolutionary strategy. He is the greatest example of unyielding, all-embracing struggle within one specific field of forces. But we are all in such particular fields. Those plagued with cosmopolitan delusions are no exception, and would do well to turn to Gramsci's analysis of the Vatican and phoney universalism in Italy's cultural past.

Gramsci was a man of the abyss. His personality, and the essence of his marathon fight with destiny, were made from the clash between Sardinia and Piedmont, between the most unredeemed, alien South and the feral new capitalism of the North. One could say, rhetorically, that this was a 'typical' plight of modern development, even on the world scale. But it means very little in political practice or theory. In practical terms the abyss is bridged differently everywhere, by a contingent state-form and political system; and there can be no easily abstractable 'theory' of these, nor any philosophical 'strategy' for transforming them. What counts, therefore, is following Gramsci's example within one's own society, employing the innumerable clues and inspirations of the *Prison Notebooks* to do so. Though not a counsel of despair, this is (obviously) one of caution and patient building. If there is an Age of Gramsci, it will be made by transfusing his pessimism of the intelligence into other places and movements. Optimism of the will, like the 'Modern Prince', should be left to take care of itself.

ON GRAMSCI'S LANGUAGE
Pier Paolo Pasolini

At the beginning of the century very few people living in Italy used Italian even as part of their daily language. Even in 1950 the vast majority spoke in dialect and learned Italian as a 'foreign' language at school. Pier Paolo Pasolini, the great Italian poet who died tragically in 1975, traces the development of Gramsci's language as he moved from a Sardinian peasant milieu to industrial Turin. He analyses the different aspects of what was a long and not always successful struggle by Gramsci to develop a new language, one no longer based on the irrationalism of the literary language current among the Italian bourgeoisie after the Risorgimento.

All of Gramsci's youthful works are written in 'ugly' Italian. Gramsci was not a precocious youth: he had to go through every phase typical of the young Southerner Italianized in Turin. On his mother's side, the contributions to his development were of a strictly particularist Sardinian kind; his father, as an employee of the state, brought a roughshod Italianization. His infancy and early adolescence were spent in a peasant milieu, in which Italian must have struck the ear as a language foreign to the Sardinians of Ghilarza, more in contact with America than Italy. Gramsci would have heard his first, resounding Italian out of the mouths of his 'self-styled' professors of literature, teachers at the private grammar school of Santu Lussurgiu. (And, given that they must prove themselves accredited, even though not required to, their Italian would naturally be a constant, caricatural effort to approximate a purist, pompous humanism.) Gramsci, as the

poor, set-apart little boy, experienced and profoundly
interiorized every event of his childhood; and since, throughout his life, he suffered from the shame, the impediment of his
early self-sacrifice, that encounter with an official Italian which
stood for culture and liberation must also have marked him
deeply.

In fact, all his writings, up to and even partly including
Ordine Nuovo, bear the stamp of that absurd acquisition, that
fake liberation. It seems impossible that a man of Gramsci's
stature was unable to shrug off a language expressive of only
the tritest sentiments. Someone with Gramsci's devotion to
reason, the very presence itself of that vocation, it strikes us,
would at once drop the bombastic expression of literary
Italian. Yet, from 1914 to 1919, his language lacks any capacity
other than to grasp the emotional or passionate moment of an
idea, with some of the intensity typical of 'Vocian'*
irrationalism, though the better examples of this are rare
enough. For the rest, his language is wholly humanistic,
inclined to the romanticism which had directly, and with much
sound and fury, been appropriated from pre-socialist humanitarianism, the most immediate linguistic ancestor to which
Gramsci might reasonably turn (and which he never forgot. It
is very likely this language, purified and turned into myth, that
Gramsci returns to perhaps unconsciously when he comes to
consider a possible language of communist hegemony; and it is
again this very one, the language of Marxist humanism,
reinforced by the spirit of the Resistance, that many politicians
today still refer to as the hegemonic language of communism.)
One needs all the patience of a philologist, all the love which
the figure of Gramsci inspires, to read the pages written during
those five years.

A different kind of language first helped the young Gramsci
to shed the exaggerations of expressive humanitarianism, the
language of science — especially then, a non-Italian language.
Consequently, after a humanist phase (always the primary step
for the able southern youngster who chooses to move up in
Italy) there had to follow a French one. Turin, as the city of
Gramsci's Italianization, plays some considerable part in this.

---

*From *La Voce,* important literary magazine, which led a movement for the
renovation of Italian culture in a European perspective. (ed. note)

Of course, Turin's cultural tradition would have an impact on his French phase; but the main thing remains his reading, directly in the original, of the formative texts of this new cultural phase. French influence, acting upon such a fragile, inconsistent, vacant, linguistic body as Gramsci's Italian indeed was, once again produced extreme and dramatic effects. Not so much because one can point to the presence of imported French expressions, but rather because of the insecurity which French scientific communication brings out in that expressive, irrationalist sort of Italian. In two of Gramsci's pages alone, from 1919, I can underscore certain words and expressions: *interroriti* (a non-Italian formulation of 'terrorized'), *mobilizzati* ('mobilized', French form of the Italian *mobilitare*), *devastazioni irrevocabili* (literally, 'irrevocable devastations'), *non si è generata per la nostra azione politica* ('it was not bred by our political action', Gramsci's use of *per* instead of *a causa della,* 'owing to', 'on account of', is an example of imprecise syntax), *sterminate comunità di dolore e di aspettazione* ('immense (limitless) communities of pain and expectation (hope)'), *servigi* ('tasks', in old Tuscan, e.g. as used by Boccaccio, 'leave this *business* (task) to me', or also an action performed to benefit others without seeking recompense). Not to mention a word which unfailingly appears, i.e., *officina* ('atelier' or 'workshop') instead of *fabbrica* ('factory') which only becomes predominant after 1919.

Only when we come to the *Ordine Nuovo,* that is, as Gramsci's original mode of thinking begins to mature through genuine, personal experience (and timidity always drove Gramsci to live, as it were, impersonally) do we see a language becoming at first possible, and then in a certain way absolute.

Nevertheless, the awkwardness of the former, timid scholar indulging in arch, professorial jokes and word-plays, Latin tags, etc., does reappear though less often every time Gramsci clothes an idea, or rather a spent idea, with an emotional aura (hence, frequently in polemics or invectives).

By means of a persistent, quasi-religious apprenticeship to reason, Gramsci overcame the irrationalism of the literary language adopted by the Italian bourgeoisie ever since national unification, to such an extent that whenever he comes to express a thought, language disappears and turns into the transparent medium of thought. Perhaps, if examined coldly, and setting aside what it says, that language might still seem 'ugly' to a purist, to a sensitive linguist: ugly, in this sense, because debased, humiliated by drab handbooks, political jargon, translated terms, marked by an indelible professorial, Frenchified imprint. But all of that becomes irrelevant in the light of its capacity to function, a serviceability which renders it in a peculiar way absolute. Yet it only takes one of the old, compacted and feeble nerve-ends of irrationalism to crop up again, and Gramsci, not yet well-trained enough to subdue it linguistically, will fall prey to it, his language succumbing to the uncertainty and bombast of his first boyhood pages. Only in his letters from prison, nearing the end of his life, does he successfully combine irrationalism and the exercise of reason. But it is no longer a reflex irrationalism, following upon an emotional outburst or polemical rage, which imparts its halo to correct political reason. In such cases, irrationalism always conceals an ideological shortness of breath, a missing link in one's reasoning.

In his youth, in fact, the expressive weakness of Gramsci's Italian served to hide gaps of political inexperience, or, more precisely, gaps in the socialism to which he adhered.

Towards the end of his life, instead, the question becomes one of giving narrative, evocative voice to the humblest and fortuitous facts of life, to the variety of mysterious and irrational details, and what amounts to the 'natural poetry' which every life holds in abundance. Then, the force of rational habit which had so far dominated language, disregarding what it withheld, enters into contact with that controlled irrational kernel (not now a missing link, paralogism or vacuum in reason itself, but a mystery which reason acknowledges and dreams) and becomes coloured by pathos of a kind which somehow, by some miraculous osmosis or unconscious reciprocity occurring in the depths of language, makes one think of certain compassionate, lucid and *sotto voce* lines by the poet Umberto Saba:

> No, il comunismo
> non oscurerà la bellezza e la grazia!
> (No, communism
> will not obscure beauty and grace!)

I asked myself, at this point, what must Gramsci's *oral* language have been. I turned to Terracini* for information (just lately, I'd heard him commemorate his friend, in precisely the style that Saba, as the writer of the *Scorciatoie, Raccontini* or the *Autobiography*, would certainly have envied: in oral Italian, its structure steeped in dialect, its source truly mysterious and yet adding intense effect to his design), and he replied exactly as I had expected. In his writings, Gramsci definitely resorted to a 'spoken' Italian; the technical coinage kept its political origins, as terms taken from Marxist science. But such 'technicalisms', we all know, are (so to speak) inter-professional, except for syndicalist aims which require specialization. So too, as we've seen, there are rhetorical passages to be found in Gramsci, but derived from a non-Italian rhetorical tradition — Italian tradition at that time produced d'Annunzio. And we know, too, the *oral* correlative of this centralist, d'Annunzian tradition: the survivors of nationalism still continue to employ it, in hand with the military top brass, prolonging the afterlife of an authoritarian, aestheticizing 'diction'. One is confronted here with a particular *birignao**, probably born at the same time as the theatrical one.

(Inevitably I am forced to grope about in near darkness, since no series of documentary records exists to consult or add weight to what I write. Italians have never been phonologists. The little evidence there is, does not seem to precede the year in which recording instruments were invented. Precious little, in other words, with regard to the 'continuity' of Italian oral tradition, quite apart from what one might like to know about that tradition at the time of Italy's unification.)

In speaking, therefore, Gramsci employed at once, dia-chronically, two languages and two linguistic traditions.

When he had occasion to read aloud from one of his writings, Gramsci pronounced the written words orally, and they were represented as such to his listeners (their ears, at that moment, mediated the representation of the words as written

---

*A contemporary of Gramsci and Communist leader in the post World War II period. (ed. note)

*An absurd, operatic and ostentatious diction adopted by actors and singers. (ed. note)

ones to the visual imagination); equally, he would align his phonemes according to set patterns, accents, stresses of voice, etc., etc., which stood in a relation of purely formal coexistence to written language: as poor relations dressed up in the clothes of rich ones.

The three fundamental elements of Gramsci's Italian pronunciation, that is, the pronunciations of Sardinian dialect, Piedmontese dialect and the bureaucratic-professional Italian of the petit bourgeoisie which was also becoming an oral Koinè at that time created round the canons of oral Florentine — all these elements are immensely inferior to the level of Gramsci's 'written language', which takes in Hegel, Marx, progressive French culture, a deep, and in his personal way, perfect reading of the Italian classics, and so on.

The uncertainty, poverty, misery, the vague generality of Gramsci's oral language (just as it is for every man of Italian culture, then and now) is not proportionate to the security, the richness, the absolute quality of so much of his writing — or, indeed, his oral discourse, even when improvised, set down in shorthand, published and read with the eyes.

IV
CONSTRUCTING
A WORKERS' STATE

REVOLUTION AND PRODUCTION
Franco De Felice

Franco De Felice offers us a guide to reading Gramsci's articles on the factory councils. He suggests that what we should look for is not just a discussion of workers' control but a description of an alternative way of running society: the councils as the basis of a new State. The premise of Gramsci's writing on the factory councils, he argues, is the belief that a system of dual power can arise in which the proletariat challenges bourgeois state power because of the 'actuality of the revolution' in the historical period of imperialism. The revolution is 'actual' or on the historical agenda because of a long term crisis of capitalist society.

This crisis is not simply an economic one but immediately involves the political system. The traditional liberal view of the state — as maintaining minimum services but basically keeping out of a whole range of social and economic activities which remain in private hands — no longer adequately describes the modern situation. Traditional liberal democratic institutions, in particular parliament, which represents the individual as a citizen unrelated to social or economic roles, are in crisis. This is the background for Gramsci's claim that a new system of representation based on production was necessary and possible. A similar notion was put forward in Britain at the same time as Gramsci was writing by the guild socialists. Today, a crisis of parliament and the rise of a 'neo-corporatism' in which governments increasingly deal directly with pressure groups by-passing and undercutting representative institutions is obvious in a wide range of countries.

For Gramsci such a situation meant that the destiny of society was in the hands of the proletariat. Then, as now, traditional working class organizations, trade unions, the party, co-operatives were no longer sufficient to the immense task facing the working class. A new organization was needed which could unify the working class and in turn revolutionize the trade unions and the party. This, De Felice says, is the basis of Gramsci's argument for the factory councils.

The adequacy of traditional forms of working class organization has again become an urgent question. According to Gramsci it was possible for the councils to assume a particular role in running production and in forming the basis of a new state. This was so because of changes in the organization of capitalism. The individual entrepreneur is no longer important. The liberal state is in crisis. Both of these elements are related to the changed role of the state in the economy making the productive sphere a part of politics. According to De Felice it is the realization that the economy can no longer be considered the 'private sphere' that provides Gramsci with a strong argument that the factory councils could have a political role, not just an economic one.

But Gramsci's analysis of the potential of the factory councils, De Felice says, was also based on a critical examination of the experiences of the Russian revolution and the failures of the Hungarian and German revolutions. Revolution, according to Gramsci, had to be viewed as a process, not a single dramatic break, in which the destruction of the old society could only be ensured by the construction of a new one. This is a process which must begin within the heart of capitalist society – the productive sphere – and must continue long after the establishment of a new state.

But what are the limits of Gramsci's writings in this period? De Felice points out that a severe defect in Gramsci's analysis in 1919-1920 was his inability to conceptualize the problems of non-proletarian groups, such as the peasants, as special and different and therefore as not immediately reducible to the experience of the urban working class. Thus the factory councils did not easily provide a model of organization for other social groups.

Gramsci defined the problem of revolution as the creation of a new state. But how is this new state to be created? The reply came to him from the Russian revolutionary experience and the development of new forms of working class organization: the Soviets. Gramsci's whole thinking on the Factory Councils begins with the actuality of the revolution: the disintegration of the productive apparatus of the state, the decomposition of the bourgeois socio-economic formation. The existence of these objective conditions put the destiny of society and the possibility of resolving the crisis into the hands of the proletariat. But was the proletariat ready? The traditional split between political and trade union activities, and the institutions bound up with these, had made them unequal to the work at hand. A new form of organization was necessary.

> The traditional institutions of the movement . . . are not dead. Born in response to free competition, they must continue to exist until the last remnant of competition has been wiped out, until classes and parties have been completely suppressed . . . But beside these institutions, new, State-oriented institutions must arise and develop — the very institutions which will replace the private and public institutions of the parliamentary-democratic State. The very institutions which will replace the person of the capitalist in his administrative functions and his industrial power, and so achieve the autonomy of the producer in the factory. Institutions capable of taking over the management of all the functions inherent in the complex system of relations of production and exchange that link the various workshops of a factory together . . ., link together the various activities of the agricultural industry, and through horizontal and vertical planning have to construct the harmonious edifice of the national and international economy, liberated from the obstructive and parasitical tyranny of the private property-owners. (PWI 77)

When revolution is on the agenda, class struggle involves the state. The working class, in order to accomplish its task, must succeed in placing the question of the state at the centre of the struggle. The Factory Council, for Gramsci, is the appropriate instrument for this task. It is the new class institution, and it expresses the experience of the most advanced sectors of the international workers' movement, from Russia to the United States, from Germany to Britain. It puts the problem of power concretely as the order of the day: 'the present form of the class struggle for power is embodied in the Councils'. (PWI 146)

What makes the Council an instrument of struggle that is alternative to the bourgeois system, one which cannot be absorbed by it? It is the cell of the future workers' state, because its *raison d'être* lies in the labour process, in industrial production, i.e. in something permanent. It does not lie in wages or class divisions, i.e. in something transitory and, moreover, the very thing we are trying to supersede.' (PWI 100)

The Council can become the embryo of the workers' state and create a counter-government because it cuts across the divisions, stratifications, specializations according to skill produced in the working class by capitalism. And thus it permits the working class to recover its unity and autonomy and to become aware of the overall role that it performs in production.

> All the problems inherent in the organization of the proletarian State are inherent in the organization of the Council. In the one as in the other, the concept of citizen gives way to the concept of comrade. Collaboration in effective and useful production develops solidarity and multiplies bonds of affection and fraternity. Everyone is indispensable, everyone is at his post, and everyone has a function and a post. Even the most ignorant and backward of workers, even the most vain and 'civil' of engineers, will eventually convince himself of this truth in the experience of factory organisation ... The Council is the most effective organ for mutual education and for developing the new social spirit that the proletariat has successfully engendered from the rich and living experience of the community of labour. (*PWI* 100)

The immediate consequence of the development of Councils was to introduce a new counter power at the heart of modern capitalist production: the factory. This new power reflects a change in the balance of class forces in which the entrepreneur can no longer act as an autocrat. On the eve of the Piedmont general strike of April 1920, this was made clear.

> Commendatore Agnelli antagonizes the workers' administration, and within a quarter of an hour fifteen thousand workers have downed tools, gathered in two huge meetings inside the workshop, and obtained a retraction. In that moment, the first council to be born in Italy experienced its first intense and powerful taste of life in such a way as to demonstrate its viability and future line of development. (*PWI* 332)

The possibility of creating a counter power is related to the weakening of the power of the individual entrepreneur and what is the central feature of Gramsci's analysis of the actuality of the revolution: the accentuated tendency of capitalism in the era of imperialism towards the socialization of production.

The factory is not an independent entity. It is not run by an owner-entrepreneur who possesses the commercial know-how . . . to buy the raw materials wisely and sell the manufactured object at a profit. These functions have been displaced from the individual factory and transferred to the system of factories owned by the same firm. And it does not stop here: they are concentrated in the hands of a bank or system of banks, who have taken over the real responsibility for supplying raw materials and securing markets for sales.

During the war . . . was it not the State which supplied raw materials to industry, distributed them in accordance with a pre-established plan and became the sole purchaser of production? . . .

In this way the State has become the sole proprietor of the instruments of labour and has taken over all the traditional functions of the entrepreneur . . . (*PWI* 165)

What is the significance of insisting on the *factory* council as the embryo of the alternative state and, as Gramsci does, on the close relation between revolution and production? 'If the foundations of the revolutionary process are not rooted within productive life itself, the revolution will remain a sterile appeal to the will, a false mirage — and chaos, disorder, unemployment and hunger will swell up and crush the finest and most vigorous proletarian forces.' (*PWI* 93) What will the effects be on the traditional working class organizations — the trade unions and the party?

After having reasserted the Bolshevik character of the elaboration of the Council strategy, and having emphasized the use of Councils as the instrument for resolving problems of great urgency — like the relation between the party and the unions and the revolutionary transformation of these two institutions, Gramsci went on to explain why

we of *L'Ordine Nuovo* have insisted so obstinately on the factory councils . . . In Italy, in order to shake up lazy mental attitudes, in order to force the functionaries violently to take up a position, in order to concentrate attention on the concrete problems of the Revolution, we had to get the workers, the great masses of humanity, with their passions, with their caprices, their irrepressible needs, to erupt directly onto the scene; we had to get the delegates of the masses of factory workers to carry into the meetings of the Unions the voice of the thousands and thousands of workers who cannot take part in the discussions and deliberations in the course of which their action and their will is going to be committed; . . . We had to counterpose a *fait accompli* to the scepticism and lack of awareness of the leaders, we had to create the conditions in which it would be impossible to continue in the old ways and the traditional weakness of will. (*ON* 340)

A New Kind of State

The Councils, for Gramsci, could revolutionize the existing working class organizations and provide the basis for resolving the all-too-fundamental problems of building a workers' state. Not only bourgeois society, Gramsci saw, but also the institutions of the working class would be affected by the class struggle. And so, with the experience of the Russian Soviets, the new revolutionary organizations created by the working class internationally, and the failure of the Hungarian and German revolutions as background, Gramsci focussed his attention on the Factory Councils. The proletariat, Marx had said, needs an organ with a state-like form as a weapon of the class struggle. Gramsci translated this thesis into the necessity of having institutions that would in the first instance realize the unity and autonomy of the working class. Further, these institutions — the Factory Councils — would permit the political development of masses of people, not just a small élite. Technical preparation for the management of a factory was in reality training for self-government. Through the Councils, the working class would rediscover itself, acquire consciousness of its organic unity and counterpose itself as a whole to capitalism. (*PWI* 263) This, Gramsci saw, was the way to acquire the psychology of a dominant class:

> The laws of the workers' State need to be executed by the workers themselves: only in this way will the workers' State avoid the danger of falling into the hands of adventurers and political intriguers, of becoming a counterfeit of the bourgeois State. (*PWI* 171)

This is not just the traditional concept of a radical workers' democracy based on the rejection of the delegation of political functions to a staff of bureaucrats. It is far wider-reaching: Gramsci sees that the working class can become the dominant one only if it has acquired a consciousness of the necessity and legitimacy of its own state. The reorganization of the working class becomes a necessary condition for overcoming economistic corporatism. Through the work in the Factory Councils, people's daily existence becomes linked to more general questions and this engenders the possible transformation of the whole of society.

The Councils also provide the basis for considering how the working class can lead other classes. A purely capitalist society, Gramsci is well aware, consisting of a handful of employers and an endless mass of wage-earners, does not exist. In reality we find a whole variety of floating intermediate social strata, incapable of expressing anything but an eclectic compromise ideology as they try to mediate between the capitalist class and the proletariat. In a period of crisis, even these intermediate groups begin to move and indeed, play an essential role in disorganizing the entire framework of the bourgeois state. Yet they must have a radicalized working class capable of providing them with leadership, if the crisis is to result in a move towards socialism. Otherwise one has the kind of insubordination and disruption which occurred during the Italian peasant revolt. When broad non-proletarian social strata are shifted onto subversive bases, the working class has to intervene to organize and lead them. Given the position that these groups occupy within the fundamental relations of production, they cannot play any real alternative role and are therefore bound to be subaltern to one of the two determinant social-historic forces. What can guarantee that their revolt does not lead in a counter-revolutionary direction is the working class's capacity for leadership, the fact that this class is not simply one element of the revolt but constitutes its organizing principle. This is how Gramsci interprets Marx's classical formula: by liberating itself, the working class liberates the whole of society.

But the working class can only achieve this political leadership if it succeeds in unmasking the bourgeois concept of politics. One of the essential coordinates of the framework of the bourgeois state and its preservation is the distinction between civil society and state-political society; between class identity and one's role as a citizen. The abstract equality of relations between citizens conceals the material origins of relations between people who belong to different classes. This is Marx's great lesson in *The Jewish Question*. And so in order to overthrow the underlying structure of bourgeois domination, make the working class the ruling class which organizes around itself all the other oppressed social strata, there is only one possible point of departure: the relations of production, since therein lies the basis of class divisions in capitalist society. To say, as Gramsci maintains, that production is the source of power and sovereignty (*PWI* 91) means that economics is not only the production of goods but of social relations too.

> Capitalist production, therefore, under its aspect of a continuously connected process, of a process of reproduction, produces not only commodities, not only surplus-value, but it also produces and reproduces the capitalist relation; on the one side the capitalist, on the other the wage-labourer. (*Capital*, I, London, 1967, p. 578)

Marx's now classical and graphic definition is retranslated by Gramsci in these terms:

> The revolutionary process takes place in the sphere of production, in the factory, where the relations are those of oppressor to oppressed . . . where freedom for the worker does not exist, and democracy does not exist. The revolutionary process takes place where the worker is nothing but intends to be all, where the power of the proprietor is unlimited, where the proprietor has power of life or death over the worker, and over his wife and children. (*PWI* 261)

Herein lies Gramsci's and the *Ordine Nuovo*'s feat in recharging economics with a dialectical relationship to politics.

> At the basis of every serious problem of production, there lies the political problem, i.e. that of social relations, of the organic functioning of society. If we wish to organize production seriously, we must first, or better still, simultaneously, organize the whole of society, which finds its most general and direct expression in production, in relation to it and for it. Production is the essence of society, its most comprehensive and immediate 'symbol'. (*ON* 24-31)

Gramsci's reflection on the relation between politics and production, between revolution and production served to underline that it was only by starting from this reality that the working class could identify itself as an alternative. Only by defining the intermediate social strata in the light of the position they occupy in the productive process and with respect to the working class could the working class organize and direct them. Thus Factory Councils are a basis for a new *political* organization.

> . . . the construction of *communist* political soviets cannot help but follow in historical terms the emergence and primary systematization of the Factory Councils. In the first instance, the Factory Council and the system of Councils assay and demonstrate empirically the new positions which the working class has come to occupy in the field of production. The Councils give the working class an awareness of its current value, its true role, its responsibility and its future. The working class draws conclusions from the quantum of positive experience amassed personally by individuals, acquires the character and mentality of a ruling class and organizes itself as such; in other words, it sets up political Soviets and establishes its dictatorship. (*PWI* 162)

The concrete problems of the relationship between Factory Councils and soviets based in the community was not resolved — either by Gramsci or the Factory Council movement itself. But Gramsci's originality lay in the fact that he posed the problem of how a political, class and mass movement could — beginning with the factory — go on to encompass and reorganize the entire structure of the city and the nation. In the second place, the experience gained was that every state may be characterized as an array of different, subaltern class forces, organized by and under the direction of a leading class. This was also true of the workers' state. It differs from the bourgeois one, however, because it unifies society on the basis of an objective and permanent factor like that of production, rather than on an abstract 'contract' as bourgeois political theory would have it. In the Factory Council, wrote Gramsci, 'the worker participates as a producer, i.e. as a consequence of his universal character and of his position and role in society, in the same way that the citizen participates in the democratic parliamentary State.' (*PWI* 295)

The Council is therefore a representative institution 'that develops morphologically not arithmetically and, in its higher forms, has the effect of impressing a *proletarian* pattern on the apparatus of production and exchange that *capitalism* created for the purpose of making profits'. Gramsci went on to hypothesize a restructuring of the national and international economy that would follow the lines of a long series of closely interlocking links, and then to pose the problem of the withering away of the state by means of the progressive absorption of politics into economics. (*PWI* 263)

Revolution as a Process

Undoubtedly, the construction of the workers' state delineated by Gramsci has a strong futuristic slant to it. But it would be mistaken to read these notes of his on the communist state as though they were immediate operative criteria. He was attempting to focus on the essential point of the supersession of the bourgeois distinction between economics and politics: this is the element of continuity between the revolutionary phase of the 'conquest' of the state and the transitional phase. The Councils had to challenge this distinction from within capitalist society and create the basis for a transformation of politics which would be completed during the transition to communism.

> . . . the revolution as the conquest of social power on the part of the proletariat can only be conceived of as a dialectical process, in which political power makes possible industrial power and vice versa. The Soviet is the instrument of revolutionary struggle that provides for the autonomous development of the communist economic organization from a system of Factory Councils to a Central Economic Council . . . (it) is the instrument for the final struggle to the death with the capitalist order, in that it creates the conditions in which class-divided society is eliminated and any new class division is made 'physically' impossible. (*PWI* 308)

What then is the main problem with Gramsci's elaboration of the construction of the new state? With the exception of a few brief notes, the problem of the link between the working class and the non-proletarian social masses is not posed, let alone resolved. In other words, it is not clear to what degree the category of 'producer' does not constitute another example of treating the non-proletarian social masses as simply equivalent to the proletariat. To what extent, in point of fact, does Gramsci's conception of the revolution and the state really overcome the view that the revolution was a purely proletarian creation — a view typical of the tradition of the Second International even in its revolutionary sectors, as with Rosa Luxemburg?

These important criticisms aside, what must be reasserted conclusively is that Gramsci's conception of the state as a weapon of class struggle — and therefore of revolution as the process of the construction of a new and alternative state — does not mean that the socialist state simply *continues* the bourgeois one, but on the contrary, that there is a *break*. The 'leap' is made by overturning the balance of power between the classes. This is the result of an alternative process of organizing the masses that strongly conditions the type of state that is being created, its capacity to resist the return of reaction: its durability. For Gramsci, then, there is no doubt whatsoever that alternative institutions have to be created before the leadership of society passes to the proletariat; their creation is, indeed, the condition for this passage. The old state will fall only if the new state is already in the process of being created. This is Gramsci's interpretation of dual power. The old society will be destroyed only if a new one is built.

We have seen all these historical developments in Germany, Austria, the Ukraine and Hungary. The revolution as a destructive act has not been followed by the revolution as a process of reconstructing society on the communist model. The presence of these external conditions — a communist party, the destruction of the bourgeois State, powerful trade-union organizations and an armed proletariat — was not sufficient to compensate for the absence of another condition: the existence of productive forces tending towards development and growth, a conscious movement on the part of the proletarian masses to substantiate their political power with economic power, and a determination on the part of these proletarian masses to introduce proletarian order into the factory, to make the factory the basic unit of the new State as an expression of the industrial relations of the factory system. (*PWI* 306-7)

This is the fundamental thesis that is sustained throughout 1919-1920 by the *Ordine Nuovo*.

The lesson that Gramsci drew from various experiences was that the principal task of a revolutionary social formation is to prevent there being two revolutions: to guarantee that the popular revolt finds the working class and proletarian forces organized and capable of transforming the productive apparatus into an instrument of liberation. The revolutionary process for Gramsci, is a continuous one and herein lies its significance for us today.

THE FACTORY COUNCILS
Mario Telò

Mario Telò goes beyond De Felice's analysis to criticize another important aspect of Gramsci's ideas on the factory councils. In a far-reaching article, only one section of which is included here, Telò argues that in the Ordine Nuovo *period Gramsci falls into the trap of 'productivism' or production for its own sake. During this time Gramsci was prevented from thinking through the problems of a qualitatively different kind of development by his 'productivism'. According to Telò, in arguing for the generalization of the productive system of capitalist factories as the basis of a new proletarian state power, Gramsci failed to question the structure or context of capitalist development. He simply maintained that the working class should control it. He thus unconditionally accepted 'scientific management', as promoted by the American Frederick W. Taylor in his work on the organization of labour in the factory.*

This productivism is overcome in the Prison Notebooks, *Telò says, when Gramsci suggests that the working class must provide the leadership for a new type of development which does not just copy that of capitalist society. As a result of Telò's discussion, Gramsci's development of the concept of hegemony and his notes on* Americanism and Fordism *appear much more clearly as a self-criticism of his earlier belief in Taylorism. The* Notebooks *also represent a critique of the productivism of Leninism, of many of the discussions in the Comintern in the 1920s, and a fundamental aspect of the course of development of the Soviet Union – all based in an uncritical faith in the benefits of economic 'progress'.*

The usual reasons given for the defeat of the Factory Council Movement were, as Gramsci himself insisted, its geographical limitation to the industrial North and its lack of successful political links with other social strata, above all, with the struggles of the agricultural labourers and peasants. However, above and beyond subjective factors which certainly counted — such as the lack of a revolutionary party or the lack of a revolutionary will in the socialist leadership — the isolation of the Factory Council Movement was certainly not accidental. It was part and parcel of the *Ordine Nuovo* group's own 'productivism'. This productivism made it difficult for them to grasp the complex social stratifications which existed in Western capitalist societies. They failed to recognize the way in which divisions between classes and groups were maintained and further reproduced, and how, in effect, the industrial North was related to the backward agricultural South precisely as a result of capitalist development.

Under Gramsci's guidance in 1923, the more prominent members of the group began a process of self-criticism. They then connected the failure to generalize the Turin experience, its 'factory-ism' and local character with the primacy they themselves had attributed to the 'technical element' in the factory. What they had left out of their thinking was the essential discussion of the general nature of social relations which the organization of production implied and reproduced. The *Ordine Nuovo's* view had been that the working class would become a ruling class because of its roots in the factory where it was an element of the impressive productive apparatus abandoned by the capitalist bourgeoisie with the death of the figure of the entrepreneur-captain of industry. In prison, Gramsci was able to move beyond the limits inherent in this view. In developing the concept of hegemony, he examined the factory council experience in the context of a *critical* analysis of capitalist development and of the strategic model of revolution in the West.

Organization of the Productive Process: An Uncritical View

For the *Ordine Nuovo* group in its early years, the dictatorship of the proletariat organized in Councils in the factory meant that the proletariat would extend the idea of the rationalization of the enterprise; they would generalize the productive system of the capitalist factory to the whole social structure. In short, the content of the revolution, of what it actually accomplished, was identified with management by the proletariat of the process of industrialization or economic development. The structure of capitalist development was not questioned; nor was the social content of industrialization criticized.

This is clear in the unconditional acceptance of the Taylorist organization of labour supported by various articles in the review. Examples of support for anti-productivist demands made by the Turin working class remained secondary. The autonomy of the *Ordine Nuovo*'s position, the impossibility of its being incorporated into a capitalist position, was thought to be guaranteed by the connection with the Soviet experience and communist ideology. Piero Gobetti, a liberal intellectual greatly influenced by the work of the *Ordine Nuovo*, notes that the Councils ended up by regarding the hierarchies of the capitalist organization of labour as 'natural'. 'Moving outside the factory, they adopted the specific legacy of bourgeois tradition, not proposing to build a new economy from nothing but rather to take over and continue the progress of productive techniques achieved by the industrialists.'[1]

The conflict was hard and uncompromising. The Councils were opposed to any form of co-management or acceptance of the employer's discipline in the factory. However, what was missing was any clarification of the connection between economic and political struggle. The revolutionary perspective was not grounded in any organic policy whereby demands at the factory level could raise the question of the *quality* of the productive forces and establish a new identity of the worker as 'producer'. (*PWI* 73 ff and 114 ff) In fact, the longer the economic and political crisis lasted, the more the group had to concern itself with the general problem of production in the revolutionary process and move beyond the idea that there would be a single dramatic break. The Council, as the basic organization of the producers, that is of workers and technicians, took on the aspect of an institution whose main aim was to control the process of spreading the productive apparatus created in Turin and in Piedmont on a national scale. (*PWI* 150 ff)

The Russian experience demonstrated that only management by Soviets of the development of the productive forces could provide a way out of the crisis. It seemed the only exception in a picture of a collapsing world economy. But this catastrophic view of the world situation, the widespread idea that the 1917 revolution would lead to revolution in the West because capitalism was unable to develop any further, was far too mechanical and deterministic.

Capitalism Can Develop No Further

The revolutionary movement of the time seemed convinced that capitalism did not have the margin to expand the productive forces. This very development was presented as the proving ground of the working class movement. Thus the problem of socialist revolution was seen as that of *the political management by the working class and its party of the development which the bourgeoisie was no longer able to complete.* The implicit notion that the productive forces are neutral and that their expansion leads unilinearly towards socialism is an evolutionary residue of the Second International. It recalls the positive judgement made by Lenin in 1899 of the development of capitalism in Russia — the theme of 'production for production's sake' — and projects it, insufficiently mediated and transposed, onto the tasks of the international communist movement.

On the one hand, the acceptance by the *Ordine Nuovo* group of Leninist strategy constituted a powerful factor in its maturation. The relation with Leninism deprovincialized the group culturally and provided a key to understanding the global dimension of the revolutionary process. On the other hand, it ran up against the fact that the Italian social formation was not readily adaptable to the strategy which had succeeded in Russia. The insistence on the 'productive' worker — modelled on capitalist efficiency rather than any hegemonic alternative — set up a barrier against non-working class social strata. Simplistically labelled 'non-productive', these were thus thrown back into the arms of the bourgeoisie. Productivist rationalization could hardly relate in a positive way to social strata like the intellectuals of the public service. The expansion of this group was understood as 'a chaotic increase in incompetent bureaucracy, . . . and the consequent creation of endless parasitical bodies' (*PWI* 165) typical of the degeneration of the state which has taken on the role of entrepreneur as it intervenes increasingly in the economy.

The inadequacy of this analysis of the situation, its failure to see the specific contradictions of the middle class, and of the proletarian and semi-proletarian strata in city and countryside, contributed to the overall failure of attempts to construct agricultural and urban soviets, as well as district committees (aimed at establishing relations between industrial and service sector workers). It also had repercussions on relations with technicians and white collar factory workers and imposed an isolation on the working class even within the factory.[2] At the start of the Council movement, the strength of the workers had led these groups to think about their links to the working class. As Gramsci wrote, 'The technician too is reduced to the status of a producer, linked to the capitalist by the wicked and savage relationship of exploited to exploiter. His mentality sheds its petty bourgeois incrustations and becomes proletarian, revolutionary in outlook.' (*PWI* 164) But the elimination of unproductive petty bourgeois strata appeared as a necessary phase and instrument of the proletarian revolution conceived of as the completion of the rationalization of production. Before the seizure of power, the petty-bourgeoisie had to be driven out of society 'in the way a plague of locusts is driven from a half-devastated field — with steel and fire'. This would have the effect of 'relieving the national apparatus of production and exchange of a leaden harness that suffocates it and prevents it from functioning. It would have the effect of clearing the social atmosphere and bringing the workers face to face with their real adversary: the class of capitalists . . . ' (*PWI* 135) Gramsci later explicitly criticizes this productivism in the *Notebooks* when he comments on the strategy of war of movement or of frontal attack.

After the seizure of power, the repressive state activity in the economic sphere (production and distribution) and in the political sphere (to prevent any possible reactionary reversal) would guarantee the necessary economic conditions to enable the working class to increase production. (*PWI* 325) Thus we have a much reduced notion of the dictatorship of the proletariat stemming from a conception of revolution limited to the working class.

The picture which emerges is thus a highly problematic one: exaltation of a working class productivism based in an already existing industrial apparatus; separation of the working class from intermediate social strata; an accentuation of its distance from non-working class proletarian and semi-proletarian strata. Then, too, the problem of an alliance with the proletarian and peasant strata in the countryside remained unsolved. It was assumed that the agrarian strata and their parties (especially the Catholic Popular Party) were like their Russian counterparts. The *Ordine Nuovo*'s perspective was, after all, one intent on repeating the pattern of the Russian experience. (*PWI* 84) Thus no analysis was undertaken of the specific roots of Italian backwardness in comparison with Russia. Relations with the peasant strata were placed in the reductive perspective of the industrialization of agriculture and the South. The group's general plan aimed at a permanent solution in which the relationship with other social strata would be resolved as socialism succeeded in completing the bourgeois revolution.

Gramsci's Criticism of the Capitalist Productive Process

From the first prison notebook, Gramsci interweaves reflections on new phenomena in American society with crucial aspects of his strategic elaboration. The attempt to rationalize industry — begun above all in the Ford factories — and the accompanying plan of a general transformation of American society produced a basic problem which neither Gramsci in the *Ordine Nuovo*, nor indeed the entire revolutionary movement at the time, perceived. What repercussions on labour organization and the structure of productive forces would capitalism's new ability to answer the problem of expansion have? What should the attitude of the working class be? (*PWI* 279-80; 311-12) On this, the *Notebooks* constitute the start of a process of rethinking which had begun in the Communist International in the mid-1920s. Discussions had been centred on new facts about the consolidation of capitalism and evaluation of the nature of and prospects for rationalizing production.

Gramsci's approach to these problems is much richer because he did not want simply to note new facts in capitalist societies. Rather he wants to investigate these facts to arrive at an understanding of their implications for the theoretical problem of *prediction*. He sees American rationalization as a response to the objective requirements of a 'planned economy'; and as a counter-force to the rate of profit's tendency to fall. Rationalization pinpointed the possibilities, wide margins and limits of a phase in the development of productive forces. It led to uncovering changes in the structure of capitalist society, but changes which simultaneously left constant basic social and power relations. (*SPN* 308-13)

Gramsci's examination of the new dynamic of American society forms part of his comparative study of the various types of consolidation of ruling class hegemony which took place after 1917 and the defeat of the revolution in Europe. The parallels he found between America, Western Europe and especially Fascist Italy not only pointed to the obstacles facing a general application of Fordism. They also added to the understanding of the role of the state in this new phase of development; and of the reasons behind the enormous expansion of intermediate social strata in the context of the general extension of the state's activities. (*SPN* 301-6 for example)

This theoretical framework is important in order to grasp the way in which Gramsci went beyond a 'crisis theory' of the downfall of capitalism; and consequently beyond the traditional *Ordine Nuovo* conception of the relation between Councils and production. The working class's will to make a complete break is translated into its real ability to pose the question of the development of the productive forces in the process of creating a new hegemony. It is not by chance that the theme of hegemony becomes the keystone of the critique of Ford-type rationalization and even explicitly the principal element for solving the problem of development in a society's transition to socialism.

Hegemony and the Role of the Working Class

The new hegemony is based on criticism of what exists and on a defence of what is crucial to guarantee its class character. Consequently the processes by which 'rupture' develops in the structure and above all in the factory are fundamental. It is important that the capitalist vision of the worker as 'trained gorilla' in the end fails completely. However, an abstract alternative model of rationalization is not the answer. Instead, Gramsci points to the working class as direct judge and participant in the choices required 'to find for themselves an "original", and not Americanized system of living, to turn into "freedom" what today is "necessity".' Thus the refusal of part of the working class to adjust to 'the highest degree of automatic and mechanical attitudes' (*SPN* 317) emerges as something which cannot be reduced to a mere defensive, trade-union resistance to the process of rationalization. Given technological innovations cannot simply be applied in a different way. The class itself decides on the identification of the 'rational kernel' to be preserved and imprints its mark on a process of development which reflects in its very depths the leadership of one class rather than another. (*SPN* 279-80; 302)

In this perspective, the role of the Councils changes markedly. The 'collective worker' (*SPN* 201-2) becomes the link between *autonomy* and the growth of the *new hegemony* within the productive process. This involves the awareness that 'technical requirements can be conceived in concrete terms, not merely separate from the interests of the ruling class, but in relation to the interests of the class which is as yet subaltern', and which for this very reason shows a tendency to go beyond its subordinate position. Here the Councils have moved from a union phase to become institutions directed towards a general alternative to productivism, that is, an alternative to the organization of production for its own sake, for the production of exchange value. This represents 'the factory as a producer of real objects and not of profit', and thus corresponds to the analysis in the first volume of *Capital*.[3] In this way (and only this way) the Councils are 'a movement to exploit the factory'. (*SPN* 286; 292)

Criticism of Soviet Productivism

Gramsci's re-examination — after the defeat of the working class movement in Italy — of the link between the working class and the development of the productive forces does not simply concern the strategic theme of 'revolution in the West'. The theme of Taylorism provides the opportunity for one of

his most significant and radically critical remarks concerning
the building of socialism in the USSR. Here Gramsci goes
beyond his initial distinction between East and West — which
rooted different strategies in different historical realities.
Instead he posits common ground between the two, especially
as regards responses to the problem of the relationship
between revolution and development.

Gramsci's criticism hinges on the Soviet Union's uncritical
adoption of Fordian methods of industrial development,
expressed in the markedly 'productivistic' formulas used by
Trotsky. This marked a fundamental choice — one taken over
by Stalin, and stemming from Lenin's own failure to solve the
problem.[4] The transfer of Fordism to the USSR, though
initially accompanied by a false concern with moral aspects,
ended up by slipping into 'profoundly mistaken practical
solutions', and a form of 'Bonapartism'. The charge of
'Bonapartism' echoes that of 'permanent Jacobinism', which
Gramsci habitually used to describe Trotsky's positions. (*SPN*
301) In both definitions, the polemic is based on Trotsky's
failure to understand the *specific* nature of the political
dimension inherent in the development of the working class
and the socialist revolution. This in turn becomes the failure to
resolve the question of the link between economics and politics
and a wavering between economism and reproducing the
model of bourgeois revolution.

Hegemony and Passive Revolution

By contrast, the penetrating formulation of the category of
passive revolution provides a basis for a political theory. The
notion of capitalism collapsing as a result of a crisis belongs to
the war of movement, just as the prospect of the survival of
capitalism through passive revolution requires the notion of
hegemony. A definitive break is made here with economism.
Gramsci constructs his theoretical base in such a way that the
central position of the political sphere is not juxtaposed to civil
society, thus losing sight of the complexity of the rupture
taking place in the socio-economic structure. The achievement
of state power by the working class can at last be seen as the
projection of its special vocation: to establish an expansive
hegemony capable of assimilating the vast majority of the

population.

Gramsci did not completely work out the political terms for achieving this goal, but he argued that it was necessary to examine the terms in which the tendency towards crisis in capitalist societies and their primary contradictions are constantly reformulated. This tendency towards crisis arises within the processes of rationalization. There can be no simple linear movement towards capitalist crisis and from there to socialism. The passive revolution — in the historical period of the transition to socialism — does indeed present a more advanced terrain, a terrain made more favourable by the past and present struggle of the workers and popular masses. However, Gramsci rejects evolutionism, convinced that development does not necessarily lead to socialism and even in some ways hinders it. This is because there is a tendency, derived from the continuous development of the productive forces, towards the growth of 'ever-increasing areas of social passivity', that is, of waste and parasitism as complementary to capitalist rationalization in the occupational structure, consumption, etc. It is also caused by the reproduction of class divisions in an increasingly complex and marked form and the deepening of inequality through the division of labour. There is also less and less social control over politics with an implicit weakening of the proletariat.

The young Gramsci did not fully develop this theoretical picture in the *Ordine Nuovo* and his strategy in that period was in some ways fundamentally different from his view in prison. Yet he developed two notions in those years which were exceptionally important and which were the basis of subsequent theoretical developments: that the working class's task of creating a new state is now on the historical agenda and that this new state would be established through a process of transformation starting with the factory and the productive forces.

NOTES

1   P. Gobetti, *La rivoluzione liberale,* Einaudi, Turin, 1969. p 114.

2   P. Spriano, *'L' Ordine Nuovo' e i Consigli di fabbrica,* Einaudi, Turin, 1971. p 120.

3   *Ibid.*, p 202.

4   C. Bettelheim, *Class Struggle in the USSR*, Harvester, Hassocks 1976.
    pp 352-356.

V
POPULAR CULTURE

GRAMCSI'S OBSERVATIONS
ON FOLKLORE
Alberto Maria Cirese

An area where Gramsci's influence has been particularly felt is in the study of popular culture. Historians, sociologists, linguists, anthropologists and others have been inspired by Gramsci to study the culture and ideology of the mass of the population. Few seem to realize, however, that while Gramsci argued that such work was vitally important, he was fundamentally critical of popular culture. But how then could the hegemony of the working class be based on popular ideologies? What was the relationship between beliefs held in an apparently spontaneous way and a conscious revolutionary leadership? What is the relationship between popular ideas and a coherent philosophy? These are some of the questions addressed by Alberto Maria Cirese's analysis of Gramsci's notes on folklore. According to Cirese, Gramsci is able both to criticize the limitations of popular ideology and to maintain a solidarity with those classes which are at the moment subaltern because he takes the ideology of the mass of the population as the starting point for a transformation of things as they are.

But there was no romantic quality about Gramsci's interest in folklore. His childhood in Sardinia had been too painful. Folklore and ideology in a wider sense had to be analyzed seriously and critically because it was a factor influencing people's daily lives. Nor was Gramsci's focus on the people utopian. It was rooted in his conviction that for the first time in history the mass of the population had the potential to intervene to transform society. But this mass carried within it little of structured concepts and many views of the world. The question to be asked was how could the positive elements within these views be harnessed to become the foundation of a new hegemonic influence on society?

According to Gramsci, the content of popular conceptions of the world is mostly backward. The conceptions themselves are unsystematic, lack coherence, and are subject to the influence or hegemony of official culture. They make up a kind of mosaic of the remnants of high or official culture, past and present, which is able to keep in check any threatening aspects of popular world views. In a thorough analysis of Gramsci's texts, Cirese examines his attempt to disentangle the positive qualities of official culture which allow it to be hegemonic. The subaltern classes lack precisely these hegemonic qualities. What concerns Gramsci is the process of going beyond a world view which is at the moment 'folklore' so that the popular classes are able to produce an autonomous culture and to select elements from the culture handed down from above to use for their own, opposite ends, incorporating spontaneous elements which go against the morality of the ruling strata.

How then can what is now 'folklore' become hegemonic? Cirese maintains that Gramsci sees the difference between official culture and popular culture as one of quality, *rather than* quantity. *Yet he also maintains that there are* quantitative *differences, saying that there is a kind of continuum between 'spontaneous' and 'scientific' philosophies. What does he mean? Gramsci sees every human being as an intellectual. Each of us has a potential for systematic or philosophical thought. The skills of intellectuals are not innate but simply techniques acquired through training, much as a skilled joiner or computer operator acquire their skills. Thus logical, coherent thought could be acquired by many people. When Gramsci writes that he is not using quantitative differences in a mathematical sense but is referring to a 'quantity of qualitative elements', he is indicating the acquisition of a number of skills which are qualitatively different from the thought processes of most people.*

Looking at Gramsci's discussion of folklore in the most general terms, we find: firstly, that he expressly rejects the view that folklore is of no importance (it should not be thought of 'as something strange or peculiar or colourful'); secondly, that he is no less explicit in claiming that it *is* important (though only as an object of study). He not only makes the point generically (folklore is 'something very serious that must be taken seriously'), but argues it from the statement that the whole phenomenon of folklore contains or expresses a 'conception of life and the world' which can be *precisely located in socio-cultural terms* in relation to other conceptions of the world.

This conception of life and the world, as Gramsci makes clear, is characteristic of certain strata of society, namely the 'people'. The people is taken in the sense of 'all the subaltern and instrumental classes in every society that has existed up to now', and its conception of the world is not only different or very different from official conceptions of the world, but is in opposition or contradiction or conflict with them. Alternatively, 'official' conceptions, characteristic of 'the cultured sectors of historically determined societies' or the ruling strata or the 'state', are, like 'official society' in general, in competition and conflict with folklore.

All of this leads to the crucial observation that 'folklore can only be understood as a reflection of the conditions of the people's cultural life'. This is the reason why research into folklore must 'change its approach, as well as becoming more extensive and more thorough'. Thus, pure scholarship must give way to more adequate research-criteria, notably the principle that 'the people is not a culturally homogeneous group, it presents a large number of cultural stratifications, in various combinations' which can be identified to a certain extent on the basis of the greater or lesser isolation of particular historical popular groups.'

What Gramsci does then is to *validate* an object or area of study on the basis of a *definition* of the object itself. But, though they do not preclude it in principle, neither Gramsci's validation nor his definition add up to an endorsement either of the view that folklore, or the conception of the world which it contains or expresses, or the ways in which it goes against official conceptions of the world are valid in themselves; or of the possibility that they might be put to valid politico-cultural uses.

In other words, Gramsci's statement that folklore is 'something very serious' cannot be applied to the politico-cultural uses that might be made of folklore. Not only is this statement limited to folklore as an object of study, but it comes in a context where Gramsci stresses the need to bring about 'the birth of a new culture among the great popular masses', i.e. to do away with 'the gap between modern and popular culture or folklore'.

All that we can say for the moment is that Gramsci is raising research into folklore from the level of pure scholarship to that of science or knowledge; as well as promoting folklore itself from being a curiosity to being a *conception of the world*. And he takes the further step of locating it socially and culturally 'in the framework of a nation and its culture': *characteristic of the subaltern classes* on one hand, and *in opposition to official conceptions* on the other.

And closer examination of these three cardinal features of Gramsci's definition of folklore will show that his endorsement cannot be extended to the politico-cultural sphere.

If we now go on to analyze the three key-concepts, at least as far as they emerge from the passages referred to so far, and try to bring out the general principle underlying them, we find the following:

1 Describing both folklore and official, or, more broadly, cultured intellectual products as *conceptions of the world* puts them on the same *generic* level, but there is still obviously a *specific* difference. It is indicated verbally by the distinction, and opposition, between 'official' and 'popular'. If we agree, for the sake of clarity, to use the adjective 'folkloric' instead of 'popular', the generic equivalence and the specific difference can be represented thus:

Folkloric v. official
conception of the world

This formula is only partially satisfactory, but we can make do with it for the time being.

2 As well as the fact that the folkloric conception is in *opposition* to the official one, Gramsci explicitly makes the point that the inverse relation obviously obtains as well, and that official conceptions of the world are in *competition* or *conflict* with those of folklore.

What is not clear for the moment is which of the two conceptions is active and which is passive — a provisional uncertainty which can be represented equally uncertainly thus:

(active or passive) v. (active or passive)
opposition

3 The socio-cultural location of the two specific kinds of *conception of the world* is shown by the use of a series of

semantically oppositional pairs. Generally speaking only one term of each pair is stated explicitly while the other is left implicit, though it is immediately obvious. Here the implicit term is indicated by an asterisk: subaltern/*hegemonic; instrumental/*non-instrumental; cultured/*uncultured; ruling/*ruled; dominant/*dominated, etc.

This series of pairs can be reduced in essence to just two opposites. The first has to do with the socio-political sphere, the second with the socio-cultural sphere, social class and intellectual 'sector' or category respectively.

We can represent the first as follows:

$$\frac{subaltern\ v.\ hegemonic}{\text{social class}}$$

It does not seem arbitrary to use the term 'hegemonic' here, despite its not appearing explicitly in the pages in question.[1]

The second pair could be represented by automatically employing the term 'uncultured' as the implicit opposite of 'cultured'. But the resulting contrast between *cultured* and *uncultured* could give rise to some misunderstanding. For there are reasonable grounds for believing that in Gramsci's view the usual contrast between *culture* and *non-culture* is not exactly the same thing, and does not imply the same judgement, as that between *culture* and *ignorance*, meaning the 'complete absence of any form or kind of culture'. He speaks, as we have seen, of 'the conditions of the people's *cultural* life'; he places popular song 'in the framework of a nation and its *culture*'; he uses the expression 'popular *culture* or folklore, and so on. We shall want to return to this point in due course, but, in order not to prejudge the issue, we should leave open the possibility that the opposition lies not so much between *culture* and *non-culture* as between different kinds of culture. It therefore seems right to avoid using the term 'uncultured' which we shall replace by the very Gramscian word 'simple'. Bearing these points in mind, we can represent the opposition in the socio-cultural sphere, as regards intellectual 'sector' or category, as follows:

$$\frac{simple\ v.\ cultured}{\text{intellectual category}}$$

The semantic connections and distinctions so far identified

can now be recapitulated as follows:

folkloric v. official	conceptions of the world
in	
(active or passive) v. (active or passive)	mutual opposition
located respectively in	
a subaltern v. hegemonic	social classes
b simple v. cultured	intellectual categories

Reading the table vertically, we can see at once that 'folkloric' connects with 'subaltern' and 'simple'. Neither of these terms go very well with an 'active' position, either in common usage or, still less, in Gramsci's. By the same token, the evident connection between 'official' and 'hegemonic' and 'cultured' does not square with 'passive'. In other words, even if Gramsci were not explicit on the point, the ambiguity still surrounding 'opposition' would have to be resolved by assigning 'passiveness' to folklore and 'activeness' to official conceptions. The logic of connective and oppositional coherence alone then would lead us to the conclusion that the proposition underlying Gramsci's considerations takes the following form:

The *folkloric* conception is to the *official* conception as the *subaltern* social class is to the *hegemonic* social class as the *simple* intellectual category is to the *cultured* intellectual category
as *passive* opposition is to *active* opposition

This conclusion was fairly predictable, but it is confirmed by the specific points Gramsci makes on the material of folklore itself, the conception of the world it embodies, and the opposition between both of these and official conceptions. His points are not merely statements of fact. Whether they have to do with *content* or *form* (by which we understand here mode of organization or degree of inner coherence), they are decidedly judgemental in character, and the judgement can very rarely be called positive. Even if Gramsci occasionally modifies his judgement and assesses folklore positively in certain respects, it does not seem to alter our impression that he is being quite deliberately systematic in his devaluation of folklore (beginning with those features which we have listed).

It is often hard to make out whether Gramsci is talking about folk-material as such or the conception of the world it expresses, but the attributes he assigns all point plainly in a negative direction.

Thus, in a context where the reference is definitely to the material itself, Gramsci states that there is 'nothing more contradictory and fragmentary than folklore'. Elsewhere, where the reference is less certain, he notes that 'folklore' has stayed in a 'dispersed and varied state'. Referring to the folkloric or popular conception of the world, Gramsci says that it is 'to a large extent implicit' as well as 'unelaborated', 'unsystematic', and 'above all varied':

> not only in the sense that it is different from and juxtaposed to something else, but also in the sense that it is stratified, ranging as it does from a greater to a lesser degree of coarseness. Although perhaps we should speak of it rather as an indigestible mass of fragments of all the conceptions of life and the world that have succeeded one another in the course of history, most of which indeed have survived only in the mutilated and contaminated traces we find of them in folklore. (*LVN* 216)

The negative judgement, then, affects all aspects of folklore: both the way in which it is organized and the nature or indeed the content of the elements which make it up. The way that Gramsci thinks and talks about this material, whether in general terms or through specific examples, is as something essentially debased, the spill-over of cultured conceptions. And not only is it backward in relation to the developments of science and 'cultured culture': it is even out of touch with the conditions under which the people actually live.

In addition to the passages already cited, one might look at those in which Gramsci underlines folklore's dependence on the 'culture of the dominant class', or where he talks about how 'certain opinions and scientific concepts, taken out of context, and more or less distorted, are for ever falling into the popular domain' where they are 'assimilated in strange ways'; or again where the 'Ptolemaic conception' (*MS* 55) — which elsewhere is assigned to 'common sense' (*SPN* 420) is regarded as 'typical of folklore'; or, finally, where he points out that 'certain typically folk-conceptions either continue in existence even after conditions [of the people's cultural life] have changed (or appear to have changed), or else give way to strange combinations'. The tradition, in short, is a mosaic.

Passiveness and backwardness of content are of course simply a manifestation of the fact that the material is incapable of elaboration or systemization. With everything connected in this way, what we appear to have is an entirely homogeneous series of attributes. Whether Gramsci is referring to the material of folklore or its conception of the world, its content or its form, he always attributes to it qualities that constitute the *weak* (or negative, low-value) term of an oppositional pair whose *strong* (or positive, high-value) term is reserved more or less explicitly for conceptions to be found on the side of official society and the ruling strata.

Looking first at formal qualities, we find explicitly associated with folklore: contradictoriness, fragmentation, dispersal, multiplicity, implicitness, non-elaboration, un-systematicness, difference, juxtaposition, stratification, indi-gestibility, etc. Explicitly stated qualities such as elaboration, systematicness, political organization and centralization, organic systemization, etc. are reserved for non-folk concep-tions. But it would obviously not be a distortion to extend the list to include the negation of the remaining 'weak' terms assigned to folklore (*non-contradictoriness, *non-fragmenta-tion, *non-multiplicity, i.e. *unity, *non-implicitness, i.e. *explicitness, and so on).

There are some nuances, but most of these pairs point to the fact that the manner of ordering collections of cultural phenomena and their respective conceptions of the world, and the results of that process, are in one case positive and in the other negative.

The qualities that refer particularly to the manner in which the process takes place are elaboration, systematicness, organization, centralization, organic systemization and the like, and their opposites, whether explicitly stated or not. If we agree to call the positive and negative poles 'organic' and 'unorganic' respectively, and to refer to the ordering-process as 'combination', the semantic connections and distinctions can then be schematized as:

unorganic v. organic

combination

Such qualities as fragmentation, dispersal, multiplicity, stratification and their opposites are concerned on the other hand with the results of the process. To indicate the two different kinds of internal organization we can use the terms 'fragmentary' and 'unitary', which gives us:

fragmentary v. unitary

internal organization

One pair — implicitness/explicitness — is left over, and this we can take as referring to the mode of expression or manifestation, schematized as:

implicit v. explicit

mode of expression

As regards the material of folklore — in other words what is contained in its opinions or beliefs or practices — Gramsci emphasizes above all the fact that it is a 'debased spill-over'. This is obviously in contrast to the original character of what is produced by 'culture', so that we can represent the opposition as follows:

debased v. original

content

If we now add these new pairs of attributes to those already identified, we get the following (simplified) table:

folkloric v. official
(active or passive) v. (active or passive)
subaltern v. hegemonic
simple v. cultured
unorganic v. organic
fragmentary v. unitary
implicit v. explicit
debased v. original

— which makes it increasingly unlikely that the quality of *activeness* can be attributed to folklore.

Gramsci has quite different ways of talking about the forms

taken by the opposition between folk and official conceptions, depending on which of the two aspects of the relation he is considering, and it is these explicit statements that enable us finally to decide the question of activeness and passiveness.

Looked at from the point of view of folklore, the opposition is 'for the most part implicit, mechanical, objective'. But when it is looked at from the other point of view, it completely changes character and becomes something active and organized. This is what is implied when Gramsci asks whether the 'elaboration' and 'systemization' of Catholicism wrought by 'intellectuals and the Church hierarchy' were not in fact necessary 'in order to keep folklore in its dispersed and varied diverse state'. The opposition appears even more active and organized when Gramsci refers to the state as an entity which is 'not agnostic, but has its own conception of life which it is its duty to disseminate through education of the popular masses': this 'educational activity', as Gramsci observes, 'is in competition and conflict with other explicit or implicit conceptions', amongst which is folklore which, therefore, has to be 'overcome'.

Thus, from the point of view of folklore the opposition takes the form at best of resistance. It might be a tenacious resistance, but in kind it is mechanical, implicit and objective. On the opposite side, one has an activeness which at the least is involved in 'keeping things in check', but which has the power to 'root out', 'replace', 'hammer', and so on.

Once again, then, the weak and strong terms are distributed on each side of a sharp dividing line, with the former linked to folklore and the latter to official conceptions.

There are here at least two recognizable semantic distinctions. There is the opposition between implicit, mechanical and objective, and *explicit, *non-mechanical, *non-objective; and there is that between the *aggressive* character of official conceptions and folklore's attitude of *resistance*. The first obviously has to do with the degree of consciousness or intentionality involved, and we can represent it by the terms 'mechanical v. intentional'. (Drawing on other passages in Gramsci, the terms 'spontaneity v. conscious leadership' could be used instead.[2]) The second opposition, which is concerned with aggressive capabilities and force of expansion, can be represented by the terms 'active' and 'passive' as already used.

It does not seem appropriate to run these two pairs together, so the connections and distinctions concerning the 'opposition' that Gramsci speaks about require two different schematizations. The first is to do with *consciousness*, the second with the *capacity to influence* on the outside.

If we may agree to use the term 'opposition' to link the two poles of *consciousness*, we shall have the following schema:

$$\frac{mechanical\ v.\ intentional}{\text{opposition}}$$

And if we further agree to use the term 'conflict' to link the two poles of the *capacity to influence* and expand, the relation will be represented as:

$$\frac{passive\ v.\ active}{\text{conflict}}$$

In this way we have both confirmed the straightforward hypothesis that the qualities Gramsci attributes to folklore are homogeneous in a necessarily *negative* sense, and resolved the ambiguity surrounding the 'opposition' between the two conceptions. The general proposition underlying his statements can now be formulated as follows:

> *Folkloric* conception is to *official*
> as *subaltern* social class is to *hegemonic*
> as *simple* intellectual category is to *cultured*
> as *unorganic* combination is to *organic*
> as *fragmentary* internal organization is to *unitary*
> as *implicit* mode of expression is to *explicit*
> as *debased* content is to *original*
> as *mechanical* opposition is to *intentional*
> as *passive* conflict is to *active*

Everything falls into place, then, but perhaps just a little too neatly. Presented in this way, the constant attribution of weak or negative terms to folklore and strong or positive ones to non-folk conceptions has all the marks of the deliberate systematicity we mentioned before, and can obviously look suspect. Might it not in fact be a mirage or distortion produced by the schematization and hence excessive impoverishment of an argument that in itself is a good deal more mobile and articulated?

There is no question but that Gramsci's considerations are richer than the proposition we have come up with. Apart from anything else, there are a number of 'positive' attributes which we have passed over but which need to be taken into account, as well as other qualifications and nuances. But before we go on to consider these, the point must be made that the systematic quality to which we have drawn attention is explicitly confirmed by the text as we have examined it so far.

It is Gramsci himself who says that all the negative qualities listed above *must* be assigned to folklore, *before* moving on to an examination of its concrete manifestations, and perhaps even quite separately from them. This list of negatives and their attribution to folklore are to be argued by deduction from the very concept of 'people'. If the people consists of all subaltern and instrumental classes, it follows *by definition*, as Gramsci writes, that 'the people . . . *cannot* possess elaborated and systematic conceptions which, however contradictory may be their development, are politically organized and centralized'. Elaboration, systematicness and centralization are in fact expressions of hegemony (even if not only of hegemony), which is precisely what those classes which are still subaltern lack.

So systematic a dichotomizing of the various attributes would seem to be a real characteristic rather than an arbitrary impoverishment of the text.

This being the case — at least so far as we can see — it is fairly obvious that Gramsci's treatment of folklore moves along two separate lines, and that his assessment changes radically as he shifts from one to the other. On the one hand, he considers folklore as an object of study and as such he validates it in full. But on the other, he looks at it as a force or factor in real life and its process of development, and from this point of view he characterizes it with a long, and so far systematic and unbroken, series of negative, low-value, qualities.

In other words, folklore is allowed the rank of a conception of the world, but within this category of phenomena it is placed at a lower level in the hierarchy than that assigned to the official conceptions from which it is distinguished and which stand in opposition to it. *By definition*, it is denied all the formal qualities of coherence, unity, consciousness, etc., which are typical of the hegemonic classes and their 'official' conceptions. Gramsci's esteem goes entirely to the latter, quite independently of the specific content of the conception in question or what social class it belongs to.

The upshot is a mixture of tensions and conflicts that border on the edge of ambiguity. The cultural expressions of the social classes with which Gramsci solidarizes so clearly at the political level are assessed positively to the extent that they are to be considered simply as an object of scientific research — but are judged negatively when it comes to seeing them as factors in real life and its process of development. Alternately, the cultural modes of the classes which Gramsci opposes both politically and culturally are esteemed as permanent 'values' and 'forces'.

It is precisely these tensions or ambiguities which give rise to conflicting interpretations on the question of the political use of folklore. Thus, at one extreme there is the tendency to shift Gramsci's positive judgement on folklore as an object of study onto its potential use in politics, while at the other we find his negative judgement on the modes and content of folklore extended to the object of study itself.

Everything seems to revolve around the real or apparent ambivalence of the concepts of 'subaltern' and 'official'. The text seems to allow of two different interpretations which can be summarized very roughly and schematically as follows. Depending on how they are affected by the context, both singly and in relation to each other, the two concepts may take the form of an opposition either:

(a) between 'subaltern = the modern proletariat which today is historically in the right even if it has attained power only in a few cases (for Gramsci, the USSR) and 'official = the modern bourgeoisie which today is historically in the wrong even though in many cases it still retains power'; or:

(b) between 'subaltern = those classes, past or future, that are lacking in or deprived of historical force' and 'official = those classes whose hegemony, whether past or future, constitutes real history'.

It is at this difficult point that we turn for guidance to those of Gramsci's observations that we have not yet taken into account.

These remaining observations are different from the foregoing inasmuch as they provide a more or less immediately *positive* description of folklore. Few though they are, this is not a reason for discounting their effect on the systematic distribution of strong and weak terms noted above, and we should examine them with a certain amount of care. Here to begin with is a brief list of the relevant points.

1 Some of folklore's *weak* attributes are modified quantitatively by Gramsci at the level of general definition. Thus, he writes that the folkloric conception 'is implicit *to a large extent*', and that its opposition to official world views is '*For the most part* likewise implicit, mechanical, and objective'.

2 Referring specifically to 'popular morality' — but without making it clear whether he is thinking of the conservative conceptions or the progressive innovations which he will distinguish between a little later on — Gramsci attributes a particular 'tenacity' to certain folk-convictions: 'there are certain imperatives which are much stronger, more tenacious and more effective than those of official "morality".'

3 Still in the area of morality, and also that of 'juridical folklore', Gramsci credits at least some folk-conceptions with the ability to 'adhere and correspond spontaneously' to actual conditions of life and their process of development. Hence it can happen that:

(a) they are not always necessarily just the debased, inert, spill-over of dominant conceptions. So much is clear from the passage in which he speaks of 'that mass of beliefs and opinions on the subject of one's "own" rights which are in continual circulation amongst the popular masses, and are for ever being reviewed under the pressure of the real conditions of life and the spontaneous comparison between the ways in which the various classes live'. (*LVN* 219)

(b) they can sometimes have a progressive value which the analysis of cultural stratifications must take account of; thus, Gramsci underlines the need to 'distinguish between different strata' in the sphere of popular morality as well:

some of them fossilized reflections of the conditions of days gone by, and therefore conservative and reactionary, others consisting of a range of often creative and progressive innovations, spontaneously determined by the forms and conditions of life as it is developing, which go against, or merely differ from, the morality of the ruling strata of society. (*LVN* 217)

(c) they may achieve a degree of expansive capacity that might throw official conceptions back on the defensive; thus, when discussing a certain kind of criticism levelled at 'so-called natural law', Gramsci notes that, behind its apparent objectives, 'the polemic is really aimed at *checking* the influence which "natural law" strands in popular thought might have (*and actually do have*), particularly on young intellectuals'. (*LVN* 218 and 219. Italics added)

4 Speaking about popular song — though there are indications that the point might be applied more widely — Gramsci acknowledges that, even though folklore is generally speaking dependent on official conceptions, (i.e. the process of 'cultural descent' from élites to masses is going on), the people is 'itself' able to select according to its 'own' criteria, these going more or less implicitly against official ones. Thus, he makes the point that even though popular songs 'are written neither by nor for the people', they have been 'taken over by it because they conform to its way of thinking and feeling'; they are representative of 'how it conceives life and the world, in contrast with official society'. This makes the phrases Gramsci uses elsewhere rather less generic: 'folklore has always been linked to the culture of the dominant class, and, *in its own way, has always drawn on it* for motifs which have then been incorporated and combined with previous traditions.' (Italics added)

It is fairly clear that there are two different ways in which what for the sake of brevity we shall call these 'positive' remarks operate in relation to those already examined. Either they *introduce new qualities or aspects*, not previously taken into consideration, or which have not so far come to the fore; or they *modify in a quantitative sense* certain qualities already otherwise attributed. We shall examine these two aspects separately.

The following act in the first way and introduce 'new' qualities: (a) the point about the particular 'tenacity' of some popular conceptions; (b) the acknowledgement that folklore, at least in certain cases, is able to adhere 'spontaneously' to real conditions of life as they develop; (c) the attribution of a 'progressive' political value to some of the phenomena of folklore.

We must therefore introduce these new data into our previous table. But in so doing we have to observe that the positive remarks under examination, as is clearly stated, concern only *some* features or elements of folklore, while the negative characteristics equally clearly concerned *the whole* of folklore. This means two things: firstly, that these positive attributions are not to be placed at the same level as the negative ones already dealt with; and secondly, that assigning them to folklore *does not lead to* their negations being assigned to official conceptions *as such,* but at most to their affecting some aspects of the latter.

Thus, leaving aside the fact that the 'tenacity' of popular attitudes is not always regarded 'positively' (since it is also responsible for holding back the people in a manner deplored by Gramsci[3]), the statement '*certain* popular moral imperatives are more tenacious than those of official morality' means only that *certain* official imperatives are weaker than those of folklore. The same is true of the capacity to adhere to reality: some popular opinions have it, but this does not mean that non-folk opinions do not. But were any proof needed of the particular, *non*-universal, character of these positive qualities in folklore, one would only need to look at Gramsci's acknowledgement of the 'progressive' value of certain popular beliefs or opinions. This acknowledgement rests on the creation of an explicit contrast between *progressive* and *reactionary* (or *conservative*) *inside* folklore itself — requiring, at most, an identical contrast inside official conceptions.

If, in short, we go on to fit these 'new' qualities into the system of oppositions we have set up, we find that the latter is 'extended' and also looks different on the page. Thus, if we agree to use the term 'effective' for the capacity to adhere to reality, the table would be extended in the following (simplified) way:

<u>folkloric v. official</u>

(tenacious or not tenacious) v. (tenacious or not tenacious)

(effective or not effective) v. (effective or not effective)
(progressive or reactionary) v. (progressive or reactionary)

Only one of the oppositional pairs to which the extension is
added appears to be affected in any way, and it is the one that
concerns 'content'. From the point of view of folklore,
'content' no longer appears as purely 'debased': it might be
occasionally original', or even autonomous. This points
forward to those quantitative modifications already mentioned which we shall be looking at more closely in due course.

Otherwise, the extension seems to leave the absolute nature
of the oppositions and their distribution intact. The fact that
folklore can sometimes be tenacious, effective and progressive
(or rather, *more* tenacious etc. than official conceptions
sometimes are) neither affects nor limits — if anything, to
some extent it confirms and strengthens — the implicitness of
the mode of expression, the unorganic character of combination, the fragmentation of internal organization, the passiveness of the conflict, the simplicity or elementariness of the
intellectual category, or in short the subaltern position of the
social class to which folklore belongs. All that is affirmed is
that the implicit mode of expression does not of itself preclude
the presence of (some) progressive political values, that
fragmentation or unorganicness nevertheless allow room for
(some) strata of innovations, and so on.

The real consequence of the new group of oppositions is to
be found at a different level. It is directly linked to the fact
which makes it impossible to infer any positive judgement on
folklore as such from what Gramsci wrote, the fact that the
new oppositions 'tenacious'/'not tenacious', 'effective'/'not
effective', 'progressive'/'reactionary' do not coincide with the
dichotomies 'subaltern'/'hegemonic', 'implicit'/'explicit', 'unorganic'/'organic', etc., but are added to them.

Because of this lack of coincidence, it is both possible and
necessary to rearrange the whole system, no longer taking the
opposition between 'folkloric' and 'official' as the point of
reference but rather each of the new oppositions, most
particularly that of an explicitly political kind.

The result is a complete reshuffling of the semantic
connections and distinctions. What is revealed in the long run
is that in Gramsci's text there exist implicit terms of

conceptual reference which lie beyond the straightforward opposition between 'folkloric' and 'official' as it has been presented so far.

Pedantic though it may be, it could be of some use to represent the schema constructed in function of the dichotomy between 'progressive' and 'reactionary' in diagrammatic form. The schema would then offer us not two but four possible kinds of conceptions of the world. While the vertical connections between 'folkloric' and 'subaltern', 'implicit', 'unorganic', etc., and between 'official' and 'hegemonic', 'explicit', 'organic', etc. remain unchanged, the four kinds would take the following form:

folkloric and reactionary	official and reactionary
folkloric and progressive	official and progressive

One of the most immediately obvious features of this new pattern is that the concept of 'official' is, so to speak, split in two. It is seen as capable of assuming at least one negative quality ('reactionary'), which interrupts the long and hitherto unbroken series of positive attributes — or of adding one further positive quality ('progressive') to all those preceding.

The first is hardly surprising, and it is moreover explicitly stated in the text with Gramsci describing some of the attitudes of the cultured and ruling strata as 'the most narrow-minded conservatism'. (*LVN* 219) This corrective to Gramsci's systematic acknowledgement of positive qualities is in any case perfectly consistent with the obvious gap between his own views and the 'official' conceptions of the time and place in which he is writing and working. The compatibility between 'official' and 'progressive', on the other hand, might occasion some surprise, particularly since the text under consideration does not appear to offer any immediate indications or concrete examples of a connection which we have brought out by purely formal and combinatory means. There is, however, no real reason for surprise if one reflects that the term 'official' is really just a general heading for a number of highly valued qualities. So as regards its intrinsic qualities, the expression 'official and progressive' can be translated, on the basis of the connections which we believe we have established, as: 'a conception of the world that is organic, unitary, explicit, original in its contents, intentional in its opposition to other conceptions and active in its conflict with them, and finally, progressive'. Which obviously means for Gramsci the philosophy of praxis, historical materialism, Marxism — the point of view which he himself takes up. But 'official' also means 'pertaining to the cultured sectors and the hegemonic classes': for Gramsci, both of these further conditions can be regarded as met only in the Soviet Union, whereas for the rest of the world only the first is satisfied. Thus it can be seen that, far from being produced by purely formal means, the combination of 'official and progressive' stands in fact for the *goal* in view or the *model* which is referred to.

But there is a good deal more. By inserting this new combination, which in the first instance came about by purely formal means, the static nature of the opposition between 'folkloric' and 'official' is decisively broken. The four-term pattern above has no room either for Marxism as the conception of the world belonging to social forces that are not yet hegemonic or for those workers' parties that are not yet in power. But it is that same pattern which demands their presence, based as it is on three terms denoting a given state of affairs and one which designates a goal and a model. The schema therefore represents a process, an action in time, and thus contains Marxism as not yet hegemonic, the workers' parties as not yet in power, or more precisely the class-struggle. These are present not as terms or factors, but as mediators or *agents* which effect the transition from the given state of affairs to the new situation and transform a 'progressive' that is still 'folkloric' (i.e. still subaltern, implicit, fragmentary, etc.) into a definitively 'official' (i.e. fully hegemonic) 'progressive'.

Thus our formal repatterning of the schema in function of the political assessment explicitly stated by the text has led us to recognize from within the presence of an underlying context, of unspoken but decisive conceptual reference-points. It is precisely to the tacit but active presence of these references that the ambivalence or ambiguity mentioned above has to be related, for it comes about as the result of repeated, sudden shifts, not perhaps kept entirely under control, from one level or point of view to another.

If the level concerned is that of describing a given state of affairs, and as long as the factors taken into account are limited to *bourgeois* official conceptions on the one hand and folklore as reflecting the cultural life *of the great masses of the people* on the other, the oppositional, what one might almost call alternative, value of the folkloric conception is immediately apparent, and the way is opened to a recognition of its ability both to produce its own autonomous culture and to select products handed down from above for its own, opposite, ends.

In such cases, the text authorizes us to recognize the folk conception as a spontaneous form of the 'spirit of cleavage', which Gramsci defines elsewhere as 'the progressive acquisition of consciousness of [the innovatory class's] own historical personality', (*PP* 172 and 173) and to see 'progressive' or 'protest' folklore at least as the manifestation of a *class-instinct* ('instinct' of course being understood as a 'primitive and elementary historical acquisition', not a biological phenomenon). (*SPN* 199)

But this limitation of perspective to the level of pure description and the straightforward comparison between folklore and bourgeois conceptions is short-lived. Straightaway, reference to the essential terms comes into play, the tension opens up between things as they are and the goal in view, and we move from the area of static description to that of action or process. At this point, there are at least three sides to the comparison (folklore, bourgeois conceptions, Marxist conception), and all the decidedly negative limitations of folklore come to the fore, however progressive it might be in certain respects and however significant its opposition to the official conceptions of the bourgeoisie. At the same time, the way is cleared for an appreciation of all the formal qualities which are possessed by official conceptions (whether bourgeois or proletarian) and not by folklore in its role as the cultural expression of social classes that are still subaltern. When it comes to an appreciation of those formal qualities, Gramsci contrasts folklore with the Marxist conception of the world, not with bourgeois ones: what are now in question are *class-consciousness* and class-struggle, the Communist Party, proletarian hegemony, in other words, the aims and agents of a huge transformation of things as they are.

So it seems that the constant play of light and shadow falling across Gramsci's discussions of folklore and official conceptions is to be attributed to the fact that the beam is cast from a number of different angles. But it is controlled by a single switch movement towards a goal and adaptation to a model.

We cannot, however, ignore the point that in all the criss-crossing of levels and points of view, one perspective remains constant. This is the esteem afforded to certain qualities which we shall call intellectual and which are the condition and expression of hegemony, *by whichever class it is exercised*. These qualities are presented, so to speak, as crossing class-boundaries: their possession or exercise is conditioned by class, but not their value, which is permanent. That is why one cannot be sure what hierarchical order all the terms, explicit and implicit, which the text relates to one another, should be put in, except for the entirely positive elements at one extreme ('official and progressive') and the entirely negative ones at the other ('folkloric and reactionary'). The order of the middle terms remains uncertain, since it is impossible to determine whether more value is given to what is politically positive (which would put 'folkloric and progressive' higher up the scale) or to what is formally positive (in which case it would be 'official and reactionary').

There is then a question whether a 'progressive' content which is without formal capacities or intellectual force should not be considered inert, if not indeed 'reactionary', while formal and intellectual capacities, even though their content is 'reactionary', should of themselves ultimately be regarded as 'progressive'.

A solution to this problem might be found if we look back to Gramsci's examination of other forces. His interest in folklore as an object of study is consonant with his desire for 'a more cautious and precise assessment of the forces acting in society[4]. Undoubtedly he regards folklore as one of these forces.

We have already seen him paying tribute to the 'tenacity' of folklore, and pursuing this line a little further we would find more explicit statements elsewhere, as for example when Gramsci writes:

It is worth recalling the frequent affirmation made by Marx on the 'solidity of popular beliefs' as a necessary element of a specific situation. What he says more or less is 'when this way of conceiving things has the force of popular beliefs', etc. Another proposition of Marx is that a popular conviction often has the same energy as a material force or something of the kind, which is extremely significant. (*SPN* 377)[5]

Another example would be his note on the 'fanatical granite compactness of the "popular beliefs" which assume the same energy as "material forces" '. (*SPN* 404)

These observations might obviously allow us to regard 'material forces' (and hence folklore in so far as it is comparable to material forces) as 'content' and intellectual qualities as 'form', tending thereby 'to reinforce the conception of "historic bloc" '. (*SPN* 377) As a consequence we would be authorized by the text at this point to see the positive aspect of folklore as residing in the fact that it is a 'force' or 'energy' which is made the content of a 'form' that takes shape elsewhere, *rather than* in particular items of content, however progressive they may be.

But on the other hand, the whole argument lends itself to over-simplification. Notwithstanding Gramsci's declared intention to treat this 'distinction between form and content [as having] purely didactic value, since the material forces would be inconceivable historically without form and the ideologies would be individual fancies without the material forces', (*SPN* 377) even the dialectical relationship between form and content is broken. The intellectual form is regarded as pre-existent or at any rate determining, while, if the material forces are regarded as essential, it is only at the instrumental level. Their content (as well as the 'other' forms which this content cannot but take on) is completely devoid of interest. In spite of Gramsci's statement to the effect that 'the demands of cultural contact with the "simple" ' must be 'continually felt' (and therefore satisfied), (*SPN* 330f) the only point of interest in the simple is their material force, with which contact is made in political action rather than cultural or scientific research.

So we come to a group of problems which go far beyond the specific questions which we intended to deal with in these notes: problems concerning the relation between intellectuals and masses, or between spontaneity and conscious leadership.

In fact, Gramsci's observations on folklore are one aspect of this wider batch of problems, and reflect the difficulties which arise from them. So much is clear not only from the direct mentions of 'spontaneity' which we have already come across, but also from the remaining positive comments on folklore to which we must now turn our attention.

It has already been mentioned that, as well as introducing 'new' qualities, Gramsci's positive comments on folklore modify certain previously-attributed negative qualities in a quantitative sense. A glance back to the points listed above will suffice to show that this second kind of positive comment is concerned with what we have agreed to call 'mode of expression', 'contents' and 'conflict', and that they make the association with folklore of the weak or negative terms in these three cases (implicit, debased, passive) less absolute. Essentially, what is said is that the folk conception is implicit *though not entirely so;* that its contents are debased spill-overs, *though not all of them;* and that its conflict with official conceptions is passive, *though not always.*

As a result, there are at least three cases in which the horizontal contrasts which we thought we could identify change character: being purely *qualitative* in kind, they were *discontinuous;* now they take on the appearance of a *quantitative continuity*. It emerges in short that there is a series of intermediate and continuous nuances between '*entirely* implicit, debased or passive' and '*entirely* explicit, original or active', which can be expressed verbally with phrases like 'on the whole', 'a little more', 'a little less', etc., or with the phrases that Gramsci himself uses, '*to a large extent*' and '*for the most part*'.

Bearing this in mind, we should modify the purely qualitative schematizations worked out above in at least three cases. Just to take one example, instead of:

implicit v. explicit

we should put:

implicit to a large extent v. implicit to a limited extent

or

implicit to a limited extent v. explicit to a large extent

or even, so as to include the outer limits:

implicit v. implicit to a large extent v. . . . v. implicit
to a limited extent v. explicit.

And we should do the same for 'debased' and 'passive'.

This revision is by no means a trivial one. It involves a transition from quality to quantity which is consonant with certain of Gramsci's general procedures. But could *all* the contrasting pairs we have before us be revised in the same way?

It would make sense for 'simple', 'fragmentary', 'unorganic' and 'mechanical', but a good deal less so for the contrast between 'subaltern' and 'hegemonic'. It is true that, forcing the issue a little, we could conceive of attenuations or exceptions in this case as well. Using words a little bit loosely, one could say for example that the proletariat today is *a little less subaltern* (or even, looking to the other side of a not precisely defined dividing-line, *a little more hegemonic*). Gramsci himself is basically presenting the dominant classes as *a little less* (or *not entirely*) *hegemonic* when he talks about the expansive power of certain popular beliefs. But such expressions have very little rigour about them and simply correspond to *a little stronger, a little weaker,* and so on. We know perfectly well in fact that '*a little more* power' is not '*power*', and that the difference between them is precisely 'revolution'.

It is in short extremely difficult to recast the qualitative contrast between 'subaltern' and 'hegemonic' as a simple continuous gradation of quantitative steps from '*more* subaltern' (or perhaps '*less* hegemonic') to '*less* subaltern' (or '*more* hegemonic'). But even if we did decide to do it, and push Gramsci's text in a 'reformist' direction, so to speak, we would come up against further and not inconsiderable difficulties.

For even if Gramsci regarded *all* the qualitative contrasts he presents us with as quantitative distinctions, the fact remains that *by definition,* as he puts it, he systematically and nearly always *absolutely* assigns negative qualities to folklore, and almost without exception he expresses himself in terms of quality and discontinuity (words sometimes *betray* one's thought, as is well known, but also in the sense that they *make clear* what it really is).

So we are faced with an alternative. By explicitly introducing a number of quantitative modifications we would bring about a radical transformation in the system of qualitative contrasts that seemed to be emerging from the text. But there are strong arguments against such a transformation: the fact that it is difficult to give a quantitative sense to the fundamental contrast between 'subaltern' and 'hegemonic'; Gramsci's attribution of negative qualities to folklore and positive ones to official conceptions 'by definition', and his use of an essentially qualitative terminology. All these factors indicate that his modifications should be relegated to the conceptual sidelines, and lend to his positive comments on folklore the banal character of exceptions which confirm the rule.

Once again, then, an ambivalence is created, two possible ways of reading the text.

One way might be to lay emphasis on the value of the positive comments and the quantitative modifications. But then we not only run into the difficulties which have just been mentioned, but also have to face the fact that folklore is the target of a whole series of negative qualifications which extend far beyond the terms presented here, and this is not easy to get round. Quite apart from the numerous remarks scattered through the rest of Gramsci's work, there is a rather revealing incongruence in the text of the *Observations* itself. Having just given a rigorous definition of folklore, Gramsci goes on to say that 'it could be argued that all religions, even the most cultured and sophisticated, are 'folklore' in relation to modern thought', even if there is the 'vital difference' that 'religions . . . are, as has been said, "elaborated and systematized" by (religious) intellectuals and the Church hierarchy'. With this statement, Gramsci goes against his own definition of folklore as characteristic of the subaltern classes and standing in opposition to official conceptions, and demonstrates that, in spite of the rigorous terms he himself has established, the idea that 'folklore' actually means everything that modern thought (with its apex represented by Marxism) must sweep away is firmly entrenched.[6]

One can then resolve this ambivalence in the opposite direction, and the text gives us considerable authority for so doing. But we then find ourselves having to pose a much more important question to the text itself. The reasons for his negative assessment of folklore are clear enough, and at the same time it is understandable that Gramsci should take a serious interest in the subject on more than one occasion (not only is he forced to exercise his powerful intellectual curiosity on a large number of minutiae, but there is also that element of *tenacity* that makes folklore important for the purposes of knowing and transforming reality). But we still have to ask ourselves how he manages conceptually to define so 'indigestible' a mass of debased fragments and debris as a *conception of the world*, when its essentially unorganic character is enhanced rather than diminished by the presence of a few conceptions that are progressive and effective.

Gramsci's definition of folklore as a *conception of the world* draws together into a single category phenomena that differ widely from each other, ranging from this indigestible mass to Marxism which he regards as the only truly 'original and integral conception of the world', the harbinger of 'an historical epoch', a conception that is incomparably superior to any non-Marxist official conception, however elevated, and one that will be superseded only with 'the disappearance of political society and the coming of a regulated society'. (*SPN* 381-2)

The range covered is so wide that one cannot help asking whether to speak of folklore as a conception of the world is anything more than a play on words. If not, then the common element has to be found which allows Gramsci to bring together under a single conceptual heading phenomena which he himself shows to be radically divergent from one another because they either have or do not have certain qualities regarded by him as being of decisive importance (originality, critical consciousness, organicity, centralization, etc.).

In short, what is it that makes them alike or brings them together in spite of such deep (and repeatedly emphasized) intrinsic differences?

There seem to me two different answers to this question.

The first answer is explicitly stated by Gramsci, but is the less persuasive. It is the solution he gives to the wider problem of the relations between 'spontaneous' philosophy and 'scientific' philosophy, of which the relation between unorganic conceptions of the world and critical conceptions are only a specific example. From it derives the quality of 'spontaneity' which Gramsci explicitly attributes to folklore's capacity to adhere to reality.

The second, and in my view, more valid answer is also to be found in Gramsci, but not in anything he says explicitly. Rather, it is contained in the very nature of the conceptual operation that he undertook specifically, but not exclusively, in respect of folklore.

The first solution alluded to above consists in the distinction which he makes (and it is already implicit in the *Observations*) between 'differences of quality' and 'differences of quantity'.

Discussing the relations between 'modern theory' (i.e. Marxism) and 'the "spontaneous" feelings of the masses', Gramsci asserts that there can be no 'opposition' between them because 'between the two there is a "quantitative" difference of degree, not one of quality. A reciprocal "reduction" so to speak, a passage from one to the other and vice versa, must be possible.'[7] (*SPN* 199)

If one recalls that just before Gramsci had written: 'It may be said that spontaneity is . . . characteristic of the "history of the subaltern classes", and indeed of their most marginal and peripheral elements, [which] have not achieved any conscious-ness of the class "for itself" '; (*SPN* 196) and bearing in mind the quality of spontaneity attributed to folklore's capacity to adhere to reality, and, finally, the identification of the 'people' with all the subaltern classes, it becomes clear that the *quantitative* continuity which Gramsci establishes between 'modern theory' and 'spontaneous feelings', between the highest form of consciousness and the most unconscious experiences, can immediately be transferred to the relation between folklore at its most fragmented and official concep-tions at their most organic. They are both *conceptions of the world* because the difference between them is one of 'quantity', not one of 'quality'. (*SPN* 347)

But the assertion that there is a quantitative continuity between Marxism and spontaneous feelings (in support of which Gramsci turns first to Kant and Croce and only subsequently to Marx) is simply a more specific and clearer application of a far more general principle: 'the principle that all men are "philosophers" ': this idea too is not exclusive to Gramsci, and Gramsci himself regards it as in a certain sense a commonsense truth. (*SPN* 323 & 330) What this means is that 'between the professional or "technical" philosophers and the rest of mankind, the difference is not one of "quality" but only of "quantity" '. (*SPN* 347)

Admittedly, Gramsci adds at once:

> The term 'quantity' is being used here in a special sense, which is not to be confused with its meaning in arithmetic, since what it indicates is greater or lesser degrees of 'homogeneity', 'coherence', 'logicality', etc; in other words, *quantity of qualitative elements* (italics added). (*SPN* 347)

In Gramsci's view, the difference is not limited to the fact that the 'philosopher . . . "thinks" with greater logical rigour, with greater coherence, with more systematic sense than do other men', but consists primarily in the fact that 'the professional or technical philosopher . . . knows the entire history of thought. In other words, he is capable of accounting for the development of thought up to his own day and he is in a position where he can take up a problem from the point which it has reached after having undergone every previous attempt at a solution.' For that reason, 'he has the same function in the field of thought that specialists have in their various scientific fields.'

Nevertheless, a 'qualitative' continuity between 'the specialist philosopher' and 'the rest of mankind' appears to be re-established by virtue of the fact that the philosopher is a specialist in an activity that is common to everyone, namely thought: 'it is not possible to conceive of any man who is not also a philosopher, who doesn't think, because thought is proper to man as such, or at least to any man who is not a pathological cretin'. (*SPN* 347)

These statements are clearly the realization of the programme that Gramsci sets himself in the study of philosophy and culture.

> It is essential to destroy the widespread prejudice that philosophy is a strange and difficult thing just because it is the specific intellectual activity of a particular category of specialists or of professional and systematic philosophers. It must first be shown that all men are 'philosophers', by defining the limits and characteristics of the 'spontaneous philosophy' which is proper to everybody. (*SPN* 323)

It is worth adding that Gramsci sees this 'spontaneous' (or what he also calls 'common and popular') (*SPN* 328) philosophy as being contained, not only in language and in common sense and good sense, but also in 'popular religion and, therefore, also in the entire system of beliefs, superstitions, opinions, ways of seeing things and of acting, which are collectively bundled together under the name of "folklore" '. And finally that he goes on to say that 'everyone is a philosopher, though in his own way and unconsciously, since even in the slightest manifestation of any intellectual activity whatever, in "language", there is contained a specific conception of the world'. (*SPN* 323)

There is then more than enough to establish a direct link between Gramsci's concept of 'spontaneous philosophy' and his definition of folklore as a 'conception of the world'. Folklore, as Gramsci conceives it, is in fact a special form of 'spontaneous' philosophy; thus, considerations about the latter could, it would appear in principle, be transferred to the former. On this basis, Gramsci's remark elsewhere that ' "pure" spontaneity does not exist in history: it would come to the same thing as "pure" mechanicity' (*SPN* 196) may also be applied to the folk conception of the world.

This is further confirmation of the fact that elaborated and critical conceptions on the one hand and on the other the indigestible mass which folklore might be defined as can both be placed in the same category because the difference between them for Gramsci is one not of *quality*, but only of *quantity of qualitative elements*. The 'positive' remarks on folklore, like the modifications to its negative attributes, are the more or less explicit pointer to this underlying conceptual intention.

This would seem to be the end of the matter, were it not for the difficulties we have already outlined in connection with the transformation of the resolutely *qualitative* system of characterization attributed by Gramsci to folklore and folkloric conceptions; and were it not further for the fact that the specific differences which Gramsci insists on as soon as he has connected things at a general level are always more radical and decisive than the affinities.

In addition to what has already been noted in connection with folklore, the reader's attention is drawn to the decisive distinction between philosophy *tout court* — which alone is 'an intellectual order' — and forms of spontaneous philosophy such as 'religion and common sense', which 'cannot constitute an intellectual order, because they cannot be reduced to unity and coherence even within an individual consciousness, let alone collective consciousness'. (*SPN* 326)

The fact is that in order to maintain a link between the opposite terms of his repeated swings back and forth from identities to differences and from quantitative continuity to qualitative discontinuity, as Gramsci wished, he must be able to call on a precise, and more than purely verbal, criterion of distinction between *qualitative differences* (which would break the continuity he claims) and *differences of quantity of qualitative elements* (which on the contrary would not undermine the connection he seeks between the 'specialist' philosopher and the 'common' philosopher, 'conscious leadership' and 'spontaneity', intellectuals and 'simple people', or, to use more current and realistic terms, between leaders and masses, central committees and the rank-and-file, and so on).

But in the absence of such a criterion — and it seems to me that it is absent, at any rate in the uses which more or less frequently we have *actually* made of Gramsci's thought — in its absence, the link is broken; the subtle and indefinite dividing-line between *quality* and *quantity of qualitative elements* is erased; the constantly emphasized specific differences prove far more decisive than the attribution to a single common genus; to acknowledge the presence of a conception of the world even in the slightest intellectual activity becomes a game of words without further consequence; to assert that 'all men think' becomes a trivial banality in face of the fact that *some* men think *well* and *many* think *badly*, and does not so much as scratch the surface of the prejudice which Gramsci wanted to destroy.

All of this would matter very little if all that was involved were a few marginal questions concerning the debris of folklore. But far larger problems are involved, problems as important, precisely, as that of 'conscious leadership'. Above all it would not matter were it not that — in the process of its becoming 'the common sense of a [particular] environment', as is the fate of 'every philosophy' (*SPN* 330f) — the uneasy balance between quantitative continuities and qualitative separations was not in fact broken in favour of the second term. As a result, certain hierarchies of subject-matter and sectional interests traditional to our culture remain essentially intact. This is also meant, let me be quite clear, as a note of self-criticism.

Nevertheless, the extremely wide range that Gramsci allows to his idea of conception of the world, the way in which he extends it to include even the most bizarre, disparate and chance combinations of heterogeneous and indigestible elements, has an undoubtedly aggressive power in the face of traditional conceptions, their identification of *culture* with their *own* culture and their reduction of *history* to the history of the *upper reaches* of society.

This aggressiveness — which is active even in spite of other indications of Gramsci to the contrary — does certainly not originate from the generic principle that all men think so everyone is a bit of a philosopher. It would in any case be hard to find in this one principle any criterion whereby one might assign some form of *unity* to even the most indigestible masses of material — something that must be done if we are to distinguish one conception from another, let alone talk about a *conception of the world*.

The fact of the matter is that this aggressive drive springs from Gramsci's entire political and theoretical commitment.

It is this commitment which brings about, for example, certain sudden and even disquieting ruptures in the carefully weighted balance — whether of a didactic or a dialectical kind — between form and content, intellectuals and common people, and so on. As an example, take the passage where Gramsci asks (but only in very indirect relation to folklore): 'Is it possible that a "formally" new conception can present itself in a guise other than the crude, unsophisticated version of the populace?' (*SPN* 342)[8]

But another, and very important, part of Gramsci's political and theoretical commitment is his tendency to set up a constant relationship between cultural phenomena and the social groups by which they are conveyed. At the same time as always being concerned with formal coherence and organicity, Gramsci pays continual attention to the links between indigestible masses of material as well as organic philosophies and one or other of the 'many social groups in which everyone is automatically involved from the moment of his entry into the conscious world'. (*SPN* 323) Precisely because he is aiming for a 'more cautious and precise assessment of the forces acting in society', Gramsci does not draw up his observations on the basis of very general class-distinctions, but provides a working *scale-model,* articulated into categories, groups and sub-groups. He makes a distinction between 'the common sense of the more educated strata of society', that 'of the people' and that of the 'intellectuals' (*SPN* 330f)[9]; he emphasizes the fact that 'there is one Catholicism for the peasants, one for the *petits bourgeois* and town workers, one for women and one for intellectuals which is itself variegated and disconnected' (*SPN* 420); and still more directly he makes the point that 'in acquiring one's conception of the world one always belongs to a particular grouping which is that of all the social elements which share the same mode of thinking and acting'. (*SPN* 324f)

This 'grouping' can sometimes consist simply of dispersed and isolated individuals, whose only link with each other is that of shared conceptions. However, it can also be a concrete social or socio-cultural group: it 'can be one's village or province'. Furthermore, though the conception of the world which holds sway there and is 'mechanically' imposed on its members may be pieced together from other sources, it is born or can be born — whatever its more distant origins — from a cultural activity which is socially internal to the group and qualitatively homogeneous with it:

> it can have its origins in the parish and the 'intellectual activity' of the local priest or aging patriarch whose wisdom is law, or in the little old woman who has inherited the lore of the witches or the minor intellectual soured by his own stupidity and inability to act. (*SPN* 323)

Thus the use Gramsci makes of the idea of *conception of the world,* at least when dealing with 'spontaneous' conceptions, is constantly supported by a dense network of references to concrete social situations, however humble, whose 'way of seeing and acting' is constituted by the cultural formation with which Gramsci is engaged at the time. Thus, any judgement on the formal qualities or content of such material is accompanied by the acknowledgement that, whatever its origins or level, that particular 'combination' of cultural elements is the intellectual heritage of a particular social group. The group lives it and makes use of it from the inside, without realizing its contradictoriness, or at any rate not realizing it in the same way as somebody looking in from the outside. Thus, any combination of cultural elements which is embodied by an identifiable social group comes to constitute a kind of 'de facto unity'. It can be looked at from the point of view of the group which recognizes itself in it and so can legitimately be called a 'conception of the world' because, even if it is not so *for us,* it is *for others.* Not for nothing do phrases such as 'in its own way' recur in Gramsci.

Gramsci's continual linking of cultural phenomena and social groups — and nowhere more clearly than in the pages on folklore — seems then to provide the real explanation for the way in which he is able to bring radically different phenomena under a single conceptual heading, without the concept itself dissolving. To regard folklore too as a conception of the world is not a mere play on words precisely to the extent that, if only for a moment, judgement is suspended on its content and formal qualities, and it is acknowledged as having a unitary existence for the 'people'.

It is no less true of course that the moment of judgement is essential and decisive in Gramsci, than it is that the distinction between the two moments seems to be resolved in favour of the judgement, or rather the condemnation. For while the ways in which he uses the idea of conception of the world appear closer (with all due reservations) to the ethno-anthropological concept of 'culture' than to the traditionally selective conception of culture as an élite-phenomenon, it cannot be forgotten that in a section entitled *Hegemony of Western Culture over the whole World Culture,* Gramsci has left us one of the most inward-looking formulations both of the ethnocentric view of world cultural history and of the limitation of the European 'cultural process' to the élites, to the definite exclusion of 'popular cultures'. (*SPN* 416-417)

But to refer to this passage must not in its turn lead us to forget all the rest, that is to say, what was actually achieved. Above all, it should not lead us to ignore the tensions, some of them serious, which build up in the course of the work. It is precisely the need prompted by these tensions to identify what

Gramsci says and how, that enables him to be actively, and not just historically, present in the field of socio-cultural research today.

NOTES

Unless otherwise indicated quotes are from *LVN* 215-221. These notes are soon to be published by Lawrence and Wishart in a volume containing Gramsci's writings on literature.

1 Apart from obvious considerations, the term can be inferred without a shadow of doubt from the expression 'subaltern and instrumental classes'. Furthermore, it can be seen as a correct equivalent of 'ruling' and 'dominant', which are used explicitly in the phrases 'ruling strata' and 'dominant class'.

2 *SPN* 196-7: *Spontaneity and conscious leadership*. The term 'spontaneity' can be variously defined, for the phenomenon to which it refers is many-sided. Meanwhile it must be stressed that 'pure' spontaneity does not exist in history: it would come to the same thing as 'pure' mechanicity. In the 'most spontaneous' movement it is simply the case that the elements of 'conscious leadership' cannot be checked, have left no reliable document. It may be said that spontaneity is therefore characteristic of the 'history of the subaltern classes', and indeed of their most marginal and peripheral elements; these have not achieved any consciousness of the class 'for itself', and consequently it never occurs to them that their history might have some possible importance, that there might be some value in leaving documentary evidence of it.

 Gramsci goes on: 'Hence in such movements there exist multiple elements of "conscious leadership", but no one of them is predominant or transcends the level of a given social stratum's "popular science" — its "common sense" or traditional conception of the world.'

 For the continuation of this passage, see Note 3 below.

3 In this connection, cf. what Gramsci writes immediately after the passage cited in Note 2 above:

 This is precisely what De Man, empirically, counterposes to Marxism; but he does not realize (apparently) that he is falling into the position of somebody who, after describing folklore, witchcraft, etc., and showing that these conceptions have sturdy historical roots and are tenaciously entwined in the psychology of specific popular strata, believed that he had 'transcended' modern science — taking as 'modern science' every little article in the popular scientific journals and periodicals. This is a real case of intellectual teratology, of which there are other examples: precisely, the admirers of folklore, who advocate its preservation; the 'magicalists' connected with Maeterlinck, who believe it is necessary to take up anew the thread — snapped by violence — of alchemy and witchcraft, so that science may be put back onto a course more fertile in discoveries, etc. (*SPN* 197).

4   *PP* 172-3: *Ideological material*. A study of the actual organization of the ideological structure of a dominant class, i.e. the material organization whose purpose is to maintain, defend and develop the theoretical and ideological 'front' . . .

The press plays the most dynamic role in this ideological structure, but not the only one. Everything that has, or might have, a direct or indirect effect on public opinion is part of it: libraries, schools, the various kinds of clubs and societies, even architecture, the lay-out and the names of streets . . . If a study of this sort were undertaken properly, it could be quite important. Apart from providing us with a living historical model of such a structure, it would accustom us to a more cautious and précise assessment of the forces acting in society. What can an innovatory class set up against this formidable collection of trenches and fortifications constructed by the dominant class? The spirit of cleavage that is the progressive acquisition of consciousness of its own historical personality, a spirit of division which should tend to spread out from the protagonist-class to the classes that are potentially its allies. All of this requires a lot of complex ideological work, the first condition of which is a precise knowledge of the ground to be cleared of its element of human mass.

5   *SPN* 377. The passage goes on:
The analysis of these propositions tends, I think, to reinforce the conception of *historical bloc* in which precisely material forces are the content and ideologies are the form, though this distinction between form and content has purely didactic value, since the material forces would be inconceivable historically without form and the ideologies would be individual fancies without the material forces.

6   Another slight divergence from the more rigorous concept comes where Gramsci says that 'common sense' is 'philosophical folklore'. But elsewhere Gramsci distinguishes between 'popular' common sense, the common sense of 'the more educated strata of society' and that of 'the intellectuals' (cf. *SPN* 331). I think that this distinction *according to socio-cultural strata or levels* should be given more thought than it usually is in discussion of Gramsci's concept of common sense. In the first place, it confirms Gramsci's alertness to what I have referred to elsewhere as *connotation* (i.e. the solidarity between cultural phenomena and social groups). Furthermore, it warns us to be careful not to relate to common sense as a socially undifferentiated phenomenon what Gramsci relates, or might relate, specifically to the common sense of the cultured strata or that of the popular strata (which are in their turn internally socially

differentiated): cf. his distinction between 'different' Catholicisms.

7   *SPN* 198-9: At this point, a fundamental theoretical question is raised: can modern theory be in opposition to the 'spontaneous' feelings of the masses? ('spontaneous' in the sense that they are not the result of any systematic educational activity on the part of an already conscious leading group, but have been formed through everyday experience illuminated by 'common sense', i.e. by the traditional popular conception of the world — what is unimaginatively called 'instinct', although it too is in fact a primitive and elementary historical acquisition). It cannot be in opposition to them. Between the two there is a 'quantitative' difference of degree, not one of quality. A reciprocal 'reduction' so to speak, a passage from one to the other and vice versa, must be possible. (Recall that Immanuel Kant believed it important for his philosophical theories to agree with common sense; the same position can be found in Croce. Recall too Marx's assertion in *The Holy Family* that the political formulae of the French Revolution can be reduced to the principles of classical German philosophy.

8   *SPN* 342-3: And yet the historian, with the benefit of all necessary perspective, manages to establish and to understand the fact that the beginnings of a new world, rough and jagged though they always are, are better than the passing away of the world in its death-throes and the swan-song that it produces.

9   Elsewhere Gramsci writes:
Common sense is not a single unique conception, identical in time and space. It is the 'folklore' of philosophy, and, like folklore, it takes countless different forms. Its most fundamental characteristic is that it is a conception which, even in the brain of one individual, is fragmentary, incoherent and inconsequential, in conformity with the social and cultural position of those masses whose philosophy it is. At those times in history when a homogeneous social group is brought into being, there comes into being also, in opposition to common sense, a homogeneous — in other words coherent and systematic — philosophy. (*SPN* 419)

On another occasion, Gramsci affirms even more explicitly: 'Every social stratum has its "common sense" and its "good sense", which amount in effect to the most wide-spread conception of life and mankind.' (*Int* 148, not in *SPN*).

NOTES ON CONTRIBUTORS

NOTES ON CONTRIBUTORS

Christine Buci-Glucksmann is a feminist who has written on Lenin, Bukharin, social democracy, feminism, the state, Euro-communism, and the French Communist Party as well as on Gramsci. She teaches philosophy at the Ecole Normale Supérieure in Paris.

Alberto Maria Cirese teaches cultural anthropology at the University of Rome. He has written on Southern Italian culture, popular poetry, structural analysis of proverbs, Propp and Lévi-Strauss, folklore and anthropology.

Franco De Felice teaches history at the University of Bari. In addition to publishing various articles and books on Gramsci, he has written on the peasants in Southern Italy and on the Popular Front.

E.J. Hobsbawm is Professor of Economic and Social History at Birkbeck College, London University. Among his many publications are *Primitive Rebels* (1959), *The Age of Revolution* (1962), *Industry and Empire* (1968), *The Age of Capital 1848-1875* (1975), and *The Italian Road to Socialism* (1977).

Pasquale Misuraca has worked at the Institute of Sociology at the University of Rome. He has written articles on Gramsci, politics, sociology, and the State, and he is finishing a second book *Politica e partiti nella critica di Gramsci* with Luis Razeto Migliaro.

Luis Razeto Migliaro taught sociology at the State Technical University in Santiago, Chile, until 1973. He now teaches at the Institute of Ethnology and Anthropology at the University of Perugia. In addition to two books on Gramsci with Pasquale Misuraca, he has published books on the social sciences, social classes and institutions, and the state and political research in Latin America, as well as numerous articles.

Tom Nairn is a frequent contributor to *New Left Review* and a member of its editorial committee as well as that of the new *Bulletin of Scottish Politics*. His books include *Atlantic Europe: The Radical View* and *The Break-Up of Britain, 1965-1975*.

Pier Paolo Pasolini, born in Bologna in 1922, was — until his violent death in 1975 — one of Italy's foremost poets, novelists, political essayists and film-makers. His many prize-winning films include *Theorem, Pigsty*, and *The Gospel according to Saint Matthew*. One of his best known volumes of poetry, *Le Cenere di Gramsci*, is something of a tribute to the political thinker.

Mario Telò has done research at the Basso Foundation in Rome and has taught at the Universities of Roskilde (Denmark), Salerno and Bari. He is the author of articles about the working class movement and Marxism between the two world wars, and in particular on Gramsci, Bukharin and "plannist" socialism in the 1930s. He is now preparing a book about the policies of European trade unions after the 1929 crisis.

Giuseppe Vacca is on the board of governors of the RAI, the Italian State television network, teaches political philosophy at the University of Bari, and is on the central committee of the Italian Communist Party. He has written on Lukacs, Korsch, Togliatti, Marxist philosophy, socialism and democracy, Marxist theory of the state, and the problems and possibilities of mass communications.

BIBLIOGRAPHY

Primary Works

Direct references to Gramsci's writings have been inserted into the text using the following abbreviations. Italian editions are only indicated if the passage is not available in an English edition.

La costruzione del partito comunista 1923-1926, Turin: Einaudi, 1971. *(CPC)*

Letteratura e vita nazionale, Turin: Einaudi, 1950. *(LVN)*

Gli intellettuali e l'organizzazione della cultura, Turin: Einaudi, 1949. (Int)

Il materialismo storico e la filosofia di Benedetto Croce, Turin: Einaudi, 1948. *(MS)*

L'Ordine Nuovo, Turin: Einaudi, 1955. *(ON)*

Passato e Presente, Turin: Einaudi, 1952. *(PP)*

Political Writings, 1910-1920, London: Lawrence and Wishart, 1977. *(PWI)*

Political Writings, 1921-1926, London: Lawrence and Wishart, 1978. *(PWII)*

Quaderni del carcere, vols. 1-4. Turin: Einaudi, 1975. *(Q)*
This is a critical edition of all versions of all notes in prison.

Selections from the Prison Notebooks, London: Lawrence and Wishart, 1971. *(SPN)*
This has a very good historical introduction and, as with all

volumes of Gramsci in English, excellent annotation.

Secondary Works

This is a short list of works on Gramsci available in English.

BOGGS, Carl — *Gramsci's Marxism,* London: Pluto Press, 1976.
This is the first introduction in English to Gramsci's political philosophy.

BUCI-GLUCKSMANN, Christine — *Gramsci and the State,* London: Lawrence and Wishart, 1980.
This is an advanced book which argues that any understanding of Gramsci must concentrate on his notion of the state and hegemony. It places him in the context of the debates in the international communist movement in the 1920s and 1930s and discusses his view of philosophy in polemic with Louis Althusser.

CAMMETT, John M. — *Antonio Gramsci and the Origins of Italian Communism,* Stanford, California: Stanford University Press, 1967.
This is a history book which provides an excellent background to Gramsci's activities in the Italian labour movement before, during and after World War I. A full, although by now somewhat dated, historical bibliography.

CLARK, Martin — *Antonio Gramsci and the Revolution that Failed,* London: Yale University Press, 1977.
Clark discusses the background to the development of the factory councils, and the debate which arose about them in the context of the history of the Turin working class movement, Gramsci's political activities and the background to the founding of the Italian Communist Party in 1921.

DAVIDSON, Alastair — *Antonio Gramsci: Towards an Intellectual Biography,* London: Merlin Press, 1977.
Davidson discusses the influences on Gramsci's intellectual development and the changes in his ideas. He concentrates on the period before Gramsci was imprisoned in 1926 and is particularly good on Gramsci's youth in Sardinia and the intellectual debates in Turin.

DAVIS, John A. (ed.) — *Gramsci and Italy's Passive Revolu-*

tion, London: Croom Helm, 1979.
A collection of essays on Italian history, this book is organized around certain themes in Gramsci's work and discusses his interpretation of Italian history and his concept of bourgeois revolution.

FIORI, Giuseppe — *Antonio Gramsci*, London: New Left Books, 1977.
This is the best all-round biography of Gramsci.

JOCTEAU, Gian Carlo — *Leggere Gramsci: Una guide alle interpretazioni*, Milan: Feltrinelli, 1975.
Although this is available only in Italian, it is extremely useful for anyone embarking on any study in depth of Gramsci since it gives a full description of the various interpretations of Gramsci summarizing a vast literature.

JOLL, James — *Gramsci*, London: Fontana Modern Masters, 1977.
This examines Gramsci's ideas both when he was an active politician and when he was in prison and compares them to other socialist thinkers. It is recommended as a very good 'first book' for anyone just beginning to read about Gramsci.

MOUFFE, Chantal (ed.) — *Gramsci and Marxist Theory*, London: Routledge and Kegan Paul, 1979.
This is a collection of advanced theoretical articles translated from Italian and French.

SASSOON, Anne Showstack — *Gramsci's Politics*, London: Croom Helm, 1980.
Beginning with his earliest work and extending to the *Prison Notebooks*, this book analyzes Gramsci's writings on politics and the political party related to his view of the state and the revolutionary process.

TOGLIATTI, Palmiro — *Gramsci and Other Essays*, London: Lawrence and Wishart, 1979.
Included in this volume are pieces on the *Ordine Nuovo*, on the changes in the Italian Communist Party in 1923-1926 when Gramsci became party leader, and on Gramsci's Leninism.

WILLIAMS, Gwyn A. — *Proletarian Order, Antonio Gramsci, Factory Councils and the Origins of Communism in Italy, 1911-1921*, London: Pluto Press, 1980.

Williams studies the crisis in Italian socialism between 1911 and 1921, focussing on Gramsci and the factory council movement in Turin in 1919-20.

Articles

ANDERSON, Perry — 'The Antinomies of Antonio Gramsci', *New Left Review*, No. 100, Nov. 1976 — Jan. 1977. This criticizes the limitations of Gramsci's ideas on the state and political strategy analyzing various texts.

BATES, Thomas R. — 'Gramsci and the Theory of Hegemony', *Journal of the History of Ideas*, Vol. 36, No. 2, April-June, 1975.

FEMIA, Joseph — 'Hegemony and Consciousness in the Thought of Antonio Gramsci', *Political Studies*, Vol. 23, No. 1, March 1975.

HOBSBAWM, E.J. — 'Gramsci and Political Theory', *Marxism Today*, Vol. 21, No. 1, July 1977.
A wide-ranging article that complements the piece by Hobsbawm in this volume.

MERRINGTON, John — 'Theory and Practice in Gramsci's Marxism', *Socialist Register*, 1968.
Merrington examines various important theoretical issues.

MOUFFE, Chantal and SASSOON, Anne Showstack — 'Gramsci in France and Italy — a Review of the Literature', *Economy and Society*, Vol. 6, No. 1, Feb. 1977.
A number of the works discussed here are now available in Chantal Mouffe's *Gramsci and Marxist Theory*. This article provides an overview of various debates and interpretations of Gramsci.

SASSOON, Anne Showstack — 'Gramsci: a New Concept of Politics and the Expansion of Democracy', in *Marxism and Democracy*, edited by Alan Hunt, London: Lawrence and Wishart, 1980.

SIMON, Roger — 'Gramsci's Concept of Hegemony', *Marxism Today*, Vol. 21, No. 3, March 1977.